Oil
Monarchies

Oil

Monarchies

Domestic and Security Challenges in the Arab Gulf States

F. Gregory Gause, III

COUNCIL ON FOREIGN RELATIONS PRESS

NEW YORK

COUNCIL ON FOREIGN RELATIONS BOOKS

If you would like more information on Council publications, please write the Council on Foreign Relations, 58 East 68th Street, New York, NY 10021, or call the Publications Office at (212)734-0400.

Library of Congress Cataloging-in-Publication Data

Gause, F. Gregory.
   Oil monarchies : domestic and security challenges in the Arab Gulf
States / F. Gregory Gause III.
     p.   cm.
   Includes bibliographical references and index.
   ISBN 0-87609-151-6 (pbk.) : $16.95
   1. Persian Gulf Region—Politics and government 2. Islam and
state—Persian Gulf Region. 3. Petroleum industry and trade—
Political aspects—Persian Gulf Region. 4. Persian Gulf War,
1991. 5. Political participation—Persian Gulf Region. 6. Persian
Gulf Region—Foreign relations—United States. 7. United States—
Foreign relations—Persian Gulf Region. I. Title.
JQ1825.A75G38   1993
956.704'421—dc20
                                               93-11318
                                                  CIP

for Cindy

Contents

Acknowledgments

W HILE THIS BOOK MIGHT NOT BE VERY LONG, THE list of debts I have incurred while researching and writing it is. It is a pleasure to have the opportunity to thank those who helped me bring this project to fruition.

First and foremost is the Arthur Ross Foundation and its president, Arthur Ross. It was Mr. Ross who first suggested to the Council the need for a project on the Gulf monarchies. The Foundation generously supported the Council's symposium on the topic in January 1992, two of my research trips to the Gulf in May-June 1992 and October 1992, and the preparation and publication of this book. Mr. Ross' curiosity, honesty, and insight were invaluable to me from the beginning of the project to its completion.

I owe enormous thanks to two friends and colleagues at the Council on Foreign Relations: Nicholas Rizopoulos, Director of Studies, and Richard Murphy, Senior Fellow for the Middle East. Nick and Dick took a flier on a young and relatively untested academic when they asked me to write this book in the fall of 1991. I hope the end product justifies their confidence in me. They are also responsible for bringing me on to the Council staff in January 1993 as Fellow for Arab and Islamic Studies, where I have had the time to finish the manuscript and the opportunity to help shape the Middle East program at the Council. It has been a fascinating and rewarding experience, for which I also owe them thanks.

I could not have fulfilled my obligations at the Council without the help of two very talented young women who have served as my assistants: Jennifer Notis from January to August 1993, and Riva Richmond from August 1993 to now. James Prince, who served as Richard Murphy's assistant up until December 1992, was an invaluable help in putting together our symposium in January 1992 and in organizing my research trips. The staff at the Council's publication office—David Haproff, Judy Train, and Jessica Barist—have helped me through the publication process with wit and efficiency. Having an office just one floor above them has given me the chance to pester them to a degree unsurpassed by their other authors, and I appreciate their patience.

The intellectual basis for this project was the two-day symposium on "Political Evolution in the GCC States: Implications for U.S. Foreign Policy" held at the Council on January 23-24, 1992. The scholars who wrote the papers for that symposium provided a sound basis for our discussions and challenged me in formulating my ideas and gathering my data for the book. While the papers provided an excellent background for my research, the approach, opinions, and conclusions, along with the errors, in this book are mine alone. I gratefully acknowledge the contribution of these scholars to both the symposium and to my research: Khaldoun al-Naqeeb, Joseph Kechichian, Mai Yamani, Jill Crystal, Fred Lawson, Jerrold Green, and Emile Nakhleh.

I also want to thank the participants in the symposium and in a subsequent author's review seminar held here at the Council in May 1993 for their ideas, questions and advice: Odeh Aburdene, Gregory Aftandilian, Muhammed Abdul Ghaffar, Abdullah Al-shayeji, Aziz Abu Hamad, Michael Ameen, Lisa Anderson, John Duke Anthony, Scott Berrie, Eleanor Duomato, Mansour Farhang, Andrea Farsak, Gidon Gottlieb, James Hoge, J.C. Hurewitz, Farhad Kazemi, Judith Miller, Paul Mlotok, Ed Morse, Richard Murphy, Gwenn Okruhlik, John Peterson, James Prince, R.K. Ramazani, Nicholas Rizopoulos, Arthur Ross, Jamal Sanad, Hafedh al-Shaykh, Jean-Francois Seznec, Fouad Saleh Shehab, Gary Sick, Michael

Sterner, John Temple Swing, Jennifer Whitaker, and Dan Zanini. Hafedh al-Shaykh even gave me my fifteen minutes of fame in the Gulf by devoting one of his regular columns in *Akhbar al-Khalij* newspaper in Bahrain to the project. I appreciate it.

William J. vanden Heuvel presided over both the symposium in January 1992 and the author's seminar in May 1993 with a firm and fair hand. I thank him particularly for his contributions, and for his expressions of support for me and for the project.

Four people read the entire draft manuscript, giving me most helpful advice and editorial guidance: Lisa Anderson, Jill Crystal, Richard Murphy, and Nicholas Rizopoulos. I owe them special thanks.

During my research trips to the Gulf, I had the opportunity to conduct over 60 interviews with officials, activists, political observers, and regular citizens in Saudi Arabia, Kuwait, Bahrain, Oman and the UAE. They taught me much about the politics of their countries and their region, and I am indebted to them. I assured each of them that their remarks to me would not be attributed, so I cannot thank them by name. I look forward to the day in these countries when this kind of precaution will not be necessary. I also thank those here in the United States, at the diplomatic missions of these states in Washington and New York, who assisted me in securing visas to their countries.

My appreciation and regard go out to a number of people who had nothing to do directly with this project, but whose friendship has been a central part of my life while I was working on this book. My colleagues at Columbia University's Middle East Institute— Lisa Anderson, Henri Barkey, Richard Bulliet, Mahmoud Haddad, Vahid Nowshirvani, and David Waldner—have been a source of intellectual challenge and personal support. The squash games with Henri have been particularly welcome, even on those rare occasions when he beats me. Being a member of Columbia University's political science department these past seven years has been a second graduate education for me. The opportunity to learn from Robert Jervis, Jack Synder, David Baldwin, Richard Betts, Barnett Rubin, Helen Milner, Robert Shapiro, Joseph Rothschild, and other senior colleagues has been incomparable. My junior colleagues in the department have been both teachers and buddies to me, and thus my thanks to them goes double: David Spiro, Edward Mansfield, Sunita Parikh, Arvid Lakauskas, Charles Cameron, Hendrick Spruyt.

Finally, an inadequate tribute to my family. My son Gregory was born one month before Iraq invaded Kuwait. He watched so much CNN with me over the first nine months of his life that the first voice to which he consistently reacted was neither mine nor his mother's, but James Earl Jones'. Watching him grow up over the past three and one-half years has been occasionally frustrating, frequently amusing, and always rewarding. My daughter Emma was born shortly after the first draft of the book was completed, in the summer of 1993. Given the choice between changing diapers and checking footnotes, I'll take the diapers every time. Gregory and Emma are unmitigated blessings. My wife Cindy kept all of us together while pursuing her own career, taking care of the children on her own during my absences and keeping up my spirits when the research flagged or the writing was difficult. I cannot imagine life without her. It is to her that this book is dedicated.

A note on transliteration: I adopted a modified form of the Library of Congress transliteration system, adapted from the style notes of the *International Journal of Middle Eastern Studies*, in rendering Arabic words and names in this book. Thus a name that is usually rendered Saddam Hussein in English becomes Saddam Husayn, which is closer to the actual Arabic pronunciation. The major modification was to leave out the diacritical marks for long vowels and velarized consonants. I also used the common English spellings of the names of countries (Kuwait rather than al-kuwayt, for example). I trust that those who know Arabic will be able to tell the correct referent for the transliterated words in the book, and I hope that those who do not know Arabic will not be bothered by the occasional unusual spelling.

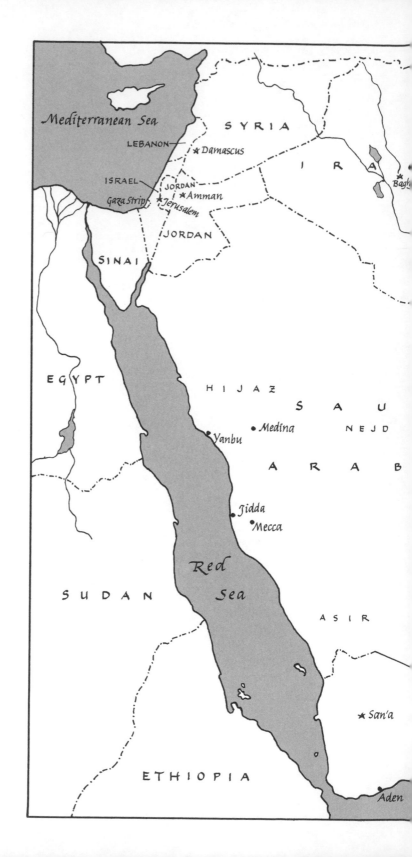

Caspian Sea

★Teheran

I R A N

Basra
Abadan
Bubiyan Is.
KUWAIT
★Kuwait

Bandar Abbas

EASTERN PROVINCE

Jubayl
Dhahran

Str. of Hormuz
Tunbs
Abu Musa

QATAR
Dubai

Riyadh

Abu Dhabi ★
Buraimi

A

UNITED ARAB EMIRATES

★Muscat

Nizwa

O M A N

Masirah Is.

Thamarit
D H U F A R
Salalah

Arabian Sea

Y E M E N
H A D R A M A W T

The Gulf Region

0   100   200   300 M.

0   100   200   300 K.   Ascherl

1
Introduction

FOUR TIMES OVER THE LAST TWENTY YEARS, THE AT-
tention of the United States—government and public, elite and
mass—has been focused on the Persian/Arabian Gulf region: during
the 1973–1974 oil embargo and 400 percent increase in oil prices,
the Iranian Revolution and hostage crisis of 1979–1981, the reflagging of the Kuwaiti oil tankers and naval deployments of 1987–1988,
and the Gulf War of 1990–1991.[1] The centrality of the monarchical
regimes of the Arab side of the Gulf (Saudi Arabia, Kuwait, Bahrain,
Qatar, United Arab Emirates, and Oman) to American policy and
American interests in each of these episodes is obvious and easy to
understand: they have the oil. In 1992, these six countries accounted for 20 percent of the world's oil production and nearly one-
half of the world's proven oil reserves. Saudi Arabia not only has the
largest proven oil reserves in the world, but also, given its small
population and thus relatively modest revenue needs, has the greatest latitude of any major oil producer in shifting its level of production. In times of supply shortfall, it has the capacity to increase
production and make up for losses elsewhere, as it did after the Iraqi
invasion of Kuwait. In tight oil markets, even a marginal decrease in
Saudi production can send oil prices shooting upward, as happened

1

in 1973 and 1979. All of these regimes have had close relations with the United States, particularly since the oil crisis of 1973–1974, but in some cases, like Saudi Arabia and Bahrain, dating back to World War II.

Unlike other countries that have played important roles in American foreign policy, these states have also been cast in high-profile and largely misleading roles in the public debate over American policy during the last two decades. In 1973–1974, they were the villains, as the stereotype of the rich oil *shaykh* entered American popular culture. In 1979–1981, they were the anachronisms, seen as the political kin of the fallen Shah of Iran, whom they would shortly follow into exile. During the reflagging operation, they were wealthy weaklings, rich enough to buy protection, but not strong enough to provide it themselves.

During the Gulf War, with U.S. opinion intensely concentrated on the Gulf for the better part of a year, the American public was exposed to a jumble of contradictory images of the Gulf monarchies. These regimes and their people, particularly Kuwait, were rightly portrayed by the Bush administration as victims of a brutal aggression. Saudi Arabia, which hosted most of the American forces sent to the Gulf, and the other states took on the public role of American allies, a stance guaranteed to elicit at least some favorable public reaction in the United States. The pictures of liberated Kuwaitis waving U.S. flags and thanking American soldiers were a tonic to a country whose troops had not received such a warm welcome elsewhere.

But negative media images were also prominent during the war. Saddam Husayn's contention that Kuwait and the other monarchies were relics of the past that needed to be swept away found some resonance in the United States. Complaints that America was fighting to defend "feudal, reactionary monarchies" abounded. Even commentators who rejected Saddam's claim to Kuwait frequently agreed with his contention that the oil monarchies were "too rich," and needed to redistribute their income to poorer Arab states. Some stories spoke of feckless Kuwaitis who partied in luxury abroad while U.S. troops fought for their homeland. The inevitable social frictions that arose between Saudis and the hundreds of thousands of American troops in their country led to numerous "clashing cultures" pieces in the U.S. media about how different American and Saudi social mores were concerning women, work, politics, and religion.

Popular portrayals of the ruling elites of these states, and by extension of their entire societies, have contributed to forming American "conventional wisdom" about how politics works in the Gulf monarchies. Such notions are based upon two general and at times conflicting assumptions. The first is that these regimes and the societies that they govern are "traditional." While traditionalism is rarely defined in any precise way, it usually means that tribal social structures and Islam are the basis of politics. In the conventional wisdom, tribalism and Islam lead to a number of consequences for the political process: institutions are meaningless, as all politics are personal; the forms of rule which exist now in these states have existed for hundreds of years, if not from time immemorial; political participation is not a serious issue; political loyalty is given and withdrawn on the basis of religious criteria; and personalistic rule by tribally-based elite families is culturally suited to the region.

The second of these assumptions is that these regimes are weak and fragile, anachronisms in a world about to enter the twenty-first century. The long-term trend against monarchies in the Middle East, with Iran providing the most recent case of the overthrow of a king, reinforces the historical American suspicion of monarchs. The social and economic upheavals of the oil boom are seen to have upset the "traditional" political order, calling into question whether the old forms can survive. The inability of the Gulf monarchies to defend themselves against larger, more powerful neighbors contributes to this sense of fragility.

The picture of politics in the Gulf monarchies that emerges from these two assumptions is basically consistent, whether put forward by proponents or opponents of close U.S. ties with these states: these are "traditional" regimes which are culturally distinct from the West but need Western help to maintain themselves. Proponents use this picture to argue that the monarchies need U.S. military and political support against their neighbors, and should not be pushed to conform to "Western" standards of democratization and human rights. Opponents of American commitment to these states portray regimes that do not share American values but need American support to maintain themselves domestically, allies that are both "politically incorrect" and unreliable because of their domestic fragility.

This book examines the bases of politics in the Gulf monarchies to see how far they differ from the conventional wisdom that dominates American public discourse about them. It argues that the role played by tribalism and Islam has changed over time, and that the importance of these concepts for the politics of the Gulf monarchies is a matter of debate and dispute in the countries themselves. The book also emphasizes that the key to understanding the domestic political processes of these countries is the enormous amount of wealth that oil revenues have placed in the hands of the state since the oil boom of the early 1970s. That wealth, and how it has been used, explains why these purportedly fragile regimes have been able to ride out the domestic and regional storms of the last two decades: the social changes occasioned by the oil boom, the Iranian Revolution and the rise of Islamic opposition movements, the Iran-Iraq war, and the combined military and ideological challenge of Saddam's invasion of Kuwait.

While the strength of the regimes has been underestimated by outside observers, so has the extent and importance of domestic political activity in the societies of the Gulf monarchies. Demands from society for governmental responsibility and popular participation have grown with the socioeconomic changes that oil wealth has brought. Paradoxically, those demands have been spurred by the same growth of state institutions that stabilized the monarchical regimes over the past two decades. Although usually hidden from foreign observers, "politics"—discussion of government performance and social goals, organization to affect decision making—are going on in these states. The tension generated by the institutionalization and growth of the state, the concomitant political demands that process creates within society, and the government's reactions to those demands are central themes of this work. Each of the regimes has dealt with these tensions and demands in different ways.

It is vitally important that Americans, both policymakers and the larger public, go beyond the conventional wisdom described above and develop a more informed understanding of these regimes and societies. Their foreign policies, whether dealing with regional challenges like Iran and Iraq or with the United States, can only be understood in terms of their domestic realities—rich countries with small populations and political systems subject to a number of pressures. The intersection of domestic realities with international political factors will determine their oil policies and their political futures. The tensions inherent in the U.S. desire both for stability in the Gulf and for reform in the monarchical regimes in the areas of human rights and democratization can only be managed through a clear understanding of their domestic politics. The most serious setback to American interests in the Gulf in the past two decades was not an international war, but a domestic political event—the Iranian Revolution—that radically altered the region's strategic balance. Misunderstanding of Iranian domestic politics contributed to U.S. inability either to avoid the outcome that occurred in Teheran or to anticipate and deal with this change in a coherent fashion.

This book concentrates on themes common to the politics of the six monarchical states on the Arab side of the Gulf. It is not intended to be a political history of each of them. They are different, with varied histories, population profiles, and political agendas. Where those differences have important political effects, they will be discussed. However, the thrust of this work is what they share, in terms of the dynamics of their politics, their reactions to their regional environment, and the challenges they face. It focuses particularly on specific events in the period immediately before and since the Iraqi invasion of Kuwait to illustrate the themes set out above. The notes and bibliography direct readers to the best sources on the modern political history of each individual state.

For the general reader, there follows a thumbnail introduction to each of the six Arab Gulf monarchies. In 1981 the six formed an international organization called the Gulf Cooperation Council (GCC), and they are sometimes collectively referred to as the "GCC states." Table 1 provides some basic statistical information about them.

SAUDI ARABIA

The Kingdom of Saudi Arabia is the largest of the six Gulf monarchies by far, with a land area about one-fourth the size of the

TABLE 1. ARAB GULF MONARCHIES—BASIC STATISTICAL INFORMATION

Country	Area Sq. Mi	Population Total	Citizen Population	Non-nationals % of Total Population	GDP US$ Billion 1990	Literacy Percent Adult Population	Oil Production 1000 Barrels Per Day 1992 Avg.
Bahrain	268	464,000	330,000	29	3.9	77	110
Kuwait	6,880	1,500,000*	625,000	60	23.0	73	1,025***
Oman	82,030	1,442,000	1,062,000	26	10.6	35	770
Qatar	4,427	413,000	141,000	66	7.4	82	396
Saudi Arabia	830,000	12,259,000**	8,066,400	34	104.7	62	8,438
UAE	30,000	1,825,000	531,000	70	33.8	55	2,328

* There are no official figures on Kuwaiti population since the Iraqi invasion. Estimates are based upon recent conversations with informed Kuwaitis.
** Saudi Arabia announced census results in December 1991, with a total population of 16.9 million, including 12.3 million citizens and 4.6 million foreign residents. *New York Times*, December 18, 1992, p. A8. The figure for citizen population differs markedly from the estimates made by Birks Sinclair & Associates, cited below. The official Saudi figure seems somewhat high.
*** Kuwaiti production by September 1993 had increased to 2.1 mbd.

Sources: Population statistics, for all countries other than Kuwait, are taken from Birks Sinclair & Associates, *GCC Market Report 1992*, Durham, 1992, as cited in Roger Hardy, "Arabia After the Storm: Internal Stability of the Gulf Arab States," Middle East Programme Report (The Royal Institute of International Affairs, 1992).
Adult Literacy: United Nations Development Program, *Human Development Report 1992* (New York: Oxford University Press, 1992).
Oil: U.S. Department of Energy, Energy Information Administration, *Monthly Energy Review*, March 1993. The figures for Bahrain and Oman are taken from *Petroleum Intelligence Weekly*, July 5, 1993, p. 1.
GDP: For Bahrain and Saudi Arabia, figure taken from official GCC publication cited in *al-Hayat*, August 10, 1993, p. 11; for other states taken from International Monetary Fund, *International Financial Statistics*, 1992 Yearbook and May 1993 monthly report.

United States. Most of the country is desert, and its population is very small for its vast extent. The citizen population is somewhere between eight and twelve million people, with about four million expatriates. Ninety percent of the population are Sunni Muslims. The Shi'i population is centered in the oil-producing Eastern province, on the Gulf coast. Other major regions of the kingdom are Nejd, the central Arabian heartland; Hijaz, the western coast of the country along the Red Sea, containing the holy cities of Mecca and Medina; and 'Asir, the southwestern portion of the country on the border with Yemen.

The founder of modern Saudi Arabia, King 'Abd al-'Aziz Al Sa'ud, known to many in the West as Ibn Saud, brought the territories that now make up the kingdom under his control between 1901 and 1934, using a mixture of military force, adept tribal politics, religious ideology, and skillful international diplomacy. Saudi territory was never under the control of any Western imperial power. The current king, Fahd, is one of the many sons of 'Abd al-'Aziz. A particularly austere and stringent interpretation of Islam, known as Wahhabism, is enforced by the state in Saudi Arabia, and the Saudi regime claims a special religious legitimacy based both on its adherence to the Wahhabi interpretation of Islam and its role as guardian of the holy places in Mecca and Medina. Oil was discovered in the kingdom in the 1930s, and commercial production began shortly after World War II. As of 1993, Saudi Arabia is the largest oil producer in the world, surpassing the combined production of the Commonwealth of Independent States.

KUWAIT

The state of Kuwait received its independence from Britain in 1961, having been a British protectorate since 1899. Its population before the Iraqi invasion of August 2, 1990, was approximately two million, less than half of whom were citizens. The population has decreased by 25 percent as a result of the Iraqi occupation and its aftereffects, with noncitizens continuing to make up over half of the total. Of the citizen population, about 75 percent are Sunni, including the ruling family, and 25 percent Shi'i.

The Al Sabah family provide the hereditary *amirs* (rulers) of Kuwait, though their rule is circumscribed by a powerful coterie of old merchant families that joined the Al Sabah in settling the country in the eighteenth century. Kuwait is the only one of the six Gulf monarchies with an active parliamentary tradition, despite the common British influence in the smaller states. That fact can be attributed to its receiving independence before massive oil revenues concentrated overwhelming power in the hands of the ruling family, and to the historical organization and cohesion of the original merchant families. It has been an oil producer since 1946.

BAHRAIN

Bahrain received its independence from Britain in 1971, having been a British protectorate since 1880 and under British influence since the mid-1800s. Seventy percent of its citizen population is Shiʿi, although the ruling shaykhs, from the Al Khalifa family, are Sunni. Bahrain was the first oil producer among the six monarchies, with production beginning in 1932, but its oil reserves are now almost exhausted. Service industries like tourism and finance play a major role in its economy. Its earlier oil wealth gave Bahrain a head start on its neighbors in developing educational and social institutions, contributing to its status as the most socially liberal of the six monarchies.

QATAR

Qatar received its independence from Britain in 1971, after being a British protectorate since 1916 and under British influence from the mid-1800s. It has the smallest population of any of the six Gulf monarchies, fewer than 500,000. Citizens make up only one-third of the total population. The citizen population is approximately 85 percent Sunni and 15 percent Shiʿi. The ruling Al Thani family is Sunni and professes the same Wahhabi interpretation of Islam as do the Al Saʿud. Oil production began in 1949; natural gas production accounts for a large share of the state income. Qatar has one of the highest per capita national incomes in the world.

UNITED ARAB EMIRATES

The United Arab Emirates (UAE) is a federation of seven emirates: Abu Dhabi, Dubai, Sharjah (al-Shariqa), Ra's al-Khayma, Fujayra, 'Um al-Qaywayn, and ᶜAjman. It received its independence from Britain in 1971, after being under de facto British control since the 1830s. Only 30 percent of its nearly two million people are citizens; of those, around 80 percent are Sunni (as are the ruling families of all seven shaykhdoms) and 20 percent Shiᶜi. The political structure of the federation is loose, with the rulers of the individual emirates preserving a large amount of autonomy. The president of the UAE, and its guiding force since inception, is the ruler of Abu Dhabi, Shaykh Za'id bin Sultan Al Nahyan.

Oil began to be produced in large quantities in the UAE, primarily in Abu Dhabi but also in Dubai and Sharjah, only in the 1960s. Dubai is a flourishing port city, the most lively and cosmopolitan on the Arab side of the Gulf, and is developing into a regional business, communications, and services center. Like Qatar, the per capita national income in the UAE is among the highest in the world.

OMAN

The Sultanate of Oman has a rich history as a commercial empire, extending its sway in the seventeenth century to Zanzibar and the East African coast. Although never formally a British protectorate, from the mid-nineteenth century British influence has been dominant. It received de facto independence in 1971, under the leadership of Sultan Qabus of the Al Saᶜid family. Most of the citizen population, comprising about three-quarters of the total population, profess the Ibadi sect of Islam, a branch of the Kharijite movement that rejected both Sunnism and Shiᶜism in the early years of Islam, although there are no political tensions between the Ibadis and the minority Sunnis. Less than 10 percent of the population is Shiᶜi. Oil production began in Oman only in the 1970s, and agriculture remains an important part of the economy. Up until 1970 the current Sultan's father kept the country largely isolated from the rest of the world.

2

The Bases of "Traditional" Politics: Islam and Tribalism

AMERICAN CONVENTIONAL WISDOM ABOUT POLITICS in the Gulf monarchies—that it is defined by immutable characteristics of Islam and tribalism—is not so much wrong as it is outdated. The founding and development of all these states depended very heavily on the ability of the ruling families to mobilize military and political support from Arabian tribes, and in some cases to use Islamic political ideologies to link various tribes (and other social groups like merchants and settled populations) in a larger political movement. Tribalism and Islam are central concepts for understanding the origins of these regimes. But the relationships between the institutions of religion and tribalism and the governments have changed markedly, particularly since the advent of enormous oil wealth in the 1970s. It is not enough to say that the political systems in the Gulf monarchies are based upon tribalism and Islam: we must look at *how* those factors affect politics now.

The power of that "conventional wisdom" to influence analysis is abetted by the Gulf monarchies themselves. They portray themselves to their own people and to the world as the embodiment of Arabian tribal values and (more in some cases than others) of Muslim piety. They have created an ideology of Islam and tribalism, based on their own interpretations of these concepts, to legitimate their rule domestically and internationally. The irony is that the symbols and rhetoric of tribalism and Islam have become more prominent at the same time that the institutions embodying these social formations have undergone drastic change. Nomadic pastoralism and the caravan trade, the economic bases of central Arabian tribalism, have virtually ceased to exist. The state now provides directly to the individual many of the benefits that in the past came from the tribe. The balance of power between the central authorities and the tribes is now squarely on the side of the former. Likewise the institutions of Islam are now much more dependent upon the state, and much more a subordinate part of the state apparatus, than was the case in the past.

These changes have not been accidental. Each of these regimes has worked assiduously to curtail the independent power of the tribes and to make tribal structures subordinate parts of their political systems. They have absorbed the institutions of Islam— mosques, schools, courts, scholarly organizations, *awqaf* (religious trusts)—into the state apparatus, to control and direct them. The versions of tribalism and Islam constructed by the Gulf monarchies have become important arms of the state, providing institutional support and ideological legitimation to the regimes. Citizens of these states are permitted to organize socially and participate politically through these sanctioned institutions. The governments supply money to support tribal and religious institutions and allow them the space to operate publicly. Such public space is largely denied to other types of social and political organization, like political parties or, with some limited exceptions, a free press.[1]

The unintended consequence of this policy, however, has been to encourage political opposition, when it arises, to organize on tribal and religious bases, both ideologically and institutionally. The regimes have no monopoly on the political interpretation of Islam and tribal values, and opponents do indict them for failing to live up to the standards they themselves profess. By limiting public space largely to tribal and Islamic institutions, it is natural that political opposition would tend to coalesce around the tribe, the mosque, or the religious school. Those movements that have operated on the fringes of sanctioned institutions, rather than those that have been driven underground, have presented the regimes with their most serious challenges.

THE TAMING OF ISLAM AND TRIBALISM

All the Gulf Arab monarchies have used Islamic rhetoric and symbols to legitimate themselves, but it is only in Saudi Arabia that the regime claims an explicitly religious justification for its rule. The origins of this claim date back to 1745, when Muhammad ibn Saʿud, ruler of a relatively small central Arabian oasis town called Dirʿiyya, formed an alliance with Muhammad ibn ʿAbd al-Wahhab, a scholar who was preaching a reform of religious practice through return to the strictest, most pristine interpretations of Islam. The alliance, cemented through generations by frequent intermarriage between the two families, was based upon the Saudi ruler accepting Ibn ʿAbd al-Wahhab's religious interpretation as the basis for his state, and the religious reformer recognizing the Al Saʿud as the *imams*, or religio-political leaders, of his movement. The fortunes of the Al Saʿud have waxed and waned in the two and half centuries since the alliance was formed, but the link between their rule and the puritanical "Wahhabi" interpretation of Islam has remained. This particular brand of Islamic ideology has been the cement holding together a polity that, before oil, had few economic resources and was subject to the competing loyalties of tribal particularism and regional identities.[2]

The relationship between Islamic institutions and political authority in Saudi Arabia has been closer than in the other monarchies. King ʿAbd al-ʿAziz Al Saʿud (Ibn Saud), the founder of the modern kingdom, relied heavily on the ʿulama (those trained in religious learning) for advice and administrative support, lacking even a rudimentary state bureaucracy. Even more importantly, ʿAbd al-ʿAziz used the Islamic ideology of Wahhabism to recruit and organize a potent military force known as the *Ikhwan* (Brotherhood) to extend the reach of his domains. Recruited from beduin tribes, the *Ikhwan* were settled in military-agricultural communes and instructed in the faith by the Saudi ʿulama. They became a powerful political force in the kingdom during the 1910s and 1920s, spearheading the Saudi conquest of the Hijaz (western part of Saudi Arabia, including the holy cities of Mecca and Medina), and encouraging ʿAbd al-ʿAziz to carry his *jihad* against the British client states to his north (Iraq and Transjordan) and east (Kuwait, Bahrain, and the Trucial Emirates). The *Ikhwan* leadership was critical of any hints that the Saudis were straying from the path of Wahhabism, or considering political accommodation with outside powers. Fearful that the *Ikhwan* would draw him into a direct confrontation with the British and alienate more moderate Muslims under his rule, ʿAbd al-ʿAziz eventually decided to confront them militarily. After receiving a favorable *fatwa* (religious judgment, plural *fatawa*) from the *ʿulama* in Riyad, he raised an army from among loyal tribal elements and townspeople and defeated the *Ikhwan* in a number of battles in 1929.[3]

The crushing of the *Ikhwan* was the essential first step to asserting the primacy of the Al Saʿud over the religious institutions in Saudi political life. With the beginnings of a bureaucratic state apparatus in the 1950s and 1960s, the *ʿulama* became marginalized politically in the kingdom, while maintaining their special, state-sanctioned role in certain areas of social policy. Secularly educated Saudis staffed many of the new bureaus and provided an alternative set of political advisers and administrative cadres. The *ʿulama* remain an important interest group within the kingdom, whose voice is heard by the rulers. Their particular role will be discussed in more detail below. Religious institutions in Saudi Arabia, however, are clearly subordinate to the political leadership.

Saudi Arabia is not the only Gulf monarchy where a religiously based political institution confronted a ruling family's desire to centralize political control in its hands. During the 1950s the Sultan of Oman faced a challenge to his control of the Omani interior from the Ibadi Imam. Ibadism is an offshoot of the Kharijite movement of the first Islamic century, which rejected both Sunnism and Shiʿism. Its Omani variant is now very similar to the Omani practice of Sunnism. Political, rather than theological, loyalties distinguished the sect. From the beginnings of the twentieth century the Sultan in Muscat and the Ibadi Imam in Nizwa had a workable *modus vivendi* dividing their spheres of influence. In the 1950s efforts by the British-backed Sultan to extend his influence into the interior, combined with the more aggressive stance taken by the new

Imam, led to armed conflict between the two. Saudi Arabia, involved in a border dispute with Oman, supported the Imam's challenge to the Sultan. In two campaigns, in 1955 and 1957–1959, the British-led forces of the Sultan put down the Imam's challenge and established direct Omani control over the interior. The Imam fled into political exile in Saudi Arabia.[4] Since that time there have been no indications of political opposition in the Sultanate based on Ibadism.

The taming of religious institutions has been a major part of state building in the Gulf Arab monarchies—in Saudi Arabia and Oman even requiring the use of military force. But, once the secular authority's supremacy was established, rulers sought to make Islamic institutions into agencies of the state. Including them in the state apparatus helped rulers, who had few resources at their disposal before oil wealth, to staff their governments, while still maintaining ultimate control over religious forces. By giving the *ulama* a role in the system, with some degree of power and status, rulers could earn their loyalty, reducing the chance of their becoming a source of opposition. The official *ulama* thus became an important element in the states' legitimation strategies, providing religious sanction to the political order.

Religious court systems in all these countries have been placed under the control of ministries of justice, with judges appointed by state authorities from among religious scholars. Secular legal institutions have been established, particularly in business and economic jurisdictions, reducing the authority of the religious courts. The governments have established or taken over financial and administrative responsibilities for religious schools and training institutions. High-ranking Sunni religious functionaries (and Ibadi counterparts in Oman) are appointed by the governments, while the leadership of Shi'i communities has remained more independent of the state. The governments designate officials, such as the Grand Mufti of Oman, or committees within their ministries of *awqaf* and religious affairs, to issue *fatawa* on major issues. In Saudi Arabia, the position of Grand Mufti became vacant in 1969. In 1970 a ministry of justice was established to supervise both religious and secular courts. The function of authoritative religious interpretation has been assumed by a state-appointed committee called the Directorate of Religious

Research, *Fatwas*, Proselytization, and Guidance.[5] It was the chairman of this body, Shaykh ʿAbd al-ʿAziz bin Baz, who issued the *fatwa* sanctioning the kingdom's call for American and other foreign troops after the Iraqi invasion of Kuwait, and the subsequent *fatwa* approving the coalition's offensive against the Iraqis.[6] Bin Baz was elevated to the position of Grand Mufti in July 1993 by King Fahd, an acknowledgment of his support for the regime during a difficult period. He is the first person to hold that office who is not a member of the Al Shaykh family, the descendants of Shaykh Muhammad Ibn ʿAbd al-Wahhab.[7]

Most of the *ulama*, be they judges, teachers, scholars, or preachers in local mosques, are now employees of the state. While the relationship between the higher echelons of the men of religion and the men of power in the Muslim Middle East has historically been close, the extent to which the state now monitors and controls lower-level *ulama* is unprecedented. In the past, a local mosque preacher in a mid-size Arabian city would have been chosen by the local notables who supported the mosque financially, or would have inherited his position from his father or uncle whom he had followed in pursuing a religious education. His salary would come from the local community or from the income generated from *awqaf* set up as bequests by wealthy patrons in the past. Now, that same local mosque is likely to have been built or refurbished with government funds, and the preacher is more likely than not to be appointed by the state as a salaried employee.[8] The administration of *awqaf* has been centralized in government ministries, removing that route to financial independence. Even in those instances where a mosque was built with private funds and hired a preacher independent of the state (particularly in the Shiʿi communities of Kuwait, Bahrain, and Saudi Arabia), the content of the Friday sermons and the activities of the *ulama* associated with it are likely to be monitored by state authorities from both the religious and the internal security bureaucracies.[9]

Saudi Arabia has seen the most extensive bureaucratization of religious institutions. As in the other monarchies, there is an elaborate system of religious courts for adjudicating personal status issues like marriage, divorce, and inheritance. The government has established Islamic universities in Riyad, Mecca, and Medina for the training of religious scholars and the large King Faysal Islamic Research Center in Riyad. Members of the *ᶜulama* have access to the state media for religious instruction and proselytization, and enjoy enormous influence over the content of nonreligious writings and programming under state auspices. The highest levels of the *ᶜulama* also enjoy direct access to the King for discussion of matters of concern to them. Certain aspects of state social policy, such as the role of women in society and some elements of educational policy, have been turned over to the *ᶜulama* by the regime.[10] The Saudi *ᶜulama's* influence is great in certain areas, but their role in other areas, such as state financial and economic affairs and foreign policy, has been limited. For the Saudi government, the trade-off is clear: power in certain areas in exchange for political loyalty and support.[11]

Saudi Arabia's special place in the Muslim world, as the home of the holy cities of Mecca and Medina, the particular legitimating role of Islam in the political system, and the vast oil wealth at the state's disposal have combined to produce a state religious bureaucracy of far greater size and power than those of the other monarchies. An entire ministry of the Saudi government is devoted to managing the annual pilgrimage to Mecca, in which the kingdom plays host to approximately one million visitors.[12] The state also supports the Committees for Enjoining Good and Forbidding Evil, whose members (known in Arabic as *mutawwaᶜin*) enforce the strict interpretation of Islamic social mores that is officially sanctioned in Saudi Arabia. The *mutawwaᶜin*, who are particularly prominent in urban areas, make sure that commercial establishments close during prayer times, guard against male-female interaction in public places, enforce restrictions against the production and consumption of alcohol, and monitor female dress to make sure that it adheres to standards of public modesty.[13]

The Saudi regime's interest in promoting its version of Islamic values and institutions is not limited to the domestic sphere. It sponsors and plays host to a number of international Islamic organizations, like the World Muslim League and the World Assembly of Muslim Youth, that promote Islamic activities and Saudi-supported interpretations of Islamic doctrine in many parts of the Muslim world.[14] The government and members of the royal family finance the construction of mosques and Islamic institutes throughout the Muslim world, and in Europe and North America. Riyad was also the driving force behind the founding of the Organization of the Islamic Conference (OIC) in 1972. The OIC, an international organization of Muslim states, holds periodic summit meetings. Its permanent secretariat is located in Jidda.

An intended consequence of the development of this vast complex of Saudi religious institutions is to produce and provide employment for a large cadre of graduates from religious educational institutions. By providing the *ulama* with salaries, social status, positions of political importance, and opportunities to spread their message outside the kingdom, the Al Sa^cud family has tried to link the ideological and political interests of the men of religion to the Saudi regime. By and large, the political leadership has succeeded in that goal. Part of the bargain, however, has been acceptance by the higher ranks of the official *ulama* of a political position clearly subordinate to the royal family. On no occasion in the last four decades have religious leaders holding high state office openly challenged the Al Sa^cud on matters of political import. Rather, they have ratified political decisions on such important issues as women's education, technical modernization (radio, television, etc.), the deposition of King Sa^cud and the succession of King Faysal in 1964, the use of force against the religious zealots who captured the Grand Mosque in Mecca in 1979, and the conduct of policy during the Gulf crisis of 1990–1991.[15]

This pattern of dealing between state authorities and religious institutions that has evolved during the twentieth century—from a position of rough equality to that of subordination of religious institutions to the state, with occasional use of force to solidify that subordination—is mirrored in the evolution of relations between the states and the tribes. In one way or another, all of the ruling families of the Gulf relied upon tribal political connections and military strength to come to power. Though generally they have been settled in urban areas for at least 200 years, if not longer, ruling families maintained their historic ties to nomadic tribes and asserted the right to rule based (to a greater degree in the smaller states than in Saudi Arabia) upon their tribal lineage. Now they all utilize tribal and other cultural symbols to convince citizens that their political systems are authentic and deserving of support.

The Al Sabah in Kuwait and the Al Khalifa in Bahrain both established their rule in the late eighteenth century, as part of a migration to the coast by segments of the Bani ʿUtub tribe of the ʿUnayza confederation. The Al Nahyan laid claim to Abu Dhabi in the 1760s, as the hereditary paramount shaykhs of the Bani Yas tribal confederation, some of whose members had moved to the coast from the interior of the Arabian Peninsula. The Al Saʿid of Oman originate from the Al Bu Saʿid tribe, which has been an important base of their support, but their claim to govern all Oman stems from the election of the founder of the dynasty to the Ibadi Imamate in the early 1700s. The Al Saʿud have their origins in the ʿUnayza confederation, but from the time of their immigration to central Arabia in the fifteenth century, and particularly from their assertion of rule in the early 1700s, they had been a settled urban clan. Extending their rule beyond the confines of their limited home territory depended upon their ability to gather tribal support around the religious banner of Wahhabism. Like the Al Saʿid in Oman, the religious appeal was essential at the beginning to expanding their tribal support base.[16]

Tribal support was absolutely essential in founding these states. With no standing armies to speak of, the early leaders had to negotiate with tribal shaykhs to raise fighting forces. What administrative mechanisms existed, outside religious institutions, were mediated through the shaykhs. The ability to play off inter- and intra-tribal rivalries was an essential element of statesmanship for Gulf rulers right up to the last few decades, and in a limited way to the present day. But the tribes were fickle supporters. They could easily shift their allegiances, either to challengers from within the ruler's family or tribal group, or to rival claimants. They were difficult to discipline, particularly to extract tax revenue from, as they could mobilize their own military forces. If sufficiently provoked, whole tribes in some cases would simply pick up and move to another jurisdiction.

Gulf rulers over the last three centuries have followed a number of strategies to lessen their dependence upon tribal loyalties to maintain their rule. They cultivated support from urban populations, some of whom still claimed tribal affiliations but could be mobilized on the basis of economic interests and urban solidarity.[17] ᶜAbd al-ᶜAziz Al Saᶜud's reconquest of central Arabia in 1901 and the Eastern province (al-'Ahsa) in 1913 was accomplished with a military force made up predominantly of townspeople, not tribesmen. It was not until 1916 that he developed the fusion of tribal and religious power in the *Ikhwan*. When, in 1929, the *Ikhwan* challenged ᶜAbd al-ᶜAziz's rule, he again turned to his urban populations for military support.[18] In the coastal emirates, the rulers came to rely on local merchants, particularly those involved in the pearl trade, for taxes and political support.[19]

As the case of the *Ikhwan* in Saudi Arabia indicates, tribes posed more direct dangers to ambitious Gulf state-builders than proving uncertain allies; at times, they were real military threats. The geographical and functional extensions of state authority, particularly in Saudi Arabia and Oman, where substantial geographical hinterlands encouraged tribal autonomy, at times elicited armed opposition from the tribes. In the case of Saudi Arabia, ᶜAbd al-ᶜAziz not only had to confront the *Ikhwan*, but previously faced the tribally based military challenge of the Rashidi dynasty of the Jabal Shammar area (defeated in 1921) and the Hashemite dynasty in Hijaz (defeated in 1924) in his geographical expansion of Saudi rule. Hashemite intrigue, aimed at stirring up tribal opposition to the Saudis, continued for decades after his capture of Hijaz.[20] Both the Jabal Akhdar revolt of the 1950s and the Dhufar revolt of 1963–1975 against the Sultan's authority in Oman raised the bulk of their forces on a tribal basis, even though the former revolt was made in the name of religion and the latter came to be led by left-wing ideologues.[21]

The rulers not only sought out local allies to balance the tribes, but also looked for international support. During the period between 1820 and 1971, the major foreign power in the Gulf was Great Britain. Under the pretext of protecting the maritime trade routes to India, Britain became increasingly involved in the politics of the Gulf coast. In exchange for ceding control over foreign and defense policy, the shaykhs who received British recognition obtained in return commitments of British defense against regional rivals, arms for their own forces, and financial subsidies. British protection was vital in maintaining the smaller emirates of the coast against the more powerful forces of the Ottoman and Persian empires and, in the first half of the twentieth century, the expansionist Saudi state.

British support lessened rulers' reliance on tribal backing. Britain provided military and police forces if rulers were challenged domestically. British subsidies lessened the rulers' need for tax revenues and gave them the ability to offer the tribes financial inducements for loyalty or, at least, quiescence. Even ᶜAbd al-ᶜAziz Al Saᶜud, who never entered into a protectorate treaty with Britain as did the rulers of the smaller emirates, benefited from his relationship with the imperial power. British subsidies and arms helped him to defeat his Ottoman-backed tribal rivals, the Rashidis, during World War I and to ride out the economic crisis of the 1930s, when the world depression severely reduced the revenues his state collected from the annual pilgrimage to Mecca.

Bahrain provides another example of how British intervention altered the relationship between the ruling family and the tribes. Prior to the 1920s, most of the important economic activity on the island was organized on an explicitly tribal basis. Individual tribes controlled pearl fishing in various coastal towns, with their own courts and armed forces to police their activities. Agricultural land was divided up and administered directly by members of the Al Khalifa family, ruling over the largely Shiᶜi peasantry. The Al Khalifa amir had no formal control over these activities, though by dint of his personal stature, he did have influence throughout the island. The urban merchant class also administered many of its own affairs, though with a more direct role for the amir.

The British Political Agents in the 1920s, Maj. H. R. P. Dickson and Maj. C. K. Daly, enforced a number of administrative and legal changes that centralized power in the office of the ruler and the new organs of the state. The tribal courts that supervised the pearl trade were abolished, replaced by a centralized court system administered from the capital. The Al Khalifa agricultural estates system was ended with the introduction of private property and laws governing landlord-tenant relations. One-third of the oil revenues accruing to the state (the first oil concession in Bahrain was granted in 1928; oil was discovered in 1932) was set aside for the ruling family, allowing many collateral members, deprived of their livelihood with the end of the estate system, to be put on pension. The right to collect taxes was reserved to the state. Military formations, particularly in the estates, were disbanded, and efforts undertaken to establish a central police force. A municipal council was set up in the capital and the Customary Council, which adjudicated commercial issues, was revamped, the Agent appointing five of its members and the ruler five.

These changes did not occur peacefully. Britain forced the abdication of the ruler, Shaykh ʿIsa, in favor of his son Hamad in 1923 because of ʿIsa's opposition to the changes. Attacks on Shiʿi villages by members of the Al Khalifa, who lost control over their estates, and by tribes hurt by the centralization led to the dispatch of British gunboats to the island to restore order. Some of the Al Khalifa responsible for the attacks were brought before state courts, an unprecedented act, and others were exiled. The Dawasir tribe, which controlled a pearling village, left *en masse* for the Arabian Peninsula, where they sought the support of the Saudis in mounting military expeditions to regain what they saw as their ancestral rights. Britain made clear that it would not tolerate such activity, lessening King ʿAbd al-ʿAziz's enthusiasm for supporting them. Their return to Bahrain was made conditional on their recognition of the state's tax collectors, police, and judicial officials.[22]

The irony of subsequent Bahraini political history, very similar to that of the other Gulf monarchies, is that the curbing of tribal and family autonomy did not end tribal and family power; it simply changed the way it was exercised. The office of the ruler and the administrative instruments of his state became dominant. Oil revenues, going directly to the state, increased its power. But once the Sunni Arab tribes and ruling family were no longer major threats, the rulers turned to them to staff many important state offices. Al Khalifa have come to control the "political" (as opposed to technocratic) ministries in the government and a number of other bureaucratic positions. The armed forces and police forces are headed by members of the family and recruited largely from Bahrainis with tribal backgrounds. During the political agitation of the 1950s, when urban Sunnis and Shiʿis were making common cause against the government, the family and the tribes provided support and, very literally, political "muscle" in the streets for the ruler. British reforms in Bahrain changed the balance of power between the ruler and these previously autonomous groups, but did not break the political alliances holding them together.

In effect, the political map of the Arab side of the Gulf, both in terms of state boundaries and ruling regimes (with the exception of the Saudis), was determined by British policy in the area during the late nineteenth and early twentieth centuries. Britain entered a very fluid tribal political milieu on the Arab side of the Gulf in the nineteenth and early twentieth centuries, where clan and tribal political entities rose and fell, and territorial boundaries were both amorphous and fluctuating. Both for their own immediate political purposes, and out of a mistaken belief that what they saw on the ground at the time must have been the case from time immemorial, the British froze the existing tribal-political map. By recognizing and protecting some families as rulers in certain territories, they interrupted the historical process of rise and decline. By strengthening the hands of the rulers, they altered the balance of political power domestically. By protecting the smaller states militarily, they halted the expansion of the Saudi state in the first half of the twentieth century. As a result, in the 1960s and 1970s they bequeathed independent sovereign states to the heirs of those ruling families.[23]

British protection, while essential to the survival of the smaller emirates, was not an unmixed blessing for the rulers. Taking the king's coin, they increasingly had to march to the beat of his colonial drummer. British officials at the 1922 Uqayr conference drew the Kuwaiti border in such a way that Kuwaitis still feel deprived of their historical territory, in favor of the British client state of Iraq and the more powerful Saudis. To lessen the power of any particular coastal emirate, the British sliced up jurisdictions like salami. In 1868 they recognized the Al Thani as the predominant clan in Doha, autonomous from Bahrain and Abu Dhabi, and in 1916 signed a protectorate agreement with them guaranteeing their rule over Qatar.[24] The fact that there are two emirates in the UAE governed by clans from the Bani Yas confederation (Abu Dhabi and Dubai) and two from the Qasimi confederation (Sharja and Ra's al-Khayma), as well as other emirates controlled by very small and

historically minor tribes, is not simply the result of tribal fractious-
ness. Britain encouraged these kinds of divisions.[25]

During the twentieth century, Britain came to control not only
foreign policy but domestic politics in the smaller emirates as well.
Bahrain was the first of the emirates in which Britain took a decisive
role in internal affairs, as discussed; in many ways, it served as a
model for subsequent policy elsewhere. British administrators ran
what bureaucracy there was, British officers commanded the police
and armed forces, British taxmen collected the customs. Rulers who
were inconvenient, because of excessive independence or excessive
incompetence, were removed from power by Britain. As recently as
1970, a year before the end of their protectorate treaty with Oman,
the British engineered the abdication of Sultan Saᶜid and the succession of his son Qabus.

While rulers used urban groups and the British to lessen their
reliance upon the tribes, it was the coming of oil revenues that
finally and decisively shifted the balance of power away from tribal
structures and toward the state. With oil money, the rulers ceased to
rely upon local groupings—tribal or urban—for financial support.
They now had money to give away, or, better, to bargain for political
loyalty and service. Tribal leaders were put on state payrolls, with
generous regular salaries replacing the irregular and less lucrative
subsidies of the past. Their ability to provide for their tribesmen has
come to depend on the state, rather than on their own and tribal
resources. Tribal shaykhs have become salaried employees of the
state.

Even more important, rulers, through the new mechanisms of
the state, can appeal directly to tribesmen, without the mediating
figure of the shaykh. Education, medical treatment, subsidized food,
housing, and state employment are granted directly to citizens,
shifting their political focus (if not always their political loyalty)
toward the state and away from the tribe. Good salaries draw
tribesmen into the regular armed forces, eliminating the need for
rulers to go through the shaykhs to recruit tribal levies. The concentration of education, state employment, and economic activity in
major cities draws some tribesmen out of the desert into urban life.
While the social importance of their tribal origins remains important (on issues such as marriage patterns, for example), their politi-

cal and economic reliance on the tribe is much reduced. In the past, tribal structures offered physical and economic security to their members; in all the Gulf monarchies, the state has now assumed that role. (Chapter 3 on oil and politics discusses these changes in detail.)

The most telling sign of the changed political role of the tribes in the Arabian Peninsula is their increasing urbanization and sedentarization. By 1970, only around 10 percent of the Saudi population lived a nomadic lifestyle, as opposed to roughly 40 percent in the 1950s.[26] The oil boom of the 1970s decreased that percentage even further. In the smaller states as well there have been sustained efforts, funded by oil wealth, to settle tribesmen. Even without direct government efforts, the move from the desert to the city has been an inevitable by-product of the economic changes brought about by oil wealth.[27] Sedentarization means that tribesmen are directly dependent economically on the state—for their houses, probably for their jobs (if they take jobs), and for social services. They are therefore easier to control politically, either through their shaykhs or bypassing their shaykhs if necessary. The prospect of armed, organized tribal opposition to state authority, the most important impediment to state building in the Arabian Peninsula over the centuries, has in effect disappeared in the Arab Gulf monarchies of today.

Perhaps the clearest indication of the changes that have occurred in the past century in the relations between the states and the tribes in the Gulf monarchies is the contrast with the situation in the other Arabian Peninsula state, Yemen. With oil discovered there only in the 1980s, and as yet in limited amounts, the Yemeni government has not had the financial resources with which to entice the Yemeni tribes into a subordinate position within the political system. Nor has it been able to muster the military capacity to break tribal autonomy in any final way. As a result, tribal forces in Yemen are still independent, in some cases well armed, actors in Yemeni politics. No tribe in the Gulf monarchies has been able to maintain an independent military capacity; many tribes in Yemen do. Though the central government in Yemen has vastly increased its capacity to deal with the tribes over the past two decades, to this day there are areas where agents of the state enter only on tribal sufferance. Tribal blockades of roads are not uncommon. Armed conflict between tribes arises, beyond the ability of the state to control. In some instances, the armed forces of the tribes confront those of the state. These manifestations of tribal independence no longer occur in the Gulf monarchies.

THE USES OF ISLAM AND TRIBALISM

The conventional wisdom about the religious and tribal nature of politics in the Gulf monarchies misses an essential fact. Establishing state authority has necessarily meant subordinating Islamic and tribal institutions to state supervision, if not outright control. However, that does not mean that those institutions, and the rhetoric and symbols that accompany them, are politically unimportant. Having "tamed" Islam and tribalism (or at least believing that they are tamed), the ruling families have appropriated these institutions, symbols, and rhetoric into an ideology of support for their rule. What most Westerners see as a "traditional" political culture is in fact a construction of recent decades, in which rulers employ a political language redolent of Islamic and tribal overtones to convince their citizens of the legitimacy of their political system. The rulers portray their system as representing the best of religious and tribal traditions, and contend that obedience to it is a religious and cultural obligation. They use these images and institutions to "forge emotive links with the populace over which [they] rule," and thus to gain legitimacy.[28] If one of the markers of "traditional" politics is the absence of ideology—a consciously articulated justification for a particular political system—then the Gulf monarchies are hardly "traditional."

A central element of this legitimation formula common to all of the monarchies is the notion of the ruler as the paramount shaykh (*shaykh al-masha'ikh*) of all the tribes in the country. In that capacity, rulers maintain very public relations with tribal leaders, meeting them not from behind Western-style desks, but in the tribal tradition of the *majlis* (council). Such meetings now rarely occur in tents, but usually in air-conditioned palaces, and are recorded so that clips can be shown on evening television news programs. But the effort to maintain ties with the symbols of the past and to use those authority structures to bolster the legitimacy of the rulers is obvious. The Sultan of Oman makes a yearly progress through the interior and southern parts of the country, receiving tribal leaders and local notables. Senior members of the Al Saʿud also visit tribal areas regularly.

Rulers also use more tangible means to encourage their subjects to think of themselves as tribesmen in a political system whose chain of loyalties culminates in the king, amir, or sultan. They dispense patronage through tribal leaders, according them a place of influence in the political system and reinforcing tribal identifications among those who eventually receive that patronage. They accept, even tacitly encourage, the prominence of personal and tribal connections in hiring practices in state agencies. In Kuwait, the only Gulf monarchy with an elected parliament, the government has drawn the districts to overrepresent tribal constituencies. Many of the tribes hold, in effect, primary elections to produce the candidates (two in each district) whom the tribe will support. While such elections are not technically permitted under Kuwaiti electoral law, they are tolerated, if not encouraged, by the government. Tribal connections can be particularly important in recruitment into the armed forces and police forces of all these states. The Saudi National Guard, a force independent of the regular army and headed by Crown Prince ʿAbdallah, has units explicitly organized along tribal lines.

Even in matters as apparently mundane as dress, there is an effort to portray rulers as true inheritors of the Arabian tribal tradition. All the Gulf rulers have continued to wear the traditional *thobe* (full-length garment) and *kuffiya* headdress (in Oman the slightly different turban). It is interesting to note that the leaders of Yemen and Iraq, who donned Western-style suits or military uniforms after their "revolutions," are now frequently pictured on official occasions and in state propaganda in "tribal" garb. In Oman all state employees on official business are required to wear the *janbiyya*, the curved dagger. Saʿud al-Faysal, the Foreign Minister of Saudi Arabia and son of the late King Faysal, in the 1970s would occasionally appear in international fora like the U.N. in a Western business suit. Now he appears in *thobe* and *kuffiya*. Bandar ibn Sultan, the Saudi ambassador to the United States, whose wardrobe is as stylishly European as any Western ambassador's, wore *thobe* and *kuffiya* at the Madrid peace conference in the spring of 1992. The only exceptions to this rule are the ruling family members who are officers in the armed services, who appear in Western-style uniforms. Sultan Qabus of Oman is the only Gulf ruler who sometimes dons a uniform for public occasions.

The issues of dress and public affirmation of tribal structures are part of a larger intellectual agenda pursued by the Gulf monarchies in the name of *turath* (heritage). State-supported projects in all the Gulf monarchies attempt to preserve or recapture aspects of economic and social life that have been in decline since the advent of the oil era. These projects are a way of affirming the cultural values and uniqueness of their society in the face of Western cultural influences. They also implicitly strive to connect the political system with these cultural manifestations, as a way of asserting the authenticity of the monarchical-tribal form of rule in these societies. Some projects are explicitly tribal in content, such as support for camel breeding and camel racing by the Saudi royal family, and some of the folklore studies promoted by the various states. In Oman the government has undertaken an ambitious program for restoring the old forts that dot the countryside. This project not only helps preserve Oman's history, but also subtly asserts the relatively recent control that the central government has established over these symbols of regional autonomy and, at times, rebellion.

Folklore is not limited to the desert. The smaller states, always more focused on the sea, have encouraged the study of the history, economics, and sociology of the pearl diving and shipbuilding industries, and the folk customs of urban settlements. National museums in Kuwait, Bahrain, Qatar, Dubai, and Oman portray aspects of pearl diving, pre-oil trade, and urban social customs. Abu Dhabi in the UAE supports an open-air "heritage village," where guests can inspect re-creations of markets and village architecture, watch tribal dances, and sample local cuisine. The state and the ruling families in Qatar, Bahrain, the UAE, and Oman subsidize craftsmen in constructing traditional Gulf sailing vessels. To coordinate and support the study of folklore, the monarchies (along with Iraq) in 1982 joined together to establish the Arab Gulf States Folklore Center, headquartered in Doha. Its board of directors is comprised of the ministers of information of the major donor states.[29] The effort to project certain cultural images is not limited to domestic audiences. Perhaps the best known example to Americans of such state-supported efforts to portray certain cultural and historical pictures of society was the exhibit "Saudi Arabia: Yesterday and Today" that toured the United States in 1989–1990. That exhibit emphasized the seamless integration of tribal traditions, Islam, modern technologies, and advanced social services in the kingdom.

Jill Crystal provides a fascinating discussion of how Qatar, the Gulf monarchy with the shortest history and least distinctive set of social and political institutions, upon independence faced the problem of creating what she terms a "civic myth." The government started with an archeological study tasked with a very specific mandate: to create a national museum. The British team that conducted the study, with the cooperation of the highest levels of the government, produced a wealth of material. The information ministry organized a national acquisition campaign for the museum, encouraging Qataris to donate items from their private collections. Older Qataris, whose life stories encapsulate the historical development of the state, were recruited for the museum staff. The centerpiece of the museum, around which the other displays are organized, is the Al Thani amir's palace from the turn of the century, asserting in a physical way the link between the country's history and its rulers. The museum, opened in 1975, has been a great success, winning international awards and, more important, becoming very popular with Qataris.[30]

Promotion of the "civic myth" in Qatar and in the other Gulf monarchies is an important government priority, primarily the responsibility of the ministries of information. They control the media in their countries, in most cases with a very firm and direct hand. Newspapers in Kuwait have the most freedom from government control in the Gulf, and in fact are frequently critical of government policies, but censorship has been imposed for long periods in the past. Newspapers in Bahrain and the UAE do not have the same freedom as those in Kuwait, but enjoy somewhat more latitude than those in Saudi Arabia, Qatar, and Oman. In all the states, television and radio are directly under the control of the information ministries. As mentioned above, they promote cultural and folklore studies and exhibitions for both domestic and foreign audiences. The ministries also support academic and popular publications, in Arabic and in Western languages, that portray the governments' preferred view of themselves, their past, and their people. In many cases they act as censors of printed and video material entering the country (in Saudi Arabia the religious authorities vet incoming material). They control access of foreign journalists and researchers to these countries.

The "civic myth" in the smaller states is based mainly upon interpretations of history and culture. It is only in Saudi Arabia that specific Islamic themes are an integral part of the ruling ideology, stemming from the historic alliance between Muhammad ibn Saʿud and Muhammad ibn ʿAbd al-Wahhab in 1745. Saudi rulers have continued to affirm the importance of this ideological basis for their rule, even as they have endeavored to bring the *ulama* more and more under state control. They enforce the strict Wahhabi interpretation of social behavior as state policy, and allow the *mutawwaʿin* wide latitude in enforcement. Wahhabi *ulama* dominate the airwaves in the state media and are sent abroad on proselytizing missions. The texts of the movement are reprinted and distributed at state expense both domestically and internationally. Saudi rulers have always averred that the Quran is the constitution of the state (and by implication that their rule is religiously sanctioned). The recent "basic system of government" promulgated by the king in March 1992 states explicitly, in its first clause, that the constitution of the kingdom remains the Quran, though for all intents and purposes the "basic system" is the functional equivalent of a constitution.[31] Long before the Iranian Revolution, and with some fervor thereafter, the Saudis have contended that theirs is the model "Islamic state."

Another aspect of the Al Saʿud's particular claim to religious legitimacy is their control of the holy cities of Mecca and Medina and their management of the annual Muslim pilgrimage. This element is more functional than doctrinal in nature. In fact, since the conquest of the holy cities by ʿAbd al-ʿAziz in 1924 (and some unfortunate incidents involving his zealous *Ikhwan* troops), the Saudis have emphasized that their custody of the holy places is a trust for the entire Muslim world, not an exclusively Wahhabi inheritance. That the government can provide the facilities and organizational wherewithal to accommodate the hundreds of thousands of Muslims who make the pilgrimage every year is a matter of great pride at home and of international stature in the Muslim world. The Saudis have undertaken numerous renovations of the holy places under explicit royal patronage. In the mid-1980s King Fahd, in a specific attempt to blunt the Iranian revolutionary contention that monarchy is an "un-Islamic" form of government, adopted the title "Custodian of the Two Holy Mosques" (*khadim al-haramayn al-sharifayn*).

The centrality of the Islamic aspect of the Saudi legitimation formula was emphasized by the king immediately after the Gulf War. There was much speculation outside the country, and some discussion inside it, to the effect that the crisis would lead to a reevaluation of political principles in the kingdom. On March 5, 1991, shortly after the liberation of Kuwait, King Fahd addressed his country in a televised speech, a rare occurrence that underlined the importance of his remarks. He asserted that the nature and duties of Saudi Arabia and its people are different from those of any other country, because of its role as the protector of the holy places of Mecca and Medina. The king went on to say:

> On this basis we will not adopt any principle of social organization except those which emerge as beneficial to Islam and to Muslims, on the condition that they do not differ from or oppose what God has made clear in His almighty Book, and what His gracious Prophet, His rightly-guided Caliphs, and the Imams of the Muslims have made clear. Therefore we are never interested in any way, shape or form with those who want to say that this country is a backward country. . . .
> Why are we backward or underdeveloped? Because we hold fast to the Book of God and the Sunna of His Prophet? This is a strength and an honor. We take pride in it. . . . I promise before God that the Islamic faith is our basis, our foundation, our starting point. What contradicts it we are not interested in and will not follow.[32]

The other Gulf monarchies rely less on explicit religious justifications in their legitimacy formulas. The Al Thani in Qatar also subscribe to the Wahhabi interpretation and enforce as strict social laws as do the Saudis. They cannot, however, claim a political inheritance from the founder of the movement himself. The Al Sa'id sultans of Oman have made no effort to reclaim the now vacant Ibadi Imamate. The other ruling families make no claim to a special religious status. Bahrain, Abu Dhabi, Dubai, and just recently

Oman, in order to encourage tourism, even permit the sale of alcoholic beverages in their countries. None of the families, however, would assert a completely secular basis for their right to rule. All claim the *shariʿa* (Islamic law) as a basis of their legal systems and Islam as the religion of the state.

The legitimation formulas used by the regimes in the Gulf monarchies have been remarkably successful. Their interpretations of tribal and Islamic values are obviously accepted by large numbers of citizens. It should not be forgotten that these interpretations are constructs, not ineffable truths. They remain contested, both domestically and regionally, as we will see below. It is clear, however, that they strike many in their societies as culturally authentic. The very fact that these regimes—written off as anachronisms during the Arab nationalist era of the 1950s and 1960s, identified as the next victims of the Islamic "wave" purportedly unleashed by the Iranian Revolution, challenged militarily and politically by the Iraqi invasion of Kuwait—have survived all these challenges means they must be doing something right. Their ideological efforts to link citizens to rulers have been at least as plausible, if not more so, than those of the Baʿthist regimes to their north and the Republic of Yemen to their south and west. Tribal heritage and Islam are extremely important in the lives of many of the citizens of these states. The Gulf monarchs are not appealing to sentiments foreign to those whom they rule.

ISLAM, TRIBALISM, AND OPPOSITION

While the Gulf monarchies may have "tamed" the institutions of tribalism and Islam, they have not completely neutralized these concepts in the political sphere. Indirectly, they may even have contributed to the growing strength of Islamic political movements in their societies. Particularly in Saudi Arabia, the rulers, by asserting an Islamic justification for their rule, have established a very strict standard against which to be held. It is harder simply to ignore and/or suppress voices claiming the rulers are not living up to their own ideals than it is to do the same to Arab nationalist and leftist opposition voices that reject the political system entirely. By legitimizing Islamic discourse in politics, regimes to some extent legitimize opposition platforms that use the same language.

Islam is a contested concept in the political realm, as the ideological competition between Saudi Arabia and revolutionary Iran demonstrates. There are those in the Gulf monarchies who interpret Islam's political implications differently from the governments. Obvious examples are offered by the Shiʿi minorities in Kuwait and Saudi Arabia and the Shiʿi majority in Bahrain. Particularly in the early and mid-1980s, inspired by the Iranian Revolution and supported by the Iranian government, underground Shiʿi organizations in Kuwait and Bahrain conducted violent campaigns against the regimes there. A coup plot in Bahrain in 1981 and an attempt to assassinate the Kuwaiti amir in 1985 were among the most publicized of these activities. Shiʿa in Saudi Arabia's Eastern province clashed with police in early 1980, when tensions generated by the Iranian Revolution were at their height. The failures of such groups to foment popular uprisings on the Iranian model, combined with the waning of revolutionary enthusiasm and more cautious policies in Iran itself, have lessened the salience of violent Shiʿi opposition in the region. In all three countries, Shiʿi organizations and leaders are now professing loyalty to the existing political systems and pressing for guarantees of their rights and an expanded role *within* the system. (This trend is discussed in Chapter 4.)

Islamic activists, however, are by no means limited to the Shiʿa. Sunni Islamic movements in Kuwait (which did well in the October 1992 elections) and in Bahrain advocate making the *shariʿa* the sole basis of law in their countries, not simply one of them, as it is now. The most prominent Islamic activist in Bahrain in recent years is not a member of the Shiʿi majority, but a Sunni professor of Islamic studies at the University of Bahrain. Dr. ʿAbd al-Latif Mahmud Al Mahmud was arrested in December 1991 after his return from a conference in Kuwait where he delivered a paper criticizing the Gulf regimes and calling for directly elected legislatures with real powers in the Gulf states. He was released shortly thereafter. Bahrainis across sectarian and political lines expressed support for his release, and he remains a popular preacher in one of the Sunni mosques.[33] The irony of the recent growth of Sunni movements in the monarchies, particularly in Kuwait, Bahrain, and Saudi Arabia, is that these movements were encouraged by the governments in the early 1980s, in reaction to the Iranian Revolution and as a counterbalance to Shi'i organizations.[34] There are other Sunni activists who agree with the official interpretations of Islam, but do not see them fulfilled by their leaders. The followers of Juhayman al-'Utaybi, who took over the Grand Mosque in Mecca in November 1979, claimed that the Al Sa'ud regime had lost its right to rule because it had strayed from the tenets of Wahhabi Islam upon which the kingdom had been built.[35]

The most interesting case of increased activism by Sunni Islamists since the Gulf War has been in Saudi Arabia. Criticism of the government has come not from suppressed groups or marginal individuals, but from 'ulama and religious activists who hold positions within the state's religious bureaucracy. While not overtly challenging the right of the Al Sa'ud to rule the country, or resorting to violence like those who precipitated the events of November 1979, they have used the Islamic rhetoric of the regime and the platforms supplied by the regime's religious institutions to question in a sharp and direct way aspects of Saudi domestic and foreign policy. In response, the regime has adopted a two-pronged strategy. On the one hand, the king has reaffirmed the close relationship between the government and the religious establishment, emphasizing the state's fidelity to the principles of Islam. On the other hand, he has pointed in no uncertain terms to limits on religious dissent, cracking down on the most vocal critics, and reasserting the government's ultimate leadership of religious institutions.

Discontent began to surface in religious circles about the presence of American and other foreign forces in the kingdom during the Gulf crisis, but it was relatively low-key.[36] The government was careful to defend its policies during the crisis in Islamic terms, soliciting and receiving *fatwas* from the kingdom's highest religious authority, Shaykh 'Abd al-'Aziz bin Baz, approving the invitation to the foreign forces and the initiation of conflict with Iraq. The government deferred to the religious establishment on a number of issues during and immediately after the crisis, including the prohibition on driving by women that became a *cause célèbre* in the West (discussed in Chapter 6). Islamic political currents came to dominate the intellectual agenda of the country's universities, to the dismay of more secular professors.[37] Over 400 members of the *ulama* and Islamic activists sent a petition to the king in the spring of 1991, in response to an earlier petition by Saudi liberals, supporting the king's announced intention to appoint a consultative council and urging him in general terms to pursue "Islamic" policy on a number of issues (this petition is discussed in detail in Chapter 4).

The limited opening in Saudi political life occasioned by the Gulf crisis led some elements in the Islamic movement to push against the outer limits of tolerated criticism. A number of university lecturers and mosque preachers castigated what they saw as un-Islamic policies on women's issues, the continued role of interest in the kingdom's banking and financial system, the country's ties to the United States, and corruption in government. Cassette tapes of many critical lectures circulated throughout the kingdom.[38] In response to these developments, the regime signaled that it would not tolerate unbridled criticism from religious circles. In December 1991 Shaykh bin Baz publicly condemned religious militants who criticized the regime, calling their assertions "lies" and "conspiracies against Islam and the Muslims." Prince Turki Al Faysal Al Saʿud, head of one of the Saudi intelligence agencies and son of former King Faysal, warned religious activists not to push too far.[39] One prayer leader in a Riyad mosque was relieved of his duties after harshly criticizing the activities of some women's benevolent organizations in which female members of the royal family were involved.[40]

King Fahd himself weighed into the public debate at the end of January 1992 with remarks publicized in the Saudi press, indicating the seriousness with which these issues were viewed. Using almost exactly the same words in consecutive meetings over two days, first with the Council of Ministers and second during his weekly meeting with senior religious officials, the king defended his policies. He stressed that the internal stability and economic strength of the kingdom were a result of "our adherence to the Islamic faith in all our affairs, religious and secular, [our] service to the two holy shrines and [our] defense of Islamic holy places everywhere." He went on to say that he was "following events with wisdom and moderation, and am working to solve them by amicable means." He was encouraged to find "with those with whom I speak that we are still able to use peaceful, moderate means to deal with certain behaviors." He ended both statements with a clear warning to the activists: "If matters exceed their limit, then for every action there is a response."[41]

The king's intervention, and his subsequent announcement in March 1992 of the new Basic System of Government and plans for a consultative council (discussed in Chapter 4) did not end the debate. In the summer of 1992 over one hundred members of the *ʿulama*, faculty at the religious universities, and other activists signed a forty-six page "Memorandum of Advice" *(muzakkarat al-nasiha)* to the king. It was unprecedented in recent Saudi history for the bluntness of its tone, its detailed critique of a wide range of government policies, and the public nature of its dissemination. Many of its general themes echoed those advanced in earlier, shorter petitions to the king: the need to curb arbitrariness in law enforcement, the need for independent oversight of government financial institutions to prevent corruption, the need for more efficient provision of government services to citizens, and the need for independent and truthful media to report on government activities. It specifically criticized judicial practices that did not safeguard individual rights and government regulation of economic and personal status which were not sanctioned by the *shariʿa*. It was unprecedented in the specificity of its criticisms and suggestions.

The Memorandum began with the assertion that the Saudi people and government displayed a "lack of seriousness" in abiding by the *shariʿa*. It complained that the *ʿulama* were being marginalized in the policy process, their *fatwas* relating to policy issues were being ignored, and their independence was being circumscribed by state restrictions and prohibitions. Foreign legal codes, particularly on business and financial issues, were being introduced and secular judicial bodies set up, diluting the role of the *shariʿa* in society and introducing "paganistic" *(al-taghut)* practices into the kingdom. "All this," the Memorandum read, "may lead to the separation of religion from the reality of the life of the people." The signers called for truly independent religious institutions, with sources of revenue independent of the state, and for the equivalent of a religious "supreme court" with the power to invalidate any law or treaty found to contravene the *shariʿa*. In effect, they advocated making the *ʿulama* a separate and coequal branch of government.

Very specific criticisms were leveled in two areas of policy where the *ʿulama's* influence has historically been limited: economics and security policy. The signers were particularly insistent that all manifestations of interest *(riba')* in the Saudi banking and financial system must be eliminated, including the investment of state funds in interest-bearing certificates from the World Bank and the U.S. Treasury, the selling of interest-bearing certificates to local banks, borrowing at interest from foreign banks, and state support for local banks that traffic in interest. They called for an end to all forms of monopoly and economic privilege, and a guarantee of equality in economic competition with judicial oversight "to prevent unfair advantage to people of influence." They condemned what they termed the kingdom's "overproduction of oil . . . on the pretext of 'supporting the stability of the world economy,' " advocating production cuts to increase the world price of oil.

In the realm of foreign and defense issues, the Memorandum challenged the policy lines set down by the kingdom in the wake of the Gulf War. It called for an end to the practice of giving loans and gifts to what it termed "un-Islamic" regimes like "Baʿthist Syria and secular Egypt," pointing to the folly of funding Saddam's Iraq during its war with Iran. It said that the Gulf crisis pointed out the "lack of correspondence between the enormous military budgets and the number and capabilities of the forces," and called for the expansion of the army to 500,000 men (an increase of at least 400 percent), obligatory military training, the diversification of foreign arms sources and the building of a domestic arms industry. The signers criticized the government for not supporting Islamic movements, but rather providing aid to states that "wage war" against such movements, like Algeria, and called for a strengthening of relations with all Islamic tendencies, be they states, political movements, or individuals. The three bases of Saudi foreign policy ought to be spreading the call to Islam, uniting the Muslims, and working for the victory of Muslim causes. In that light, the signers were very leery of the close relations the government had with Western regimes "which lead the assault against Islam," particularly of "following the United States of America in most policies, relations and decisions, like rushing into the peace process with the Jews."[42]

The Saudi government wasted no time in reacting to this un-precedented challenge from within the religious community. The Committee of Higher ʿUlama, the senior members of the religious establishment, issued a public statement condemning the contents of the Memorandum after they had leaked into the foreign press. The statement asserted that rumors to the effect that Shaykh bin Baz approved the draft and passed it on to the king were completely untrue. It questioned the motives of those who prepared the docu-ment, as they refused to acknowledge the many virtues of the state, and accused them of "planting rancor" in Saudi society to serve the interests of the enemies of the country. The statement made clear that "this action is at variance with the forms of legitimate (sharʿi) advice and the justice in word and deed it requires."[43]

Having mobilized the religious establishment to disown the Memorandum, the king asserted very forcefully his ultimate control over that establishment. In December 1992 it was announced that seven members of the Committee of Higher ʿUlama had resigned their positions for health reasons and ten younger scholars had been appointed to take their place.[44] Despite official denials of differences between the government and the religious establishment, Western news sources reported that the seven were removed from office for their failure to join in the condemnation of the Memorandum of Advice issued by their Committee.[45] A few weeks after the changes were announced, King Fahd met with senior ʿulama. His remarks were published in the Saudi press. He called on them not to use the pulpit to discuss "worldly issues" and those things not related to "the common interest." He stressed that the religious scholars have a primary place in the state, and that mutual advice (al-tanasuh) must continue among them. However, he distinguished between "superficial advice, by which a man wants to gain some external notoriety, even if it is wrong, and the advice that aims at giving counsel, which is acceptable." The King went on to say:

> Have we arrived at a point where we rely on criticisms and cassettes and on talk which brings no benefit? Our doors are open, not closed. But in recent years I think we have begun to see things we have not known, and that were never present among us. Do we accept that someone comes to us from outside our country and gives us direction? No![46]

The Memorandum of Advice incident was followed in May 1993 by the establishment of a "Committee to Defend Legitimate Rights" (*lajnat al-difaᶜ ᶜan al-huquq al-sharᶜiyya*) by six Saudi Islamic activists. The group said that its purpose was to use "legitimate means and methods" to combat injustices in the kingdom, and called on Saudi citizens to contact them with information about such injustices. The authorities reacted harshly, removing four of the founders from their government positions and revoking the law practice licenses of the other two. The spokesman for the group, a son of one of the signers, was arrested, after telling Western news agencies that demonstrations of support for the Committee had taken place in many parts of the kingdom. The Committee of Higher ᶜUlama, headed by Shaykh bin Baz, condemned the formation of the group, and senior members of the Al Saᶜud publicly defended the kingdom's human rights record. By the end of the month, one of the founders, Shaykh ᶜAbd Allah bin ᶜAbd al-Rahman al-Jibrin, renounced his membership in the group and professed his loyalty to the political leadership.[47]

These two episodes—the Memorandum of Advice and the Committee to Defend Legitimate Rights—highlight a number of important points about the relationships among state, religious establishment, and Islamic movements in Saudi Arabia. First, the signers of the Memorandum do not represent the entire Islamic tendency in the kingdom. They numbered around one hundred; an earlier, less critical, petition to the king from religious activists (discussed in Chapter 4) contained over four hundred signatures. Only six activists were involved in the Committee. Even these most critical Islamic activists did not overtly challenge the right of the Al Saᶜud to rule the country, as did their Iranian counterparts in the overthrow of the Shah. Although they seek major changes in the political system, giving them more power and independence, they still see themselves as acting *within* the system. Second, the state's institutional control over the religious establishment is still strong. It mobilized a condemnation of both the Memorandum and the Committee from the highest religious authority, and asserted its right to determine the membership of that authority.

Third, even while exerting that control, state authorities at the highest level were concerned to portray themselves as acting within

Islamic parameters in their actions. The king personally discussed the Memorandum with senior *ʿulama* on at least two occasions, acknowledging the need to consult with them. In his publicized remarks at those two meetings, he was at pains to emphasize the continued adherence of the state to Islamic principles and the important role the men of religion play in the public life of the country. He sought to delegitimize the Islamic credentials of religious critics by linking them to Shiʿi Iran, referring to ideas coming from "outside the country," and in so doing maintain the state's right to define just what Islamic politics means in the Saudi context. Similarly, senior family members defended the political system on human rights and Islamic grounds during the Committee incident. After these incidents, in July 1993, King Fahd appointed Shaykh bin Baz to the position of Grand Mufti and established a new Ministry of Islamic Affairs, *Awqaf, Daʿwa* (Proselytization), and Guidance on the recommendation of bin Baz.[48] These moves served the purposes of reiterating the regime's commitment to Islam, reasserting its right to direct the religious establishment, and rewarding those in that establishment loyal to the regime with new positions and new access to state employment.

Finally, these episodes are a clear indication that the right to define the relationship between Islam and politics, claimed by the state in Saudi Arabia on the basis of its unique history, is not unchallenged. Both the ideology and the institutions of the state can be used to challenge the policies of its government. The Saudi state can marshal considerable resources to meet such challenges, and its stability is not particularly threatened by them. But the Islamic trend in the kingdom, and throughout the Gulf, will remain an important force in political life for the foreseeable future.

Unlike Islam, tribalism does not provide a set of unifying symbols around which country-wide opposition movements can coalesce. On the contrary, individual tribal loyalties tend to separate, not unite, political movements in the Gulf monarchies. However, there are some critics who idealize tribal and village life before the advent of oil wealth, criticizing the regimes for allowing and encouraging the social and cultural changes it has brought. Perhaps the best known of such critics to the American audience is Abd al-Rahman Munif, whose novels *Cities of Salt, The Trench,* and *Varia-*

tions on Night and Day (translated into English with great skill by Peter Theroux) portray in graphic and fascinating detail the up-heavals wrought in the lives of ordinary people by the coming of the oil industry to Saudi Arabia.[49] Munif has been stripped of his Saudi citizenship and his works are banned throughout the Gulf mon-archies. While it is ironic that someone whose political affiliations are leftist and Arab nationalist would engage in radical nostalgia for the pre-industrial era, there is no denying the emotional power and pull of Munif's writing.

In a very practical way, the states' subordination and use of Islamic and tribal institutions has encouraged opposition groups to form around these organizational foci. Mosques and religious schools are among the few places in public life (as opposed to private homes) where people can openly meet and talk in these societies. There is some "social space" there, denied to other kinds of "meeting places" (political parties, free press, labor unions), that political activists can and do use to put forward their opinions and organize their adherents. It is in that milieu that the Saudi Mem-orandum of Advice originated. By contrast, in Kuwait, the one Gulf monarchy that does allow more freedom of speech and association, Islamic movements do not monopolize political discourse in civil society. They share the political field with other organized groups. Likewise, since tribal identity is encouraged by the governments, even leftist ideological political groups frequently are recruited along tribal lines. The Dhufar rebellion in Oman is a good example of how tribally organized opposition forces came under the leadership of a Marxist political movement. We will return to the general questions of political participation and representation in Chapter 4. Here it is enough to point out that the institutions of Islam and tribalism, while used very effectively by the regimes for their own purposes, can also be used by others in the political sphere.

CONCLUSIONS

This chapter began with the assertion that the "conventional wis-dom" about the tribal and religious nature of politics in the Gulf monarchies offered a distorted picture. Tribalism and Islam are important markers of personal and social identity. Tribal ties can help people politically and economically, by opening doors and linking them to those in power. The institutions of tribalism and Islam have developed into significant supports for the existing political systems in the Gulf monarchies, while losing much of the ability they had in the past to challenge those systems. Ideological constructs based on interpretations of tribalism and Islam are used to legitimize those systems to their citizens. The regimes have been largely successful in taming and using Islam and tribalism as institutional and ideological supports. However, they have not monopolized these concepts, and other political forces have emerged that contest the regimes' interpretations.

Islam and tribalism are therefore important to understanding the politics of the Gulf monarchies, but they are not the whole story. How did the regimes change the balance of power between the state and these institutions so drastically in favor of the former? Where did they get the resources to bypass tribal economic and political structures, to deal directly with citizens? How did they build the large bureaucratic structures that monitor society and control their economies? How were they able to construct and transmit their ideological messages to the citizenry through educational systems and the media? To answer these important questions, and thus to understand the nature of political power in the Gulf monarchies today, we must look at the effect of oil wealth on politics. It is to this task we turn in Chapter 3.

3

Oil and Politics

THE MOST DISTINCTIVE POLITICAL ASPECT OF THE
Arab monarchies of the Gulf is that the governments have access to
enormous wealth, particularly in light of their relatively small populations, without having to tax their societies. Oil revenues (and
other revenues from the sale of natural gas and from government
investments abroad) go directly to the state treasuries from the
international economy. Oil resources are owned by the governments; the extraction of oil is an isolated, capital intensive process
that is dominated by expatriate workers; Gulf citizens working in
the oil sector are, in effect, employees of the government. The nature
of the oil industry is such that it concentrates great power and
wealth in the hands of the governments, and its effect on the rest of
the economy as a whole is mediated through the governments in
their decisions on how to spend oil revenues.

The political effects of this kind of economy are enormous. The
relationship between state and society in such an economy is much
different from the models best known to us in the West. In our
histories, taxation and government have gone hand in hand; you
could not have government without taxation. The need to tax has,
over time, led to the recognition that taxpayers should have some

42

say in how their governments are run; the American Revolution was made under the banner "no taxation without representation." In the Gulf monarchies, since the oil boom of the 1970s, there has been no need for taxation. In fact, the central question for the rulers of these states has been how to *spend* money, not how to extract it from society. This historical anomaly has given rise in political science parlance to a new term to describe these states: the distributive, or rentier, state.[1] The rentier state is one in which government relies for the lion's share of its revenues (certainly over 50 percent, in the Gulf monarchies usually over 75 percent) on direct transfers from the international economy, in the form of oil revenues, investment income, foreign aid, or other kinds of direct payments.

A number of very specific political consequences flow from the rentier character of the Arab Gulf monarchies. First, these governments are the dominant players in their local economies. Even nominally "private sector" activities like the construction and retail sectors depend upon government spending, access to capital controlled by the government, and government licenses and permissions to do their business. By exercising such a large role in the economy, government can vest a wide array of private interests in its stability, privileging its allies and punishing those who run afoul of it. Second, governments can provide a wide array of services directly to citizens, in the form of free or heavily subsidized education, health care, housing, consumer goods, and services. Again, the intention is to provide benefits with the aim of gaining political loyalty or being able to deny such benefits (through deportation or deprivation of citizenship) to those who oppose the government.

Third, the vast resources at the disposal of most of the Gulf Arab monarchies have allowed them to build up large government apparatuses, in both the civil and military areas. Government jobs are another form of patronage that is distributed to citizens. The expanded state apparatus also provides the government with more levers to control society, through oversight functions of the civil bureaucracy, as well as through the secret police and military. Fourth, the nature of the rentier economy has, directly and indirectly weakened, if not destroyed, the economic basis of groups that in the past were sources of potential opposition to the state—most notably tribes and labor organizations. Finally, concentration of resources in the hands of the state has allowed ruling families to consolidate power and political positions in their hands to an extent unknown in previous generations.

OIL AND THE ECONOMY

It is an irony of history that the Arab monarchies of the Gulf are now rich states. For millennia, the Arabian Peninsula has been relatively poor compared to the fertile agricultural societies of Egypt, Mesopotamia, and Persia. Perhaps the richest state in Arabian history before the oil era was the state of Saba (or Sheba, of Biblical fame) in Yemen, which controlled the frankincense trade centuries before the advent of Islam. The coastal areas along the Red Sea, the Arabian Sea, and the Gulf had some important ports, and the holy cities of Mecca and Medina drew pilgrims from around the Muslim world. But the wealth of these areas was slight compared to their neighbors. Even as recently as the 1950s, the most important port on the peninsula was Aden, in Yemen. The central areas of the Arabian Peninsula were particularly forbidding ecologically and deprived economically, with very limited agricultural and pastoral economies and a small but locally important caravan trade. The economic surplus was so slight that, from the time of the Prophet Muhammad until the advent of the current Saudi state, no regime was able to unite most of the peninsula under its rule for more than the lifespan of a charismatic leader. No European colonial power evinced any interest in occupying the central areas of the Arabian Peninsula, recognizing that the costs of such an occupation would far outweigh any benefits.

Governments in this region, reflecting their societies, have historically been relatively poor. King ᶜAbd Al-ᶜAziz, the founder of modern Saudi Arabia, relied heavily upon British subventions and the royalty payments of American oil companies to maintain his treasury in the period before World War II. His major source of indigenous revenue, the pilgrimage tax, was much reduced during the worldwide depression of the 1930s, when the number of pilgrims coming to the holy cities declined sharply. The king's British adviser, H. St. John Philby, quotes him as saying during this period of financial crisis, "If anyone offers me a million pounds now, he would be welcome to all the concessions he wants in my country."[2] The governments of the smaller shaykhdoms also received financial support from the British. The amirs of Kuwait, Bahrain, and Qatar taxed the pearl industry, until it was largely destroyed by the twin calamities of the 1930s depression and the development of the Japanese cultured-pearl industry.

Poor governments provided little in the way of services to their citizens. Their most important domestic role prior to World War II was judicial, establishing a rudimentary system of courts, culminating in the ruler's *majlis*, to adjudicate disputes and some kind of police power to enforce their decisions. It was difficult for them to maintain a standing army of any size, and almost impossible to provide social services in the realms of education and health, given their financial straits. The major redistributive function of the government was to dispense subsidies to the tribes for military service and political loyalty. What government role there was in the economy was limited to a rudimentary customs system and the fact that some of the rulers, like the Al Thani in Qatar and the Al Maktoum in Dubai, were themselves merchants.

Oil changed all of this. Royalties from oil exploration concessions and then from the sale of oil provided a steady (and steadily increasing) source of revenue to the rulers of Kuwait, Bahrain, Qatar, Saudi Arabia, and Abu Dhabi, Dubai, and Sharja (in what would become the UAE) from the 1930s through the 1960s. By the 1950s, oil was the major factor in most of these states' economies; with the fourfold increase in oil prices in 1973–1974, it became the overwhelming controlling factor. The various country data in Tables 2a-f show how oil came to dominate these economies (in terms of percentage of gross domestic product [GDP] accounted for by oil exports) during the past two decades. At the peak of the oil boom, in the early 1980s, oil exports accounted for more than 50 percent of total GDP in each of the states.

In Bahrain, where oil reserves have been diminishing for decades, oil revenue still made up, as of 1988, over half of GDP. Where oil has decreased in recent years to account for less than 50 percent of GDP, oil-related revenues from state petrochemical concerns, other state industries built with oil money, investment income, and

TABLE 2A.   GDP, OIL REVENUE, AND GOVERNMENT EXPENDITURE
IN BAHRAIN (IN MILLIONS OF BAHRAINI DINAR). PERCENTAGES
OF GDP IN PARENTHESES

	GDP	Oil Revenue	Gov. Expend.
1970		78.5	
1971		97.4	
1972		106.5	
1973		132.4	
1974		430.3	67.0
1975	452.9	391.8 (86.5%)	112.3 (24.8%)
1976	593.5	463.2 (78.0%)	190.9 (32.2%)
1977	770.0	572.5 (74.4%)	242.5 (31.5%)
1978	907.6	585.9 (64.6%)	285.3 (31.4%)
1979	1,018.2	772.5 (75.9%)	254.5 (25.0%)
1980	1,158.1	1,205.7 (104.1%)	317.2 (27.4%)
1981	1,303.9	1,459.6 (111.9%)	380.2 (29.2%)
1982	1,370.8	1,182.1 (86.2%)	473.7 (34.6%)
1983	1,404.4	972.0 (69.2%)	535.1 (38.1%)
1984	1,468.5	1,062.1 (72.3%)	538.6 (36.7%)
1985	1,392.9	959.6 (68.9%)	508.5 (36.5%)
1986	1,198.2	687.3 (57.4%)	495.1 (41.3%)
1987	1,191.8	756.5 (63.5%)	418.0 (35.1%)
1988	1,262.9	688.2 (54.5%)	445.5 (35.3%)
1989	*	800.5	471.5

*Figure unavailable

Source: IMF, *Government Financial Statistics Yearbook*—1991 (Washington, D.C.: IMF, 1992), pp. 216–17.

other sources demonstrate the continuing importance of the oil sector. Even the non-oil aspects of the economies of these states, such as the mercantile, service, and construction sectors, rely on oil, as they depend upon government spending and on general regional economic health. Both Saudi Arabia and Oman, which continue to have substantial agricultural sectors, support agriculture with subsidies and price supports made possible by oil money. Revenues fluctuated throughout the 1970s and 1980s with changes in the world oil market, reaching their heights in the early 1980s and their depths (post-1973) in the late 1980s. Despite the fluctuations, the centrality of oil (and other forms

TABLE 2B.   GDP, OIL REVENUE, AND GOVERNMENT EXPENDITURE
IN KUWAIT (IN MILLIONS OF KUWAITI DINAR). PERCENTAGES
OF GDP IN PARENTHESES

	GDP	*Oil Revenue*	*Gov. Expend.*
1964	740	409.3 (55.3%)	227 (30.7%)
1965	751	174.6 (23.2%)	321 (42.8%)
1966	854	189.1 (22.1%)	382 (44.7%)
1967	962	186.9 (19.4%)	386 (40.1%)
1968	951	201.8 (21.2%)	283 (29.8%)
1969	989	214.1 (21.6%)	284 (28.7%)
1970	1,026	569.9 (55.5%)	303 (29.5%)
1971	1,382	763.0 (55.2%)	347 (25.1%)
1972	1,464	779.5 (53.2%)	379 (25.9%)
1973	1,604	1,043.9 (65.1%)	458 (28.6%)
1974	3,812	3,046.9 (79.9%)	895 (23.5%)
1975	3,485	2,443.3 (70.1%)	
1976	3,837	2,617.7 (68.2%)	
1977	4,052	2,515.4 (62.1%)	1,272 (31.4%)
1978	4,264	2,591.6 (60.8%)	1,612 (37.8%)
1979	6,862	4,634.6 (67.5%)	1,632 (23.8%)
1980	7,755	4,778.3 (61.6%)	2,147 (27.7%)
1981	7,039	3,884.4 (55.2%)	2,577 (36.6%)
1982	6,214	2,541.5 (40.9%)	3,028 (48.7%)
1983	6,083	2,837.9 (46.7%)	3,089 (50.8%)
1984	6,425	3,179.6 (49.5%)	3,047 (47.4%)
1985	6,450	2,952.4 (45.8%)	3,077 (47.7%)
1986	5,141	2,138.8 (41.6%)	2,975 (57.9%)
1987	6,154	1,925.4 (31.3%)	2,646 (43.0%)
1988	5,586	1,783.2 (31.9%)	2,698 (48.3%)
1989	6,779		2,901 (42.8%)

Source: IMF, *International Financial Statistics Yearbook—1991* (Washington, D.C.:
IMF, 1992), pp. 480–81.

of rentier income, like natural gas proceeds and investment income)
has solidified in the economies of the Gulf monarchies—for good
and ill. The steep decline in absolute GDP figures in all the states
(except Kuwait, buffered by an aggressive diversification and investment strategy) in the mid-1980s, with the dramatic fall in world oil
prices, bears witness to their oil dependency.

TABLE 2C.   GDP, OIL REVENUE, AND GOVERNMENT EXPENDITURE
IN OMAN (IN MILLIONS OF OMANI RIYAL). PERCENTAGES
OF GDP IN PARENTHESES

	GDP	Oil Revenue	Gov. Expend.
1971	125.1	87.7 (70.0%)	46.0 (36.8%)
1972	140.8	88.2 (62.6%)	69.4 (49.3%)
1973	169.4	114.8 (67.8%)	91.7 (54.1%)
1974	568.5	392.4 (69.0%)	329.3 (57.9%)
1975	724.2	497.1 (68.6%)	466.5 (64.4%)
1976	884.3	539.5 (61.0%)	551.0 (62.3%)
1977	946.8	541.8 (57.2%)	497.7 (52.6%)
1978	946.9	519.1 (54.8%)	498.7 (52.7%)
1979	1,289.9	743.3 (57.6%)	548.8 (42.5%)
1980	2,047.3	1,133.2 (55.4%)	794.9 (38.8%)
1981	2,491.5	1,520.7 (61.0%)	1,028.0 (41.3%)
1982	2,614.6	1,415.8 (54.1%)	1,176.5 (45.0%)
1983	2,740.9	1,451.6 (53.0%)	1,308.1 (47.7%)
1984	3,047.7	1,316.3 (43.2%)	1,501.0 (49.3%)
1985	3,453.8	1,536.0 (44.5%)	1,731.1 (50.1%)
1986	2,800.4	949.7 (33.9%)	1,587.2 (56.7%)
1987	3,002.6	1,307.4 (43.5%)	1,330.1 (44.3%)
1988	2,925.9	1,102.0 (37.7%)	1,363.4 (46.6%)
1989	3,230.6		1,425.4 (44.1%)

Source: IMF, *International Financial Statistics Yearbook—1991* (Washington, D.C.: IMF, 1992), pp. 480–81.

The centrality of oil can best be demonstrated by looking at the role of government spending in the overall economy. Tables 2a-f show government spending as a percentage of GDP in the six states.[3] (For comparative purposes, in 1979 federal government spending accounted for 20.5 percent of U.S. GDP, and 23.1 percent in 1989.) It is particularly interesting to note that, even when oil revenues tumbled in the late 1980s, the governments of the Gulf monarchies maintained high levels of spending to cushion the blow to the local economies. As the proportion of oil exports to total GDP fell in Oman, Saudi Arabia, and Kuwait, government spending rose to keep the economy afloat. Saudi Arabia has run budget deficits since

TABLE 2D. GDP, OIL REVENUE, AND GOVERNMENT EXPENDITURE
IN QATAR (IN MILLIONS OF QATARI RIYAL). PERCENTAGES
OF GDP IN PARENTHESES

	GDP	Oil Revenue	Gov. Expend.
1966	848	855 (100.8%)	
1967	974	963 (98.9%)	
1968	1,082	1,007 (93.1%)	
1969	1,220	1,056 (86.6%)	
1970	1,313	1,099 (83.7%)	505 (38.5%)
1971	1,850	1,441 (77.9%)	690 (37.3%)
1972	2,172	1,673 (77.0%)	959 (44.2%)
1973	2,615	2,444 (93.5%)	1,542 (59.0%)
1974	7,895	7,811 (98.9%)	1,931 (24.5%)
1975	9,877	6,893 (70.0%)	5,302 (53.7%)
1976	13,017	8,470 (65.1%)	5,809 (44.6%)
1977	14,322	8,134 (56.8%)	7,318 (51.1%)
1978	15,709	8,955 (57.0%)	6,473 (41.2%)
1979	21,783	13,398 (61.5%)	8,270 (38.0%)
1980	28,631	19,728 (68.9%)	10,937 (38.2%)
1981	31,527	19,331 (61.3%)	14,743 (46.8%)
1982	27,652	14,840 (53.7%)	12,619 (45.3%)
1983	23,542	11,132 (47.3%)	
1984	24,404	15,943 (65.3%)	
1985	22,398	12,147 (54.2%)	
1986	18,393		
1987	19,825		
1988	21,979		
1989	24,208		

Source: IMF, *International Financial Statistics Yearbook—1991* (Washington, D.C.: IMF, 1992), pp. 618–19. (Qatar ceased reporting its government expenditure and oil revenue information in the years indicated on the chart.)

1983–84, drawing down its foreign reserves, and in 1988 began to issue government bonds on the domestic market, despite opposition from Islamic activists, who object to even a hint of government involvement in financial dealings involving interest.[4] The other Gulf states also maintained a high level of spending during the oil bust of the late 1980s, cutting back on some expenditures but drawing down reserves and running budget deficits to avoid having the full

TABLE 2E.   GDP, OIL REVENUE, AND GOVERNMENT EXPENDITURE
IN SAUDI ARABIA (IN BILLIONS OF SAUDI RIYAL). PERCENTAGES
OF GDP IN PARENTHESES

	GDP	Oil Revenue	Gov. Expend.
1963	8.67	3.91 (45.1%)	2.69 (31.0%)
1964	9.32	4.15 (44.5%)	3.11 (33.4%)
1965	10.40	4.83 (46.4%)	3.96 (38.1%)
1966	11.94	5.84 (48.9%)	5.03 (42.1%)
1967	13.14	6.23 (47.4%)	4.94 (37.6%)
1968	14.66	9.09 (62.0%)	5.54 (37.8%)
1969	15.98	9.48 (59.3%)	5.97 (37.4%)
1970	17.40	10.88 (62.5%)	6.38 (36.7%)
1971	23.42	16.66 (71.1%)	10.78 (46.0%)
1972	28.26	22.71 (80.4%)	13.20 (46.7%)
1973	40.55	28.92 (71.3%)	22.81 (56.3%)
1974	99.32	126.46 (127.3%)	45.74 (46.1%)
1975	136.60	104.05 (76.2%)	110.94 (81.2%)
1976	164.53	135.91 (82.6%)	131.30 (79.8%)
1977	205.06	153.47 (74.8%)	134.25 (65.5%)
1978	225.40	127.11 (56.4%)	144.56 (64.1%)
1979	326.89	197.02 (60.3%)	185.82 (56.8%)
1980	490.94	337.40 (68.7%)	245.00 (49.9%)
1981	561.14	377.30 (67.2%)	298.00 (53.1%)
1982	458.12	251.16 (54.8%)	313.40 (68.4%)
1983	373.88	147.89 (39.6%)	260.00 (69.5%)
1984	351.40	120.73 (34.4%)	260.00 (74.0%)
1985	313.94		200.00 (63.7%)
1986	271.09		200.00 (73.8%)
1987	275.45		170.00 (61.7%)
1988	285.15	75.67 (26.5%)	141.20 (49.5%)
1989	310.82	90.24 (29.0%)	140.46 (45.2%)

Source: IMF, *International Financial Statistics Yearbook—1991* (Washington, D.C.:
IMF, 1992), pp. 640–41 (for GDP and Oil Revenue figures); Kingdom of Saudi Arabia,
Ministry of Finance and National Economy, Central Department of Statistics, *Statistical
Yearbook*, 1990, 1985–1986, 1980, 1971 (for Government Expenditure figures).

TABLE 2F.   GDP, OIL REVENUE, AND GOVERNMENT EXPENDITURE IN
UAE (IN BILLIONS OF UAE DIRHAM). PERCENTAGES OF GDP IN
PARENTHESES. (GOVERNMENT EXPENDITURE FOR FEDERAL UAE
GOVERNMENT ONLY, NOT FOR GOVERNMENTS OF INDIVIDUAL EMIRATES.)

	GDP	Oil Revenue	Gov. Expend.
1972	6.6	4.872 (73.8%)	0.164 (2.5%)
1973	11.4	6.953 (61.0%)	0.390 (3.4%)
1974	31.1	25.050 (80.5%)	0.734 (2.4%)
1975	39.5	26.962 (68.3%)	1.157 (2.9%)
1976	51.0	33.140 (65.0%)	2.144 (4.2%)
1977	63.4	36.138 (57.0%)	5.068 (8.0%)
1978	60.7	33.529 (55.2%)	6.815 (11.2%)
1979	80.0	49.078 (61.3%)	8.132 (10.2%)
1980	109.8	71.886 (65.5%)	13.332 (12.1%)
1981	121.1	68.870 (56.9%)	18.666 (15.4%)
1982	112.4	58.573 (52.1%)	19.980 (17.8%)
1983	102.9	47.783 (46.4%)	16.310 (15.9%)
1984	101.6	44.189 (43.5%)	15.669 (15.4%)
1985	99.2	42.661 (43.0%)	15.939 (16.1%)
1986	79.3		13.368 (16.9%)
1987	87.0		13.258 (15.2%)
1988	86.9		13.185 (15.2%)
1989	100.1		13.264 (13.3%)
1990	123.6		14.208 (11.5%)

Source: IMF, *International Financial Statistics Yearbook—1991* (Washington, D.C.:
IMF, 1992), pp. 744–45. (UAE ceased reporting its oil revenue information in the years
indicated on the chart.)

effects of the oil downturn reverberate through their economies.[5] In
the wake of the devastation of the Iraqi invasion, the Kuwaiti
government has taken on spending commitments that some calculate to be as high as $65 billion, nearly two-thirds of the country's
estimated foreign reserves.[6]

There are various ways the governments' dominant position in
their economies is manifested. First, these governments own many
of the major industrial concerns in their countries. Most important,
they own their national oil companies. None of the Gulf monarchies
formally nationalized the Western companies working in their terri-

tories, a political move made by other Middle Eastern oil-producing states. However, all have gradually taken over full control of production and investment decisions, employing outside concerns to provide technical and marketing services. Kuwait has gone furthest in acquiring a direct stake in "downstream" operations like refining and distribution, including a chain of European gas stations operating under the "Q8" logo. As is the case in most other countries, the states own their national airlines (including Gulf Air, a cooperative venture among some of the smaller monarchies).

The influx of capital in the 1970s led many of these states to create public companies in oil-related industries. The Saudi government built the industrial cities of Jubayl (on the Gulf coast) and Yanbu (on the Red Sea coast), an enormous capital investment, and created the Saudi Arabian Basic Industries Corporation (SABIC) to develop a petrochemical sector in the kingdom. The government retains 70 percent of the shares of SABIC, having privatized 30 percent during the late 1980s. Among other companies with either majority or 100 percent government holdings in Saudi Arabia are the national oil and gas marketing company (Petromin), the regional electric companies, some of the major hotels, a steel concern, the maritime facilities company working in the oil industry, and the national cement company.

The extent and sectoral concentration of government ownership in the other monarchies differs, but in all there are major industrial and financial concerns either wholly or partially owned by the government. In Kuwait the government owns 40 percent or more of the following companies: Burgan Bank, Bank of Kuwait and the Middle East, Kuwait Investment Company, Kuwait Foreign Trading, Contracting and Investing Company, Gulf Insurance, Warba Insurance, National Industries, Kuwait Fisheries, United Real Estate, Kuwait Hotels, General Warehousing, and Mobile Telephone Systems. The total capitalization of these concerns in 1988 was nearly $1.5 billion (U.S.).[7] In Qatar the state is primary owner of Qatari Petrochemical Company and the Qatari Steel Company, and holds a half-share of the Qatari National Bank. Various governments in the UAE have complete ownership of the following: Development Bank of the UAE, Arab Heavy Industries Company, Gulf

Mineral Water, and Safi Company for Trading and Cold Storage. They also hold part interests in a number of other concerns.[8]

In Oman, the state sector includes the Public Authorities for Stores and Food Reserves, the Public Authority for Marketing Agricultural Produce, the Oman Cement Company, the Oman Newspaper House (publishing), the Central Bank of Oman, and specialized banks for housing, development, and agriculture and fisheries.[9] Even in Bahrain, which by the 1970s had practically exhausted its oil reserves, the state moved aggressively to obtain controlling interest in major industrial concerns. In 1974 and 1975 it acquired 60 percent interest in Bahrain Petroleum (BAPCO) and 78 percent interest in Aluminum Bahrain. In 1983 it took control of United Building Factories, a local construction company experiencing financial problems, though it was leased back to a private consortium in 1985.[10] There are also a number of joint ventures among the Gulf monarchies, including the Arab Shipbuilding and Repair Yards and the Gulf International Bank (owned equally by the governments of Bahrain, Qatar, and the UAE), both headquartered in Bahrain. In 1979 Saudi Arabia bought a 20 percent share in Aluminum Bahrain.[11]

The issue of privatization has been raised by economic elites in the Gulf monarchies, particularly during the late 1980s in conjunction with the downturn in the world oil market and the popularity of privatization measures in other parts of the world. Some tentative steps in that direction were taken—for instance, the Saudis floated a minority percentage of shares in SABIC and some other government concerns for private investors. In June 1993, the Kuwaiti government, facing the financial consequences of the Iraqi occupation, announced that it was selling most of its shares in ten state-owned companies and disbanding four others.[12] Oman has drawn up serious plans for significant state withdrawal from the economy. The government has turned over to private concerns a number of agribusiness projects and Oman National Fisheries; other privatization plans have not reached the implementation stage.[13] Privatization would require governments giving up, in some cases, lucrative revenue earners and ceding a greater measure of economic autonomy, and thus political power, to civil society.

Even in the private sectors of the Gulf monarchies' economies, the indirect role of governments is extremely important. The major privately owned sectors in these economies are construction, real estate, banking and finance, agriculture, international trade, and services. In all these areas, government spending and government policies are crucial. The ruling elites can privilege certain sectors, and certain companies within sectors, through letting of state contracts, control over access to capital, policies on import of labor, and the writing of government regulations. Government spending drives the construction industry, as the major source of construction contracts throughout the Gulf is the state. Importers need government licenses to bring their products in. Many of the biggest trading concerns in the Gulf got their start by being granted monopolies in the import of certain products by the state. Agriculture, an important sector only in Saudi Arabia and Oman, depends heavily in the former country upon government subsidies of inputs (like water) and outputs (such as government-supported prices for local wheat). Both countries have state-supported agricultural banks to provide subsidized capital to farmers.

The state's role in the real estate market has been central. In all the Gulf monarchies, rulers have made grants of land to political allies and important personalities, and then the states have bought or leased that land back from the private sector at very high prices. This kind of redistribution method was extremely important in Kuwait, where in the 1950s it was the major channel for the Al Sabah to filter oil revenues to the merchant elite and tribal notables. Qatar and the UAE adopted a similar policy. In Saudi Arabia, the practice of land gifts has been in force since the early days of the kingdom. With the Saudi real estate boom in the 1970s, the beneficiaries of royal family land grants could convert their gifts into substantial fortunes.[14] In the wake of Desert Storm, with the departure from Kuwait of many foreign workers, particularly Palestinians, the government has proposed to buy hundreds of empty apartment buildings from landlords.[15]

Even where the state has left the banking and financial sector open to private capital, the state's role remains crucial. The Bahraini government pioneered the development of offshore banking units (OBUs) in the 1970s, in an effort to make the island the financial center of the region. The OBUs flourished in a permissive regulatory atmosphere in Bahrain for nearly a decade, helping to develop the service sector of the local economy. Their importance, however, has begun to fade. The development of modern financial institutions in other Gulf countries reduced local demand for OBU services. The downturn in world oil prices in the mid-1980s meant that there was less capital in the region for investment. Finally, the Iraqi invasion of Kuwait raised political risk questions for foreign firms in Bahrain. Many OBUs have closed and others are downsizing their operations. Saudi Arabia's banks, all in the private sector, rely principally upon deposits from the Saudi Arabian Monetary Agency (SAMA—the Saudi equivalent of the Federal Reserve) to maintain their liquidity. If oil revenues decrease, as they did in the mid-1980s, SAMA deposits less money in local commercial banks, increasing their vulnerability to general economic downturns.[16]

The Kuwaiti government has stepped in on two occasions in the past fifteen years to compensate investors in Kuwaiti financial markets after speculation led to crashes. In 1977 the government propped up prices on the "official" stock market (which is limited to Kuwaiti public shareholding companies) by purchasing shares, and reduced interest rates and extended repayment periods for cash-strapped investors. In 1982–1983, the government again acted to protect unwise investors, this time in the "unofficial" Kuwaiti stock market, known as Suq al-Manakh. This unregulated exchange became notorious for postdated checks, companies that had no assets save some letterhead and unscrupulous sponsors, and overheated price spirals. When it crashed, the government set up a fund to compensate what it termed "small investors" (those who owed no more than $6.75 million U.S.), issued decrees reducing the value of debt, and bought stocks and real estate from debtors to allow them to meet their obligations. Some of the most high-flying speculators were brought down through government confiscation of property and freezing of assets, but most of those involved in the scandal emerged poorer, but not ruined.[17] Suq al-Manakh has been a cautionary tale to other Gulf states, which began to keep a closer eye on securities trading. The Saudi Arabian Monetary Agency closed down the unofficial Saudi stock market in the late 1980s, allowing it to reopen only under stricter rules and tighter government supervision.

With the Kuwaiti economy reeling from the destruction wrought by the Iraqi invasion, the government again intervened with an offer to buy back the debt owed by Kuwaiti businessmen to local banks and investment companies. The cost of such a buyout has been estimated at between $20 and $25 billion (U.S.). The proposal elicited criticism from a number of political organizations in Kuwait, which charged that the bailout represented use of public money to benefit a small, wealthy slice of the Kuwaiti elite. However, the Kuwait Chamber of Commerce, a center of opposition to many government policies over the past few years, strongly supported the move.[18] The new Kuwaiti parliament has modified the government's original proposal, setting out various options for major debtors to either reschedule debt repayment or reduce their debt burdens.

Government policies in the financial sector have obviously worked to benefit certain individuals and groups. Persistent rumors surrounding each of the Kuwaiti government's bailouts (1977, 1982–1983, 1991–1992) point to members of the ruling family and highly placed businessmen as primary beneficiaries of government intervention. In trade and industrial policy, the Gulf states also act to protect certain economic interests and to accomplish political goals as well. The difficulties that have been encountered in negotiating a single tariff structure and a common market among the Gulf monarchies through the GCC are attributable in large measure to individual governments' efforts to protect certain industries and interests in their countries. Just before the Iraqi invasion, in January 1990, Kuwait placed tariffs of up to 25 percent on goods of which local producers supply up to 40 percent of local demand; imports of some goods, for which 75 percent of market demand was met locally, were banned outright.[19] Protection has nurtured local agriculture in Saudi Arabia and Oman and some key industries throughout the Gulf.

Kiren Aziz Chaudhry details how Saudi government policy since the oil boom has created a new business class in the kingdom, of Najdi (central Arabian) origin like the Al Saʿud, to balance the influence of more established commercial elites in Hijaz (the western area of the kingdom) and al-Ahsa (the Gulf coast).[20] This was accomplished not by impoverishing the other groups, who also benefited from the oil boom and had their own economic interests vested much more closely in the Saudi regime, but by directing a large portion of the enormous financial surpluses of the 1970s and early 1980s to bolstering new Najdi business interests. Similar stories can be told of the other Gulf states, where governments have had enough money *both* to benefit the established merchant families *and* to encourage new individuals and groups to get into business.

One group that is new to business in some of the states is the royal family itself. The privy purse of the ruling families, separate from the formal government budget and shielded from bureaucratic and public scrutiny, is considerable. Private investment and spending decisions by senior family members can have important economic effects, for example in the construction and financial sectors. In Saudi Arabia, Kuwait, Bahrain, and Abu Dhabi, family members had historically kept their distance from the commercial sector (at least in comparison with the Al Thani of Qatar and the Al Maktoum of Dubai, who have mixed politics and business since coming to power). Now, however, more and more members of the Al Sa'ud, Al Sabah, Al Khalifa and Al Nahyan are getting into the "private" sector. Many princes are brought in by foreign concerns that want to do business in their countries and gain a ruling family partner as political insurance. Some local concerns are also following this practice. Family members are acting as consultants and brokers for companies in the bidding process and are involved in the foreign labor market, since they have access to the licenses necessary to bring expatriates into their countries. Rarely, if ever, will the family name be attached to a business interest, but the movement, particularly of the younger generation of princes, into the business world is noticeable.[21]

The dominant position of the state in the local economy in the Gulf monarchies makes it imperative that businessmen maintain access to decision makers. Jill Crystal has documented how, in the cases of Kuwait and Qatar, major merchant families have worked to place their members in strategic places in the growing state bureaucracies.[22] The same is true in other Gulf states. The names of established merchant families like Al Zamil, Olayan, Alireza, Al Qusaybi, Al Mu'ayyad and Fakhro are frequently found in ministerial and subministerial positions in Bahrain and Saudi Arabia. In Oman, where the royal family is relatively small and not integrated into business ventures, government ministers are not only legally permitted but even tacitly encouraged to engage in private business while they are serving in government.[23]

It is generally recognized by private sector businessmen through-out the region that the motor driving the Gulf economies is the government.[24] The government has the capital because it collects the oil revenues; it redistributes that capital through its budget, its capital expenditures, and its purchasing power; it decides who will profit and by how much through its spending and regulatory poli-cies. The political effects of this dominant role in the economy are enormous. It is impossible to succeed in business without the tacit, if not active, approval of the political elite. The economic levers in the hands of governments are such that they can irreparably harm any individual or firm perceived to be disloyal or dangerous. Con-versely, governments can handsomely reward those in favor, and can even create socioeconomic interest groups that then become supporters of their regimes. In such a situation, the incentives for the business community to "go along" politically are enormous, and the costs of active political opposition to these governments are extremely high. In a word, important economic interests are vested in the state, and while business might find itself opposed to particu-lar state policies, it is all but unthinkable (in current circumstances) for it to challenge the regime or the political system.

OIL, CITIZENS, AND THE STATE

Oil wealth has allowed the governments of the Gulf monarchies to establish more direct and varied ties with their citizens than ever before in Arabian history. What is unusual about these ties, as was discussed at the beginning of this chapter, is that they are almost completely one-way—from the top down. Usually, governments can provide services to citizens only if citizens provide taxes to the government. In the Gulf monarchies, a vast array of services and benefits is now available to citizens, at little or no cost. The only requirement for receiving them is keeping your political and social behavior within the limits set by the government. As is the case with large business interests in the economy as a whole, individuals find their personal economic interests vested directly in the state.

One very important direct tie between Gulf citizens and the state is employment. The government has become the employer of last resort, and in many cases first resort, for citizens. Official statistics indicate that in Kuwait in 1988, 42 percent of the citizen workforce held jobs in the civil service. That number did not include employees of the central bank, the Public Institution for Social Security (which has a budget larger than half of the government ministries), a number of government-sponsored research agencies, Kuwait Airways, Kuwait Petroleum Company, or other government-owned corporations. Nor did it include the military.[25] It is clear that well over half Kuwait's citizen workforce earns its livelihood directly through state employment.

A similar picture of the workforce is presented by official Omani statistics. In 1990 nearly 60 percent of the employed citizen population in Oman was classified as engaged in "community services." The next highest category is agriculture and fishing, with nearly 20 percent; other categories like construction, manufacturing, and "trade, restaurants, hotels" claim less than 10 percent.[26] In other tables, the number of Omani citizens working in the civil service and for public corporations is given as 53,447, while the number of Omanis working in private sector concerns that might be grouped under "community services" (oil companies, banks, insurance companies, and hotels) totals less than 6,000.[27] It seems safe to assume that of those listed under "community services," the vast majority are government employees. Again, it appears from statistics that the military is excluded from these calculations. The conclusion that well over half Oman's citizens are direct employees of the state is a reasonable one.

The picture in Saudi Arabia is somewhat harder to discern from recent government statistics. However, a rough calculation can be made from the figures given for Saudi citizen employment in private sector establishments. In late 1988, 338,572 Saudi Arabians were working in the private sector. In the same year, total civil service employment was given as 344,020, which would not include employment in state corporations or the military.[28] It seems clear that well over 50 percent of citizens employed in the kingdom—at least as accounted for by government statistics—are in the public sector, broadly understood.

Roughly similar numbers would be generated from looking at the three smaller monarchies. If anything, the percentage of citizens working directly for the state—civilian and military—in Qatar and the UAE is probably about 75 percent, based on anecdotal evidence. The political implications of state employment are not entirely clear. It would be a mistake to assume that everyone employed by the state is absolutely committed to it, the rulers, and every policy they enact. Were such the case, military coups would never occur. However, we can deduce that those whose livelihood depends upon the state are more likely to hesitate before engaging in political activities that could threaten their positions. At a minimum, the state exerts a powerful lever over them. In the case of the Gulf monarchies, that lever applies to over half the citizen workforce. Employment may be viewed as a benefit provided by rulers, or it can be seen as a right due to citizens. In either case, it is a direct link between the individual citizen and state authority.

In the Gulf monarchies the state also provides direct and indirect financial benefits to its citizens. It is difficult to quantify the extent of such distributions, because they are accounted for in official budgets through a wide range of ministries and public organizations, and some never get into the official figures at all. In all the states, the rulers have at their disposal considerable personal fortunes, some of which are used to answer specific petitions from their subjects. But that kind of personal beneficence, shaykhly noblesse oblige in the Arabian tradition that the rulers like to emphasize, has become less prominent as populations have grown and bureaucracies have expanded. The benefits of oil wealth are now much more likely to be mediated through some government agency than conferred directly by a member of a ruling family.

The ways such mediation occurs are varied. Employment in the public sector is the most important. Other direct methods are provision of free education through the university level (and in some cases beyond, for postgraduate study abroad), and free health care. Subsidized housing is provided to many citizens, as well as grants, low-interest, and no-interest loans for purposes ranging from starting a small business to getting married and building a home, though to differing extents in different states. All six states provide social security pensions to the aged, widows, divorcees, and the disabled— again to differing degrees depending upon size of population and revenues.[29]

The states indirectly support citizens through an extensive system of subsidies on consumer goods and public services. The price of most food staples like bread, rice, sugar, flour, and meat are either controlled by the government, subsidized by the government, or both.[30] State-sponsored cooperatives operate in Saudi Arabia and Kuwait to provide food products at subsidized prices. Gasoline, needless to say, is sold by state marketing companies at prices reminiscent of the golden age of the American automobile—the 1950s and 1960s. The states also provide, either free of charge or at subsidized prices, public utilities like water, electricity, and telephone service.

Provision of all these economic benefits has a clear political intent: to convince the citizenry that their personal well-being is tied up with the existing political system. In times of political crisis, the Gulf monarchies instinctively spend more money on their populations. This "usual sort of wisdom," as one Kuwaiti intellectual put it, was on display during and immediately after the Gulf War. The three states closest to the crisis—Kuwait, Saudi Arabia, and Bahrain—all acted to reduce the economic burden on their citizens, despite the serious financial straits they found themselves in.

The Kuwaiti government in April and May 1992 wrote off telephone, water, and electricity bills that had accrued during the crisis, and suspended the current costs to consumers of those services. All government employees were paid in full for the period of the occupation. A large number of mortgages owed to government banks and state agencies were forgiven. Under pressure from the National Assembly, the quasi-parliamentary body formed in 1990 before the invasion, the government also agreed to provide each Kuwaiti family that remained in the country during the occupation with the equivalent of $1,750 (U.S.).[31] During the crisis the Saudi government lowered fodder prices charged to Saudi farmers and pastoralists and canceled two years of government mortgage payments. After the crisis, in March 1992, the government reduced or eliminated a number of charges on state services provided to consumers: gasoline was reduced in price by 37 percent, water by 50 percent, natural gas by 20–28 percent; electricity costs were reduced; costs of local telephone calls were canceled; the cost of business licenses and port and port storage fees were reduced.[32] In

May 1992, Bahrain announced a large reduction in electricity and
water rates to smaller customers, reduced government housing
rents, and increased social service grants.[33] These increases in government subsidies occurred despite the fact that each government
was, and still is, running a substantial budget deficit.

OIL AND THE GROWTH OF GOVERNMENT

As stated at the beginning of this chapter, before oil, government in
the Arabian Peninsula was a very limited thing. The "state" con-
sisted of some ruling family members and a few trusted advisers of
the shaykhs. British colonialism brought a measure of bureaucratization to the smaller states, particularly in the area of customs
collection and the military, but even at the turn of the twentieth
century, you could assemble the entire "civil service" of these states
in one large reception room, and still have space left over for the
British advisers. That is no longer the case. Particularly since the oil
boom of the 1970s, the apparatus of government in all the Gulf
monarchies has grown enormously. Employment as a state benefit
to citizens has already been discussed. Here the emphasis is on the
growth of government as a political tool, increasing the leverage that
the state holds over society. It is a tool that may be used as a carrot in
some areas, and a stick in others. Larger governments allow state
elites to provide important services, like health and education,
directly to citizens. Larger governments also permit state elites to
monitor and control their citizens to a greater extent than has been
possible in the past, particularly through the expansion of their
coercive apparatus—the military, the police, and the intelligence
services.

The growth of government in the Gulf monarchies did not
actually begin with the oil boom of the 1970s. Kuwait established a
centralized Planning Board in 1962 and adopted its first five-year
plan in 1967. In Saudi Arabia, then Crown Prince Faysal's 1962 ten-
point reform program led to administrative growth, as the government sought to make good on its promises to foster educational,
economic, and infrastructural development. Four major ministries
were created in the 1960s: Oil, Information, Labor and Social
Affairs, and Pilgrimage and Islamic Endowments. In January 1970

Bahrain implemented a new administrative structure, replacing twenty-one separate departments which had grown up during the 1950s and 1960s with a thirteen-member cabinet. However, before independence in 1971, it was hard to speak of "government" in the bureaucratic sense in Qatar, the Emirates, or Oman, outside of British advisers and British-organized military and police units.

The oil boom of 1973 spurred the growth of government in all six states, so that by the end of the 1980s they had built up large, if not bloated, administrative apparatuses. In Saudi Arabia, seven ministries were created in the 1970s: Justice, Higher Education, Industry and Electricity, Municipal and Rural Affairs, Planning, Housing and Public Works, and Post, Telephone and Telegraph. In Kuwait the size of the civil service more than doubled between 1966 and 1976, and then increased another 25 percent by 1983.[34] In 1975 four new ministries were created in Bahrain: Transport, Housing, Commerce and Agriculture, and Public Works, Electricity and Water.[35] Between 1971 and 1986, the size of the civil service in Qatar almost tripled.[36] The entire federal structure of the United Arab Emirates was developed after independence in 1971, along with the expansion in the bureaucracies of each of the seven emirates themselves. A formal Council of Ministers was established in Oman only in 1971, but has grown since then to include eighteen formal ministries and a number of independent development organizations reporting directly to the Sultan.

It is in the areas of education and health that the governments' provision of services to citizens through large and elaborate bureaucracies is most evident. Education through the university level is provided free of charge for every citizen of the Gulf monarchies. The increase in the availability of education at primary- and secondary-school levels over the past twenty-five years in all the states is remarkable. That increase has been the result of a vast expansion of their educational bureaucracies. The states have built the schools; have hired the teachers (in many cases expatriate Arabs, though over time a larger percentage of teachers are citizen graduates of these expanded educational systems); and have made education through secondary school, if not mandatory, at least strongly encouraged and officially valued. Table 3 shows how state investment in education has widened its availability to citizens. This is partic-

TABLE 3.   PERCENTAGE OF CHILDREN OF SCHOOL AGE IN SCHOOL
(PRIMARY AND SECONDARY LEVELS)

	1960	1970	1975	1980	1988
Bahrain			77	85	98
Kuwait	72	74	77	89	94
Oman		3	25	40	75
Qatar			83	88	100
Saudi Arabia	7	28	42	48	63
UAE			72	74	87

Source: UNESCO, *Statistical Yearbook*, 1975, 1980, 1991 (New York: United Nations Educational, Scientific, and Cultural Organization, various years), Table 3.2.

ularly noticeable in the two states with wider geographic extent and larger populations—Saudi Arabia and Oman.

All of the Gulf monarchies have established national universities, paying tuition and most fees for enrolled citizen students. The investment in physical plant for university expansion alone has been considerable, and the facilities constructed are in many cases very impressive. The increase in the number of university students throughout the Gulf over the past twenty years has been startling; it is almost exclusively the result of the commitment of these states to providing higher education. All of the states also provide grants for their students to continue their studies abroad, though fewer students are doing that now than fifteen years ago, as the local university infrastructure has developed. Table 4 gives the evidence of that increase. The political effects of the increasing availability of higher education, and of education generally, are mixed for the regimes. Just as the local universities are turning out educated citizens who can replace expatriate officials in both the private and public sectors, they are also producing an expanded, generally more literate and politically aware elite with which the regimes have to deal. But the commitment of all the governments to state education programs is clear, and the provision of educational opportunities is always cited by government officials as among the most important benefits provided by the regimes to their people.

TABLE 4. NUMBER OF STUDENTS PER 100,000 INHABITANTS
AT UNIVERSITY LEVEL

	1975	1980	1988
Bahrain	259	551	1,175
Kuwait	804	992	1,384
Oman		2	308
Qatar	455	991	1,763
Saudi Arabia	364	662	951
UAE		269	506

Source: UNESCO, *Statistical Yearbook*, 1991 (New York: United Nations Educational, Scientific, and Cultural Organization, 1992), Table 3.10.

Similar statistical advances can be observed in the field of public health, as Table 5 demonstrates. Infant mortality rates have declined markedly in all the states over the last three decades, and life expectancy rates have increased. These advances result in large part from commitment by these states to provide health care to their citizens, from the most basic level of services to expensive experimental procedures performed overseas, free of charge. As in all systems of socialized medicine, there are constant complaints about quality of service, and those with more money get better care because they are able and willing to pay for it. In some cases, the oil bust of the late 1980s led to decreases in absolute spending on health care, which translated into fewer doctors and longer waits for service. But it is undoubtedly true that all Gulf citizens have access to better, more modern health care than has been the case in the past.[37]

The provision of educational and health services is mediated through very large government bureaucracies in all the states. In Kuwait in 1989, the Ministry of Education had the fourth largest budget of any cabinet department, after Finance, Electricity/Water (which has a public health aspect), and Defense. Public Health ranked sixth, just after Public Works. The ministries of Education and Public Health ranked first and second in total civil service employees, with 53,674 and 32,372 employees in 1988, respec-

TABLE 5.   PUBLIC HEALTH INDICATORS
(FIRST LINE: INFANT MORTALITY PER 1,000 LIVE BIRTHS;
SECOND LINE: LIFE EXPECTANCY AT BIRTH)

	25–30 years ago	*15–20 years ago*	*most recent*
Bahrain	90.8	44.8	24.3
	58.8	64.6	68.5
Kuwait	63.8	27.4	14.8
	62.9	68.6	73.7
Oman	194.0	121.0	36.3
	43.5	51.4	64.9
Qatar	103.0	50.4	29.0
	57.3	64.3	69.8
Saudi Arabia	148.0	108.0	67.7
	48.3	56.3	64.0
UAE	108.0	45.6	24.3
	57.4	65.1	71.1

Source: World Bank, *Social Indicators of Development*—1990 (Washington, D.C.: IBRD/World Bank, 1991).

tively.[38] At the other end of the scale, in terms of oil wealth and development progress, lies Oman. The pattern of expenditure and employment on education and health there follows a similar pattern. Aside from defense and security allocations, which are not listed in official budget statistics, the Ministry of Education and Youth ranks first among the ministries in expenditure for the 1990 budget, and the Ministry of Health ranks fourth, behind Electricity/Water (again, this has a public health aspect) and the Royal Court. In 1990 the Ministry of Education and Youth employed the highest number of civil servants (10,160), and the Ministry of Health the second-highest (6,085).[39]

Oil revenues have allowed these states to build large bureaucratic infrastructures to provide services to citizens. These same oil revenues have permitted the states to create an infrastructure of control, limiting the political space available for their citizens to discuss issues and organize politically. The control mechanism is most obvious in the development of the armed and police forces of all six states. Defense and security expenditures (including budget allocations for ministries of defense and interior and national guards) are the single largest category of expenditure in the budgets of Oman, the UAE, and Saudi Arabia. In Saudi Arabia, these expenditures amounted to 33.2 percent of the 1990 budget and 30.0 percent of the 1992 budget; in Oman, 43.2 percent of the 1989 budget; in the UAE, 57.4 percent of the 1989 budget. In both Kuwait and Bahrain, the percentages were much lower (Kuwait, to almost 16 percent of the 1988–1989 budget; Bahrain, 15.6 percent of the 1989 budget), but defense expenditures in each country are rising—in Kuwait after the Iraqi invasion and in Bahrain as a result of its renewed border dispute with Qatar.[40] (For comparative purposes, during the Reagan defense build up in the United States, defense spending never rose above 26 percent of the federal budget. The average percentage of the national budget devoted to defense and security spending in developing countries for 1988–1989 was 13–14 percent.)[41] Figures for Qatar were not available. The amount of money devoted to security, in both absolute terms and relative to other government spending, is enormous. The military establishments of all the states have grown over the last twenty years, in many cases more than the increase in population (see Table 6). Even more

TABLE 6.   TOTAL ARMED FORCES
(INCLUDING ACTIVE PARAMILITARY FORCES)

	1975	1980	1990
Bahrain		2,500	3,600
Kuwait	10,200	12,400	21,800
Oman	16,100	17,500	29,400
Qatar		4,700	7,000
Saudi Arabia	69,500	73,500	75,700
UAE		25,150	43,000*

* 30% of that force is believed to be expatriates.

Source: International Institute for Strategic Studies, *Military Balance*—1975–76, 1980–81, 1990–91 (London: Brassey's for the IISS, various years).

noticeable is their acquisition of massive amounts of technologically sophisticated weaponry and military equipment.

In all these states, the function of the armed forces is officially given as defense of the country against foreign attack. Their mission in reality, however, is equally focused on maintaining *domestic* security. That is certainly clear in the case of Oman, where the military fought a prolonged insurgency in the Dhofar province from 1970 to 1975. It is equally clear in the UAE, where federal troops intervened in an internal struggle in Sharjah in 1987 to restore the rule of Shaykh Sultan al-Qasimi, who had been deposed by his brother ᶜAbd al-ᶜAziz. Most observers see the Saudi National Guard, a large, technically sophisticated military force completely separate from the regular army and organized largely along tribal lines, as a guarantee against internal upheaval, either in society or from the regular military. The armed forces of Kuwait, Bahrain, and Qatar are so small in relation to potential enemies (except perhaps each other) that they can only be viewed realistically as internal security forces. The performance of the Kuwaiti army in August 1990 was sad but clear evidence of that small country's inability to defeat its major enemy with its own resources.

It is comparatively easy to chart the growth of the regular armed forces. It is harder to document from public sources the growth of local police forces and domestic intelligence services, the first line of defense for the state against internal political opposition. But it is clear, from anecdotal evidence and the testimony of citizens of these states, that the specifically domestic parts of the coercive apparatus have also grown in size, power, and sophistication over the last two decades.[42] All the states cooperate through Gulf Cooperation Council structures and bilaterally on internal security questions, while cooperation on other issues, like defense and economic coordination, remains elusive.[43]

The success of the monarchies in establishing internal security organizations that can prevent domestic discontent from escalating into movements threatening to the state was evident during crises arising from the Iranian Revolution and the Iraqi invasion of Kuwait. Authorities in Kuwait, Bahrain, Saudi Arabia, and Qatar all confronted popular upheavals of various kinds related to the Islamic revolution in Iran: a coup plot in Bahrain in 1981; a plot to blow up the Doha Sheraton, where the 1983 GCC summit was held; riots in Saudi Arabia's Eastern province in 1979 and 1980; an assassination attempt on the Kuwaiti amir in 1985, and a number of terrorist bombings. Yet all the regimes survived the combination of military pressure, propaganda, and domestic unrest related to the Revolution and the Iran-Iraq war.[44] During the most recent crisis, Saddam Husayn used Arab nationalist and Islamic propaganda to foment discontent in the Gulf states. Despite the unsettling presence of the American and other foreign forces in Saudi Arabia and the smaller states, the domestic scene in all of them remained remarkably quiet. In part, that can be attributed to the bankruptcy of the messenger, and perhaps to the fading appeal of the message, but the effectiveness of internal security organs cannot be discounted.

That effectiveness comes at a price paid by civil society, however. Political "space," particularly in the forms of mediating institutions between society and government, tends either to get coopted or suppressed by state security authorities. Thus, we see in the Gulf monarchies that political parties are formally illegal, and when they do exist are underground. Independent labor unions are also illegal. Professional syndicates and chambers of commerce are permitted, but are usually closely supervised by the state. Broadcast media—television and radio—are completely under state control. Print media are frequently controlled directly by the state or are in the hands of private concerns close to state authorities. Independent newspapers and other publications are subject to strict censorship. Even sports and cultural clubs tend to be brought within the state's ambit, formally through a state licensing process and informally, in many of the states, through ruling family members assuming their chairmanships. Given the central role such clubs played as foci for political activity during the 1950s and 1960s, the states' interest in them is not surprising. One of the strengths of local Islamic movements is that the mosque provides some measure of protection against direct government supervision and interference, permitting political organization to occur.

There are differences among the Gulf states in the degree to which the state imposes itself on civil society. Kuwait has the greatest freedom of political and social organization, with an elected parliament, political groupings that are parties in everything but name, professional groups like the Chamber of Commerce and the Graduate Society that jealously maintain their autonomy from the government, and the freest press in the Gulf. But even there, it took the Iraqi invasion, which weakened governmental authority and prestige, to revive many of these institutions. From the dissolution of the Kuwaiti parliament in 1986 right up to the invasion, the government used its financial and coercive powers to limit the relatively greater political rights that Kuwaitis had enjoyed. In Bahrain and Dubai there is comparatively more social freedom, in terms of public entertainment and the role of women in public life.

The general trend, dating especially from the oil boom of the 1970s, for the state to exert greater control over society, is incontrovertible. Oil revenues have given the states the bureaucratic and coercive capacities to exercise that control. Fifty years ago, perhaps even thirty years ago, citizens in the Gulf monarchies could lead their lives mostly without coming into contact with the state. Now such contact is a regular part of daily life. The pervasive role of the state in the everyday lives of people is well captured by anthropologists Soraya Altorki and Donald Cole in their study of 'Unayzah, a town in Najd, the central part of Saudi Arabia:

> Births, deaths, marriages, and divorces must now all be registered with its [the state's] agencies. Landownership involves registration and must conform to guidelines set by the state, as do commercial establishments. The importation of a laborer requires approval by an agency of the state, and rules and regulations concerning that laborer must be followed once he is employed. The state provides the police force, and there is now a jail. The state provides education, not only in the form of facilities and personnel but the curriculum that is taught. The state is the main provider of health facilities and a contributor to social welfare programs, which it supervises. It has provided roads, the airport, telephones, mail service, and telegraph, which link the community to the wider world. The state also provides a major source of entertainment and the news through its radio and television networks. It has also become the major source of loans and subsidies to build houses or develop agricultural enterprises. . . . The state has become the single most important employer in the community. Furthermore, it maintains the religious establishment, including the courts.[45]

OIL AND POLITICAL GROUPS

The effect of oil (and the concomitant growth of state size and wealth) on political groups in the Gulf monarchies has been enor-

mous. Oil wealth undermined the economic base of Arabian tribalism, and allowed the governments to turn the shaykhs into salaried
employees of the state. The concentration of economic power in the
hands of the state has limited the economic autonomy and thus the
political freedom of Gulf businessmen. Two other groups of political importance have had their fortunes substantially affected by oil,
one for the worse and the other for the better.

Organized labor has, in effect, been destroyed as a political
force in the Gulf monarchies as a result of the oil boom. The
combination of the movement of citizen laborers into white-collar
(or perhaps better put, *dishdasha*—the full-length, usually white,
garment worn by most Gulf men) jobs in the government, the influx
of foreign labor into these countries, and the expansion of the states'
abilities both to police and to buy off local labor unrest has removed
indigenous labor issues from the political agenda. Those unions that
now exist are officially sponsored (and controlled) by the states. The
social basis for an autonomous, indigenous, organized labor movement has disappeared.

Viewed from the perspective of recent history, the disappearance
of labor issues and labor movements from politics in the Gulf
monarchies is centrally important. Labor once played a major political role in many of these countries. In Bahrain, labor unions,
particularly in the oil industry, were the backbone of the nationalist
movement of the 1950s, ameliorating if not erasing the sectarian
differences in the population. Major strikes occurred in Bahrain in
the 1960s and early 1970s among oil and aluminum workers. The
social base of the more radical leftist opposition groups in the
country was the labor movement, though most of the leadership
cadres came from the professional and intellectual classes.[46] Since
the oil boom of the mid-1970s, labor unrest has decreased markedly, and the leftist opposition has been marginalized.

In Qatar, strikes in the 1950s against Petroleum Development
of Qatar, Ltd. (PDQL)—a subsidiary of Shell—helped to define
Qatari identity against expatriate workers. These strikes frequently
had the tacit support of the amir and other important members of
the Al Thani family. In 1963, when disputes among the Al Thani on
succession questions spilled over into popular protests, Qatari oil
workers sustained a politically motivated strike for nearly three

weeks in support of the opposition faction. Shaykh Ahmad responded with promises of reform, some of which were actually implemented. By the mid-1960s, labor troubles receded as oil and gas revenues began to be more liberally distributed throughout society and as the leadership, chastened by the 1963 events, began to take a dimmer view of labor activity.[47] In Saudi Arabia, strikes by ARAMCO workers in 1953 and 1956 were met with physical suppression and with promises of better conditions for Saudi workers, including opportunities for training and advancement to positions occupied by expatriates. The kingdom's labor code, promulgated in the 1960s, forbids the right to strike and collective bargaining, while providing rules for proper treatment of workers and for arbitration of disputes.[48] As in Qatar, labor incidents and the leftist, underground political movements that sought to mobilize indigenous labor support have receded from the Saudi political agenda.

Another reason why labor is no longer a major player in the politics of the Gulf monarchies is because few citizens now work in those sectors where labor unions once flourished. Labor issues are still important, though now they bear upon immigrant rather than indigenous labor and thus have much reduced political consequences for these systems. The issue of foreign labor will be handled in Chapter 6, in the discussion of the challenges facing these regimes. While the oil boom eliminated indigenous labor movements, it provided vastly increased resources to another important group in the political history of these states—the ruling families. As a result, the families themselves, as corporate groups tied to but distinct from the person of the ruler, have developed a much larger role in the political life of these states.

In the past, the ruling families have been important for Gulf politics in two ways: as the pool from which the amir, sultan, or king is drawn, and as the major source of potential opposition to the ruler once in office. Each of the countries has experienced, during the twentieth century, serious internal disputes over succession. In some cases, such disputes have led to violent confrontations and to the exile of some family members.[49] In the years before the oil boom, the rulers in the smaller states relied much more on expatriate advisers—British and Arab—and on local notables to staff their small government bureaucracies than they did on their families.

King ᶜAbd al-ᶜAziz of Saudi Arabia conferred on many of his sons prominent government roles, but also looked to subsidiary branches of the family and to outsiders for political advice and for local governors. Since the early 1970s, and even before in Kuwait and Saudi Arabia, where independence came earlier than elsewhere, rulers have turned more and more to family members to staff sensitive and important government posts.[50]

A brief look at the composition of the governments in the six countries indicates the extent to which ruling family members have extended their influence into the apparatus of the state. In all six states, the prime minister is a member of the ruling family. In the cases of Oman and Saudi Arabia, the head of state himself is prime minister; in Bahrain, Qatar, and Kuwait, either brothers, cousins, or sons of the amir serve as prime minister; in the UAE the president is the amir of Abu Dhabi and the prime minister is the amir of Dubai. The ruling families supply a large number of ministers in each state. The highest proportions are in Bahrain (6 of 15) and Qatar (9 of 17), with Oman, where the ruling family is the smallest in terms of size, having the lowest proportion (5 of 30, though the Sultan himself holds the Defense, Foreign Affairs, and Finance portfolios, as well as the prime ministership). In the Kuwaiti cabinet formed after the October 1992 elections, 4 out of the 15 ministers are from the Al Sabah. In Saudi Arabia, 5 of 21 ministers are Al Saᶜud. In the UAE, 9 of 24 ministers are members of the various ruling families. The ministries controlled by family members are usually among the most sensitive and most powerful. As of the end of 1992, in four of the six states, family members held the interior portfolio; in all six, they held the defense portfolio; in five of the six, they held the foreign affairs portfolio.

The ruling families' reach into the state bureaucracy is not limited to ministries. Particularly in the cases of relatively large families, like the Al Saᶜud, Al Thani, Al Khalifa, and the various UAE families, family members are to be found throughout the civilian bureaucracy and the officer corps. For example, while the Qatari Monetary Agency is headed by a technocrat, the deputy governor is a member of the Al Thani. A similar situation holds true in the Saudi Ministry of Petroleum and a number of other ministries and agencies throughout the Gulf. In November 1991 there was a shake-up in the Abu Dhabi municipal council aimed at bringing "new and younger faces" into the shaykhdom's administration. Eight of the sixteen members appointed were from the Al Nahyan.[51] At the end of December 1992, Shaykh Za'id, president of the UAE, appointed two of his sons as chief of staff of the armed forces and head of the state security agency.[52] In most Gulf monarchies, ruling family members are also taking high-profile positions in civil society that had, in the past, been informally considered off limits—posts in private business, sports and cultural clubs, and state financial institutions that had previously been reserved for technocrats. A common complaint among many in the Gulf is that the ruling families are transgressing well-established informal lines of what is "theirs" and what is "ours." It should be noted that this particular complaint is not common in Oman, where the family is small, and was more prominent in Kuwait before the Iraqi invasion and during the occupation than after.[53]

The increased prominence of the ruling families as corporate groups is due to various factors. First, the families are larger than they were a few decades ago, and newer members want a role in ruling, which after all is the "family business." Second, families are richer than they were before. Such wealth gives members the opportunity to work in government without experiencing financial hardship. Control over the disbursement of wealth also gives the amir and other senior family members more control over their sons and cousins, strengthening family discipline and political reliability. Finally, and most importantly, oil revenues have given rulers the means to reduce their dependence upon other social groups, like merchants and tribes, to maintain their regimes. Relying on the extended family to support and maintain the regime helps safeguard its autonomy from other political forces.

The new prominence of ruling families as corporate groups in these states brings with it a number of problems. Issues of succession and the extent of the families' role in government, particularly the younger generation's, are not yet settled in all the states. The large family presence in government makes the implementation of rational legal bureaucratic standards of decision-making and administration more difficult. Along with formal lines of authority, there is a competing authority structure based upon family and client ties. The most extreme example is in Qatar, where as recently as 1983 it was reported that the amir himself had personally to sign any check over $50,000 (U.S.).[54] This problem is not limited to the ruling families; technocratic ministers are just as capable of developing family and client networks in the bureaucracy. Also, many ruling family officials are very competent and successful in running their offices by any standard. But the strong presence of ruling family members does set a tone for how government operates.

Finally, as the corporate identity and power of the ruling families grow, they run the risk of setting themselves apart from their societies, somewhat on the model of European nobilities of the feudal and monarchical periods. These families, particularly in the smaller states, had always been rather "first among equals" than birthright superiors to their neighbors in the social sphere. Taking on airs socially, particularly when coupled with a sense that the families are getting more than their "fair share" of oil revenues, could contribute to popular dissatisfaction. These sentiments, while present, are not widespread in the Gulf states now; they could become a source of political problems in the future, however.

CONCLUSIONS

The oil revolution of the 1970s profoundly affected politics in the Gulf monarchies. Continuity at the top has been accompanied by enormous changes in the structure of the state, in state-society relations, and in the political economies of all these countries. Rulers stayed the same; the bases of their rule changed in important ways. Ruling families and the states they built became much more powerful in their local economies. Other social groups—merchants, tribes, *ulama*, labor—found themselves with less bargaining power vis-à-vis the state than they had in the past. Oil revenues coming directly into the hands of the state, unmediated by the local economy, meant that the personal interests of many more people came to be vested directly in the state and the ruling family. Because of oil revenues rulers were able to build up large bureaucratic apparatuses, to distribute benefits to society, and to control political behav-

ior. The state became stronger relative to potential domestic competi-
tors and constituencies than it had ever been in the past.

That strength, however, was of a particular nature. Citizens did
not have to pay for increased services through taxation. These states
did not have to engage in the kinds of political bargains with society,
worked out over centuries and with no small amount of violence,
that produced representative governments in the West. The terms of
the exchange, from the rulers' point of view, were simple: citizens
would receive substantial material benefits in exchange for political
loyalty, or at least political quiescence. But the connections between
state and society in this situation are unidirectional: they all run
from the top down. Gulf governments have to a great degree reversed the famous American dictum: citizens are adjured to ask not
what you can do for your country, ask rather what your country can
do for you.

It is interesting to note in this context that only one of the six
states, Kuwait, requires military service of its citizens, and even
there, so many exceptions and loopholes exist that most citizens
who want to bypass the draft can do so. According to the International Institute of Strategic Studies, 30 percent of the UAE armed
forces is expatriate (see Table 6). That number might be higher;
Qatar's armed forces are also heavily expatriate. In Kuwait a large
portion of the armed forces and police consist of Kuwaiti residents
who do not hold citizenship—the "biduns", from the Arabic *bidun
jinsiyya* (without citizenship).[55] They are the descendants of people,
usually of tribal background, who were either out of the country or
chose not to apply when citizenship was formally offered. Saudi
officials have discussed the doubling of the size of their military in
the aftermath of the Iraqi invasion of Kuwait. That would probably
require a draft, and no steps have yet been taken to implement these
plans.

The states are stronger, but that strength is not based upon a
tightly knit network of affective loyalties, rights, and obligations
between state institutions and citizens. Gulf monarchs run the risk
that their strength and autonomy will in the future lead to isolation
and disconnection from society. The rulers recognize these risks.
They have attempted to meet them through conscious efforts to
develop state ideologies that increase citizen identification with

their country and its political system. They have also, to very differing degrees, responded to popular calls for greater participation in the political system. Those calls have resounded more loudly since the Iraqi invasion of Kuwait, and rulers have paid more attention to them. It is to the issue of popular participation that the next chapter turns.

4

Representation and Participation

THAT OIL HAS SUBSTANTIALLY ALTERED THE RELATION-
ship between state and society in the Arab monarchies of the Gulf is
a fact that most analysts of the region will not dispute. The effects of
this change, particularly on the nature of political demands emanating from society, is a matter of more contention. The dominant
interpretation is that the increased wealth of the general population,
combined with the increased power of the state to bestow or withhold that wealth, has reduced demands for political representation
and participation. Whether the argument is a nuanced interpretation of how merchants negotiated a trade with state elites of great
wealth for political withdrawal, or a cruder assertion that rich
people are not so interested in rocking the political boat, the result is
that oil wealth has lessened the need for rulers to include their
populations in the decision-making process. One of the foremost
interpreters of the rentier state puts the issue bluntly:

> Democracy is not a problem for allocation [rentier] states. Although
> they might find it expedient to set up some kind of representative body
> to vent and control some of the resentment that even court politics
> generates, these bodies inevitably have a very tenuous link to their
> apparent constituency. Their debates are followed with indifference by
> the public and the ruler can disband them and meet practically no

resistance whatsoever. . . . The fact is that there is "no representation
without taxation" and there are no exceptions to this version of rule. It
is only in the case that an allocation state fails, or is widely believed to
fail, to take full advantage of the possibility of receiving income from
the rest of the world that substantial political opposition may develop.[1]

The history of representative institutions in the Gulf monarchies seems to bear this assessment out. The heyday of populist,
labor, and Arab nationalist movements in the Gulf, which sponsored strikes and political demonstrations in every country except
Oman, was the 1950s and 1960s, before the oil boom. The one
enduring representative institution, the Kuwaiti parliament (*majlis
al-'umma*—assembly of the nation), was founded at independence
in 1961. It has been suspended twice, once in 1976 and again in
1986, without shaking the stability of the regime. The legislative
assembly in Bahrain, elected in 1973, was suspended in 1975 and
has not been reconvened. There have never been directly elected
representative institutions in Saudi Arabia, Qatar, the UAE, or
Oman.[2]

Yet it would be a mistake to assume that there are no impulses
from society in the Gulf monarchies for representative and participatory institutions. Demands for a say in decision making have been
mediated through numerous institutions, a few of which have been
discussed in previous chapters. Some are "traditional" social formations like tribes and religious institutions, which have adapted extremely well to representing the interests of their constituents before
government. Others are more self-consciously "modern" institutions, based on class, functional, and ideological interests. Chambers of commerce are the most prominent and enduring of such
"lobbies," but others include professional syndicates, labor unions
(less powerful now than in the past), social clubs, and organizations
of the intelligentsia. Political parties, of both leftist-nationalist and
Islamist leanings, have even operated in a semipublic way in Kuwait
and Bahrain, the two states with some experience in elected assemblies, though they have never been able to declare themselves formally. The press in Kuwait and the UAE has had the independence
to reflect points of view critical of these governments. Islamic groups
like the Muslim Brotherhood and the *salafi* movement (similar to
the Saudi Wahhabi movement) on the Sunni side and various Shi'i

groups have been increasingly important political actors in many of the countries.

Organized social movements have never been absent from the political life of the Gulf. But through the 1980s, they operated largely on the fringes of the political system, and their influence was based to a great extent on personal, client relations with important members of the government and ruling families. Both "traditional" and "modern" forms of mediation relied upon personal ties of family, marriage, and friendship to gain access to the councils of decision-makers. Recently, the capacity of the political systems to meet society's demands for representation and participation through these informal and uninstitutionalized channels has been severely strained. Since 1990 political groups and social institutions throughout the Gulf have called for more regular and formal access to the decision-making process. Governments have responded with promises of reform and change, some of which have been partially fulfilled already. This chapter examines the roots of these changes and the governments' reactions to them.

POLITICAL PARTICIPATION IN RENTIER STATES

The basis of the contention that rentier states are immune to serious public pressure for a role in the political process is the issue of taxes. In the dominant models for understanding political development in the West, the connection between rulers' needs to extract revenue from society through taxes and society's right to constrain rulers through elections and legislative bodies is direct: "No taxation without representation." Since rentier states do not have to tax their citizens, they do not have to deal with serious demands for participation. Those groups that in the past did have a substantial political role, like merchants and tribal shaykhs, "trade in" their political power for a share of the state's newfound wealth. The citizen population, having experienced the relative penury of the pre–oil boom period, are happy to be receiving jobs and benefits from the government, and credit improved conditions to the ruling families. They therefore do not see the need for political participation. Those few who, for ideological reasons, call for radical reform or political change are easily marginalized.

This account of the effects of the rentier state on demands for political participation was largely accurate for the Gulf monarchies during the 1970s and 1980s. Absence or weakness of elected, representative political institutions did not affect the stability of these regimes, despite social upheavals accompanying the massive changes oil wealth brought and the political pressures of the Iranian Islamic Revolution, the Iran-Iraq War, and the Iraq-Kuwait crisis. Citizen populations did generally appreciate the improved lifestyles that came with the oil boom. Given the small populations of all these countries (as opposed to Iran, for example), a very large proportion of the citizenry did see real improvement in their material conditions. They credited their rulers, at least in part, with that improvement. The small educated elite could easily be absorbed into responsible, high-paying government positions, mitigating their desire for formal participatory institutions.

These stabilizing and "de-politicizing" effects of the rentier state are real, but the overall impression they give is static. This is more a snapshot of the first effects of the rentier state phenomenon than a model of the dynamics over time of rentier state development. As the role of the state in these countries has grown, it has begun to call forth new demands for representative institutions and responsible government from society. Those demands spring from the very processes of state growth and expansion occasioned by the oil boom. The recent upsurge in political activity in the Gulf monarchies is not only consistent with the realities of the rentier state and its relationship to society, but is in fact generated by those realities.

The state has become the motor of economic development, the major employer, and the provider of numerous services in all the Gulf monarchies, and thus is central to the everyday life of its citizens, to an extent that would have been literally unimaginable even four decades ago. It is natural that citizens should seek some control over an institution that so powerfully affects their lives for good and ill, if only to reduce the chance of drastic and unexpected changes in its policies. Much as taxpayers want responsible governments to spend their money, the beneficiaries of rentier states want responsible governments to sign their checks. Their financial dealings with the state are as important to their daily lives, if not more important, than those of taxpayers in Western democratic countries. A sudden change in state policy in the Gulf monarchies could mean higher rents, mortgage payments, health care costs, food bills, and utility bills; it could mean loss of one's job and livelihood.

After twenty years of state benefits derived from oil, a substantial part of the citizenry has ceased to regard these benefits as temporary benefices from their rulers, and has come to see them as rights of citizenship. The fact that each of these countries has a substantial number, in some cases a majority, of noncitizens who do not share in many of these benefits reinforces the notion that citizens are different, in part because governments have an obligation to provide certain economic rights to them. Along with obligations to individual citizens, the Gulf monarchies have also taken on, over the last twenty years, a more general obligation to encourage economic growth and safeguard the health of the economy as a whole. On both personal and national levels, citizens increasingly hold the state accountable for economic conditions. It is the urge to institutionalize that accountability that leads people to demand some role in the political process. It is precisely because the state has become so important and so powerful that people want a say in it.

The process of state growth is generating these new participatory demands at the same time that other avenues of interest mediation are becoming less practical. Having a personal tie with top decision-makers is still the best way to get one's voice heard in the Gulf states (or anywhere else, for that matter), but large population growth and high birth rates in all the Gulf monarchies mean that a steadily declining percentage of the population are able to claim such ties. This is particularly true in Saudi Arabia, with the largest population of the Gulf monarchies and the most far-flung geographical expanse. But it is also the case, albeit to a lesser extent, in the smaller states, where citizen populations are increasing at among the highest birthrates in the world. Patron-client ties work most effectively when the number of clients relative to patrons is not too great. That ratio is growing and will continue to grow in the future in all the Gulf monarchies.

At the same time that populations are increasing, the oil boom has ended. Oil prices peaked in 1982 at around $41 per barrel, declined drastically in the mid 1980s, at one point to below $10 per barrel, and remain below $20 per barrel after Desert Storm. The dizzying expansion of both the economy and the government, which provided employment opportunities to all school graduates in the 1970s and early 1980s, has been replaced by a leveling out. Bureaucracies are no longer expanding dramatically; measured economic growth has replaced the "black gold" rush. It is no exaggeration to say that, in some of the smaller states, twenty years ago any talented citizen with political aspirations who was willing to work within the system could get a very responsible job (or at least a responsible-sounding title) in the state apparatus. That is no longer the case. Meanwhile, more school graduates are finding it difficult to obtain jobs of any kind, in the public or private sectors, and are looking to the state to help them.

The increased complexity of the state sector also reduces the efficiency of patron-client avenues of access. With so many ministries, departments, and bureaus dealing with every aspect of daily life, it is harder to get something done just by knowing someone. Certainly, if one knows a high-ranking member of the ruling family, or the right person in a specific ministry on a specific issue, such ties are still very beneficial. But having family or friendship ties with officials in one ministry will not necessarily help one in dealings with another ministry. The kind of patronage influence that cuts across government ministries has become limited to a few, top-level officials as the size and role of government have grown and as the bureaucratic apparatus has ramified and specialized.

As the efficacy of other avenues of political influence and participation has declined, the expansion of the state educational system in all the Gulf monarchies, funded by oil money, has produced a growing number of citizens who have the intellectual resources and proclivity to voice their political demands in general terms. High school and college graduates can read and write, and so have the capacity to be better informed about political issues in the country at large and to express themselves on those issues. They have developed personal networks that cut across family and tribal lines and can draw on these contacts for mobilizing people on political issues. They have been exposed to critical approaches for analyzing political issues, if not in the classroom, then outside it among their peers. They have certainly been taught in state curricula to take a country-wide, as opposed to a tribal or clannish, view of their political allegiance and responsibilities, even if these curricula have not encouraged thoughts of direct political participation. Islamic groups, frequently identified as "traditional" by Westerners, have been as affected by these changes as more liberal and secular political groups, in terms of how they are organized, how they pose their issues, and how they address the general public.

The impact of the educational changes in these countries is evident in the prominent role petitions have played as a means of expressing demands for a greater role in decision making. Such petitions circulated in Saudi Arabia, Bahrain, and Qatar in 1991 and 1992, and in Kuwait before the Iraqi invasion. (Their content will be discussed in more detail below.) Petitions require literate writers who think in terms of general issues and general responses to them. In framing their requests in general policy terms, as opposed to personal patronage terms, they assume the existence of a literate audience, both in the ruling elite and among the public, that is responsive to this kind of appeal, that views policy in a more rational-bureaucratic than "traditional" light. Finally, the signatures on the petitions indicate that activists have created networks that gather people together on functional and ideological, as opposed to family and tribal, lines. At least some of this networking was done in schools.

While massive oil wealth did reduce demands for participation in the early years of the oil boom, or at least gave rulers the resources to divert what demands there were, the processes of state growth and educational expansion have led to a new wave of participatory demands from society in the Gulf Arab monarchies. These demands are the unintentional, but in many ways inevitable, result of state policies pursued over the last two decades. It is a mistake to assume that oil wealth has once and for all "depoliticized" the citizenry in these states.

CULTURE, SOCIETY, AND POLITICAL ORGANIZATION

Does the importance of Islam and tribalism in the political and social life of the Gulf monarchies, what has been referred to as their "traditional" political culture, inhibit the development of participatory politics? Certainly, the regimes use the symbols and rhetoric of tribalism and Islam (particularly in Saudi Arabia) in their legitimation formulas to argue that their systems are culturally and politically authentic and truly represent the wishes of the people, even without formal participatory institutions. But these symbols and rhetoric are open to other interpretations.

The strength of tribal social structures does not preclude citizen demands for a role in politics. In fact, tribes have been particularly adept at using electoral processes in Kuwait to advance their interests. Some Kuwaiti tribes conduct primaries to pick legislative candidates whom the entire tribe supports in the general election, to maximize their electoral power (a process common in other countries where tribal structures remain strong and elections are allowed, like Jordan and Yemen). Tribal primaries before the October 1992 elections yielded some candidates who expressed a clear ideological platform (most often Islamist of some type), while also emphasizing their tribal roots. The Kuwaiti example gives clear evidence that even social structures believed to be as "traditional" as tribes can readily adjust to and take advantage of more "modern" forms of political life.

Islamic groups throughout the Gulf states point to the Quranic injunction that rulers practice consultation (*shura*) in governance to support their calls for representative institutions that can act as a check on the arbitrary power of the executive. Islamic social and charitable institutions in both the Sunni and the Shi'i communities have provided a basis for political action. For example, in Kuwait three Muslim charitable organizations—the Social Reform Society, the Heritage Society, and the Cultural and Social Society—became the organizational bases for the three Islamist blocs (Muslim Brotherhood, *salafi*, and Shi'i, respectively) that fielded candidates in the 1992 elections.[3] In Bahrain, the Shi'i social-religious institution called *ma'atim* (funerary societies that plan the yearly 'ashura celebrations commemorating the martyrdom of Husayn) have been important bases for political organization.[4] The Muslim Brotherhood in Bahrain (operating, as in Kuwait, under the name of the Social Reform Society) and the state-sponsored *salafi* (Wahhabi) organizations in Saudi Arabia have recently become more openly active players in political life.

Islam and tribalism are not immutable political facts. They are frameworks for identity. Their content is open to political debate and struggle, a process going on in the Gulf monarchies and throughout the Middle East today. Regimes put forward interpretations, supported by the financial, institutional, and media resources at their disposal. Political groups and activists put forward other interpretations, in an effort to attract popular support and build legitimacy. Political "culture" in these countries is up for grabs.

It would also be a mistake to assume that the only bases of political organization in the Gulf monarchies are family, tribal, or sectarian. Other civil society groups, organized on functional and/ or ideological bases, are important elements of the political equation. In all the states, chambers of commerce are active participants in the policymaking process. In Kuwait, the chamber joined other groups after the Iraqi invasion in pressing the government to restore constitutional life. In Saudi Arabia, the Council of Chambers of Commerce coordinates the activities of the nineteen regional chambers. There are twelve national committees organized by the Council of Chambers on industry lines. The various arms of the Council are consulted by government ministries in drafting legislation, and the Council and its regional chambers actively lobby the government and the royal family on issues of concern. The chambers played a role in convincing King Fahd to rescind the government's 1988 proposal to impose an income tax on foreign businesses and workers, and lobbied successfully on other austerity measures under discussion at that time.[5] In Riyad, the largest regional chamber, two-thirds of the members of the board of directors are elected by the membership ("the only election in the country," as was pointed out by an official of the chamber), and one-third are appointed by the Commerce Ministry.[6] The February 1993 elections to the chamber were actively contested, with open campaigning by two organized tickets, and nearly five thousand votes cast in the election.[7]

The chambers of commerce throughout the Gulf monarchies are a network through which merchants and businessmen can communicate with each other and the government, and on occasion develop common positions on issues of interest to them. They are not part of a political "opposition," nor are they threats to the regimes. As discussed in the previous chapter, business is largely dependent upon state expenditure and regulation, and the relationship between the two sectors on both a personal and institutional level is close. But the chambers, to differing degrees in the different states, provide an institutional basis for representing the interests of their constituencies. In more fluid political circumstances, they could be the basis of more overtly "political" organizations, as they have at least temporarily become in Kuwait since liberation.

Professional syndicates and social clubs are other civil society organizations that play an important role in the political life of the Gulf monarchies. Faculty and alumni associations at the national universities, lawyers', engineers', and doctors' groups, and white-collar "unions" of government employees have developed, to a greater or lesser degree, in all of these countries. Kuwait, given its relatively more open political atmosphere, has seen the development of the most autonomous and openly political of such organizations. During the Iraqi occupation, many of these groups (along with Islamic organizations) provided the organizational basis for resistance committees that distributed food, provided medical care, and conducted attacks on Iraqi forces.[8] After liberation, these groups became more outspoken in their support for the restoration of constitutional life. In Bahrain social clubs have in the past been the basis for political organization, particularly during the height of the Arab nationalist movement in the 1950s and 1960s, to such an extent that the regime began to assume a much more active regulatory role over them by the late 1950s. The major clubs, like the ʿUruba ("Arabism") Club, whose membership is largely Shiʿi, and the predominantly Sunni Bahrain Club and Ahli ("National") Club, still play an important organizational role in Bahraini society, and are the centers of political discussion, if not of overt political activity. In a more open political environment, these clubs would undoubtedly be the basis of political movements or parties.[9]

Some Gulf intellectuals have taken to heart the rhetoric of Gulf unity that accompanied the founding of the Gulf Cooperation Council in 1981 to establish organizations that cut across country borders to include members from all, or most, of the Gulf monarchies. A group of Gulf intellectuals, businessmen, and administrators has been meeting yearly since 1979 to discuss economic and social issues. In 1986, they adopted the name *muntada al-tanmiyya* (the Development Forum). Along with its more technical development studies, the group sometimes addresses broadly political issues, such as participation in the political process, the role of women in society, and the role of the media.[10] In May 1992, in the wake of the Gulf War, ninety Gulf intellectuals, academics, businessmen, and political figures established the "Gulf National Forum" (*al-maltaqa al-watani al-khaliji*) with the explicit aims of "confirming democratic values and political participation" and encouraging the development of "civil society institutions" in the GCC states. The organization committed itself to the cause of greater Gulf cooperation at the popular level, presenting itself as a "popular reserve" to support GCC efforts at the official level.[11]

Despite the fact that the state has gotten bigger, richer, and stronger over the past two decades in the Gulf monarchies, and has constricted the public "space" available for political activity, civil society organizations—be they "traditional" like tribes or religious groups, or "modern" like chambers of commerce, labor unions, or social clubs—continue to be important elements in the political and social life of these states. They strive, with greater or lesser success, to maintain some autonomy from the states, which in turn attempt to absorb, to co-opt, and in rare cases, to suppress, them. They are not "threats" to the regimes in any immediate sense, in the way that underground nationalist and Islamic groups are. In extreme circumstances, like the Iraqi invasion of Kuwait, they provide important sources of support to state and government. They lobby the government on behalf of their specific interests. They provide the organizational basis and the social space for citizens to meet, to talk, and to develop relationships that sometimes cut across family, tribal, and sectarian lines. When permitted, as in Kuwait since liberation, they can form the basis of what are, in all but name, political parties. They are proof that "culture," whether conceived in tribal or Islamic terms, is not an impediment to social or political organization in these states.

DEMANDS FOR POLITICAL CHANGE

Neither the rentier state nor cultural factors of tribalism and Islam act as absolute barriers to citizens in the Gulf monarchies seeking a greater role in their political systems. In fact, the limits on political life in the Gulf monarchies in the period up to 1990 are best understood as emanating from the states themselves, not from their economies or societies. The oil boom allowed governments to deflect most demands for participation through economic inducement or bureaucratic position; to shrink the social space available for political organizing by taking a larger role in their societies (through control of the media and regulation, co-option, or marginalization of civil society organizations), and to suppress more effectively those political elements deemed threatening to regime security. However, two important events in recent years have led to greater demands from social groups for a say in politics and to a partial loosening of the restrictions on political life by state authorities in all these countries. Those events were the oil "bust" of the 1980s and the 1990–1991 Gulf War.

The precipitous drop in world oil prices in 1986, after a steady decline from the heights of the early 1980s, triggered an economic crisis in each of the Gulf states. GDP in every Gulf monarchy, which had been increasing at substantial rates for the previous fifteen years, fell during the last years of the 1980s. Governments drew down reserves to maintain most state services, but still had to cut back on the spending that fuels local economies (see Tables 2a–2f). Some local businesses went bankrupt, unemployment emerged for the first time in nearly two decades as a problem in some of these countries, and the boom mentality of previous years came to an abrupt end. This economic shock led to a new awareness of the fragility of Gulf prosperity and thus to demands for more efficient and accountable government economic policies.

Just as the Gulf recession was ending in the late 1980s, the monarchies had to face the political crisis generated by the Iraqi invasion of Kuwait. Saddam Husayn directly challenged the legitimacy not just of the Kuwaiti regime, but of all Kuwait's GCC allies, on both Arab nationalist and Islamic bases. The presence of American troops raised questions among citizens about the ability of their governments to defend them, even after billions of dollars of oil wealth had been spent on defense. The intense international media focus on the region also led to some degree of self-examination. All these factors led the governments of the region to loosen the restrictions on political speech that usually apply, as a safety valve for the release of public pressure during the crisis.

Kuwait

It is not surprising that Kuwait, with the longest history of representative institutions and the freest political climate among the Gulf monarchies, was the first place that citizen demands for more political participation were publicly voiced. With the end of the Iran-Iraq war in August 1988, security concerns that were the stated reason for the suspension of the *majlis al-'umma* in 1986 seemed less reasonable to many Kuwaitis. Thirty members of the dissolved *majlis*, of various political orientations, had been meeting regularly since 1986; in 1989 they initiated a petition drive requesting the amir to restore constitutional rule. The organizers had hoped to get 1,500 signatures; in the end they claimed that 30,000 Kuwaitis signed the petition.[12] When the amir refused to accept the petition, public meetings organized around the Kuwaiti institution of the *diwaniyya*—a weekly open house—were held in support of restoration of the constitution. The importance of the long-established social tradition of the *diwaniyya* as the basis of these meetings was such that they became known in Kuwait as the *diwaniyya* movement. Two such meetings in January 1990, each attended by thousands of Kuwaitis, were broken up by security forces.[13] The use of violence to suppress mainstream political opinion, while not unprecedented in Kuwaiti history, was very uncommon and engendered more criticism of the government.

In response to rising public demands, in April 1990 the amir announced a compromise proposal: a National Council composed of fifty elected members and twenty-five appointed members to replace the *majlis al-'umma*. The new council would exercise oversight and consultative functions, without the legislative powers the constitution granted to the *majlis*. The amir's offer divided the *diwaniyya* movement. A number of prominent Kuwaitis agreed to serve in the National Council, and elections for the council in June 1990 achieved a respectable turnout, though below the usual 80 percent for past parliamentary elections. Most of the movement's organizers rejected the proposal, seeing it as a retreat from the 1962 constitution, and organized a boycott of the elections. The government reacted with unusual harshness toward its opponents on this issue, arresting many prominent Kuwaitis.[14] Some Gulf observers believe that the increasingly bitter confrontation between the government and the *diwaniyya* movement encouraged Saddam Husayn to think, mistakenly, that the Iraqi invasion would meet with some measure of popular support in Kuwait.[15]

The Iraqi occupation drastically changed the course of Kuwaiti politics. Stripped of much of its power while in exile and at least partially discredited by its poor performance during the invasion, the Kuwaiti government needed broad support from Kuwaitis inside and outside the country. The need to appeal to public opinion in the West, where decisions would be made about the use of military force to liberate the country, was another factor pushing the Al Sabah to present a democratic, constitutional, unified picture of Kuwait. Finally, the practically unanimous support exhibited by Kuwaitis for the country's independence and the continued rule of the Al Sabah must have reassured ruling family members about the loyalty of the populace. At a meeting of 1,200 prominent Kuwaitis from across the political spectrum, held in Jidda, Saudi Arabia, in October 1990, the amir and the crown prince agreed to restore the constitution upon liberation, amid unanimous resolutions of support for the country and its leadership.

The good feelings of Jidda largely dissipated soon after coalition forces expelled the Iraqis from Kuwait. A petition signed by political leaders from Islamist, liberal, and independent political groups circulated in March–April 1991 demanding prompt implementation of the promises made in Jidda.[16] On April 7, 1991, the amir in a televised address promised elections "sometime in 1992." The vagueness of this commitment led to a demonstration of one thousand people, organized by a coalition of groups, protesting the trend in post-liberation politics.[17]

The March–April 1991 petition was a cooperative effort among seven political groups, which had emerged long before the invasion in liberated Kuwait. One was the group of former parliamentarians who had coordinated the *diwaniyya* movement, known as the "Representatives' Bloc" (*takattul al-nawab*) and led by the former *majlis* speaker, Ahmad al-Saʿdun. Three groups emerged from Islamic social organizations: the Islamic Constitutional Movement (*al-*

haraka al-dusturiyya al-'islamiyya), a Sunni group connected to the Muslim Brotherhood; the Popular Islamic Alignment (*al-tajammuᶜ al-'islami al-shaᶜbi*), the political wing of the Sunni *salafi* movement; and the National Islamic Coalition (*al-'ittilaf al-'islami al-watani*), representing Shiᶜi Islamists. The leadership of the Kuwaiti Chamber of Commerce, representing prominent old Sunni merchant families, sponsored the Constitutional Alignment (*al-tajammuᶜ al-dusturi*). Western-style liberals and old Arab national-ists formed the Kuwaiti Democratic Forum (*al-minbar al-dimuqrati al-kuwayti*). Finally, an ad-hoc group of prominent figures not affiliated with any political tendencies but suspicious of government intentions formed the Independents Group (*majmuᶜat al-musta-qillin*). There was some overlap among the groups, particularly the Representatives' Bloc, which contained former *majlis* deputies affili-ated with a number of the other political currents. Despite their ideological differences, the seven groups remained united in their demand that the constitution be restored and that elections be held for a new *majlis al-'umma*. Representatives of the groups met weekly from the time of liberation up to the elections of October 1992 to coordinate activities and issue statements.[18]

The government's response to the political activity of these groups varied. No effort was made, as before the invasion, to strong-arm those critical of government policies. Four of the seven groups (the Islamic groups and the Democratic Forum), for all intents and purposes, were acting as political parties. Although the formation of political parties is illegal under Kuwaiti law, their actions were tolerated. In January 1992, the system of press censorship that was imposed on daily newspapers with the dissolution of the *majlis* in 1986 was formally lifted.[19] On the other hand, the editor of *al-Qabas*, a relative of the president of the Kuwait Chamber of Com-merce and member of the Constitutional Alignment, was arrested in April 1992 on charges that his newspaper had revealed state secu-rity secrets. The fact that *al-Qabas* was the most vocal daily news-paper criticizing the government convinced many Kuwaitis that the arrest was politically motivated. In May 1992, a seminar on cam-paign techniques organized by the International Republican Insti-tute, the international arm of the U.S. Republican Party, and sponsored by the Kuwaiti Graduate Society, many of whose members were critical of the government, was canceled by the interior minister. The irony that the Kuwaiti government would snub representatives of the political party headed by the liberator of the country was not lost on politically aware Kuwaitis.[20]

Much of the tension between political groups and the government came to a head in elections for the board of directors of the Kuwait Chamber of Commerce in May 1992. The chamber has been led since independence by ʿAbd al-ʿAziz al-Saqr, scion of one of the prominent Sunni merchant families who, with the Al Sabah, founded Kuwait. As indicated above, the chamber formed the basis of one of the political groups that emerged after liberation. In the May election, a slate of candidates headed by Khalid al-Marzuq formed to challenge the domination of al-Saqr and his allies. Critics of the government saw this move as an effort by the Al Sabah to put a close ally in control of a major civil society institution. They pointed to al-Marzuq's close connection with senior members of the family and his involvement in the Suq al-Manakh crisis as evidence of this plan. Supporters of the al-Marzuq list contended that this was a challenge by previously disenfranchised elements in the business community to the monopoly of the old Sunni families, pointing to the prominent Shiʿis and beduin tribal personalities on their list. They rightly pointed out that the al-Saqr list also included a number of people close to the ruling family.

Past elections to the chamber's board of directors had been desultory affairs, with few ballots cast and many members running unopposed. This contest, rightly or wrongly, came to be seen by many as a test of strength between the government and the political groups. Campaigning was intense, with nightly *diwaniyya* meetings by various candidates, considerable advertising in the newspapers, and heavy media coverage. The al-Saqr list included representatives from other political groups, including the Shiʿi Islamist group, and was endorsed by the Muslim Brotherhood.[21] The results of the balloting (one vote per commercial license for dues-paying members of the chamber, so some people had more than one vote and women who owned a business were permitted to vote) was an overwhelming victory for the al-Saqr list. It won twenty-three of the twenty-four seats, ʿAbd al-ʿAziz al-Saqr received the most votes—5,516.

The twenty-fourth seat was won by Khalid al-Marzuq, with 4,182 votes.[22]

The extent and intensity of political organization in Kuwait in the period immediately preceding and following the Iraqi invasion is clear evidence that, when permitted by the state, political groups will emerge to contest for power and pressure the government even in "Muslim tribal societies." The October 1992 elections to the *majlis al-'umma*, contested by all seven political groups and a large number of independents, were the culmination of a period of extraordinary political mobilization in Kuwait. They will be discussed later.

Saudi Arabia

While Kuwait was the pacesetter, other Gulf monarchies also witnessed an increase in open political activity in the period after the Iraqi invasion of Kuwait, at least partially tolerated by the governments. In Saudi Arabia, King Fahd's announcement in November 1990 of plans to institute a *majlis al-shura* (consultative assembly) seems to have been taken as an indication that the doors were open, at least somewhat, for Saudi citizens to present their demands in more organized ways. The first such demand came in a petition to the King, apparently circulated in late 1990, signed by forty-three Saudis identified as "liberals" or "secularists" in most of the news media. That petition, unprecedented in recent Saudi history, was couched in very deferential and supportive terms. The petition explicitly called for the maintenance of the existing regime and the "noble ruling family," praised the King's openness and devotion to the people, and strongly supported his decision to establish a consultative assembly. In the conclusion, the signers portrayed themselves as being "from the elite of your citizens—your brothers and sons, who you know well are not trouble-makers or jealous people, nor representatives of special interests, nor after private gain or ambition."

While emphasizing their loyalty to the government, the signers asserted that it is "the bounden duty of every citizen to give advice to the rulers . . . and to participate with them by word and deed in everything that he believes is for the good of the country, which belongs to all." A number of their specific recommendations dealt with the issue of representative institutions. They urged that the proposed *majlis al-shura* be given responsibility for "studying, developing, and approving procedures and regulations relating to economic, political, educational, and other matters; and for oversight of the work of executive agencies." They advocated a revival of local municipal councils and the establishment of provincial-level consultative councils, and permission for professions to form syndicates on the model of the kingdom's chambers of commerce. The petition also called for more independent and open media with "complete freedom to promote virtue and enjoin vice, and enrich dialogue in an open Muslim society."

Another major theme in this liberal petition was the importance of fairness and consistency in applying the rule of law. The signers emphasized that the basis of the legal system must be *shari'a* (Islamic law) and that efforts to implement it must be strengthened in order to achieve its "highest intentions: establishing justice, achieving equality, spreading reform, and guaranteeing everyone his rights, in order that our society be a noble picture of the modern Islamic state." But implementation of *shari'a* requires "an organized framework for issuing *fatwas*." They urged that a distinction be made between the dictates of the Quran and the *Sunna* (way, or traditions, of the Prophet Muhammad), which are infallible, and the specific interpretations of those infallible sources by the members of the *'ulama*: "What is requested is that we differentiate in our lives, in a decisive and practical way, between the dictates of *shari'a* and the views and human interpretations of the *'ulama*, which should be subject to assessment, evaluation, discussion, and response without limit or restriction."

The petition's concern with curbing arbitrariness in state action was also evidenced in other recommendations. The signers called for establishment of a basic system of government—a constitutional basis for the state (though they did not use the word "constitution"). They stipulated that the judiciary should be reviewed, its procedures modernized, and its independence insured. One recommendation dealt with strengthening the principle of "complete equality among citizens in all fields, without discrimination on the basis of tribal affiliation, family background, sect, or social status." It went on to urge reaffirmation of the principle that "no citizen will be subject to interference in his life without legal ruling." In a similar vein, the petitioners asked for "complete reform of the committees to promote virtue and forbid vice (the *mutaw-wa'in*) . . . to insure a style of wisdom and proper religious exhortation in the performance of duties." The signers also indirectly criticized the interference of some royal family members in administrative and judicial proceedings, saying that the family must not become "a means by which rules and regulations are rendered meaningless and superseded."[23]

The liberal petition elicited a response from the Saudi religious establishment and personalities associated with Islamic intellectual and political currents in the kingdom. That response took the form of their own petition addressed to the king, a shorter document than the "liberal" petition, and a subsequent amplification of the recommendations in that petition. In contrast to the first petition, which had only forty-three signatures, the "Islamist" petition was signed by over four hundred people, including the senior religious figure in the kingdom, Shaykh 'Abd al-'Aziz bin Baz, and a number of his senior *'ulama* colleagues. Given the privileged and secure position in the Saudi political system of religious institutions and the *'ulama*, the sharper, more direct tone of this second petition should not be surprising. Its preamble was very short, devoid of the extensive professions of loyalty to both the political system and Islam found in the liberal petition. It referred to "this critical period in which all people have realized the dire need for change," and requested the ruler to consider a number of circumstances in need of "reform."

The Islamist petition, like its liberal counterpart, supported the idea of the establishment of a *majlis al-shura*, emphasizing that it must be "completely independent, without any pressure that could affect the conduct of [its] responsibilities." It went somewhat further than the other document in calling for the *majlis* to play a role in both domestic and foreign policy. The Islamist petition also addressed specific criticisms of government policy in a number of areas. It called for strengthening the system of accountability for state officials, and "purging the state apparatus of everyone proved to be corrupt or unable to perform their duties, regardless of any other consideration." It criticized the government for its management of financial affairs, advocating "establishing justice in distributing the public wealth to all classes and groups in society," canceling taxes and lessening fees for government services, abolishing state-supported monopolies, lifting the ban on Islamic banks and purging public and private financial institutions of practices involving interest (*riba'*). Similar to the liberal petition, the Islamist version urged that the Saudi media be "guaranteed its freedom to increase awareness through honest reporting and constructive criticism," but also emphasized that the media must represent Islamic values and eliminate all aspects of programming contradictory to those values.

⌐ Judicial and legal issues dominated the Islamist petition. The signers called for the establishment of a commission, presumably made up of prominent *ʿulama*, to examine every state regulation and edict in light of *shariʿa* and to cancel those found to conflict with it. They urged unification of the judicial system, which currently consists of both *shariʿa* courts and secular authorities empowered to adjudicate administrative and commercial cases, under the authority of the religious law courts. The petition also called for justice and equality for all members of society, with "no favoritism to the elite or prejudice against the weak," condemning those who use their "sphere of influence" to escape their duties or violate the rights of others. The final recommendation of the petition advocated safeguarding "the rights of the individual and of society" in such a way as to guarantee "human dignity."[24]

In a country where organized political activity is severely limited, and criticism of government policy is expected to be offered on a personal basis and kept confidential, the circulation of these two petitions represented a substantial departure from the past. They touched off what in Saudi terms can only be seen as a wave of political expression. Islamic activists began to be more vocal in their criticism of aspects of political life in the kingdom, from the *minbar* (pulpit of a mosque, from which the Friday sermon is delivered) and in cassette tapes circulated through Islamic bookstores and religious institutions.[25] The Memorandum of Advice and the Committee to Defend Legitimate Rights discussed in Chapter 2 were part of this increased activism among Saudi Islamists.

Yet another petition to King Fahd appeared in late 1991, from leaders of the Saudi Shiʿi community, which is located in the country's Eastern province. They praised the king's promises made in November 1990 to establish a *majlis al-shura* and undertake other reforms, and expressed their conviction that he would not countenance any efforts to exclude any group or sect from participating in these reforms or to deny their rights. In that light, they raised four specific issues that they were "absolutely sure . . . would be taken care of by your Excellency." The first dealt with harassment of Shiᶜa in the performance of their religious rites and lack of financial support for the building of Shiᶜi mosques and religious institutions. The second complained of discrimination against Shiᶜa in hiring practices by the government and state companies, specifically mentioning SABIC and Saudi ARAMCO, much of whose activities are centered in the oil-rich Eastern province. The third dealt with "obstacles . . . being deliberately placed to prevent them [Shiᶜa] from admission" into Saudi universities. The final issue is their allegation of a "quarantine at the entrance to any branch of the army" for Shiᶜa, though many in the community wish to "discharge our duty of defending the soil of this country."[26]

Other States

The "petition fever" which started in pre-invasion Kuwait and gathered momentum in Saudi Arabia after the Gulf War also spread to Bahrain and Qatar. In December 1991, fifty-four prominent Qataris addressed a petition to the amir, saying that "the obstacles facing us have reached a point that threatens" the achievements of his twenty-year reign, and can only be confronted by the rulers and citizens together "through cooperation, consultation, and the rule of law." The signers criticized absence of freedom of expression in the media and confusion surrounding citizenship rights and the naturalization process, a major issue in a country where noncitizens outnumber citizens by almost three to one. Their specific recommendation to the ruler was in the area of institutions, not policies: the establishment of a consultative body "that has wide legislative and investigative authority, and through which actual political participation is provided." The first duty of that body should be to draft a permanent constitution "that guarantees the establishment of democracy."[27] This recommendation was a sharp if implicit criticism of the existing Qatari consultative council, appointed by the amir, which has been in existence since 1972. The provisional Qatari constitution, adopted in the same year and still in force, called for elections to the council. The amir has chosen to extend the life of the original appointed body over the past twenty years rather than permit such elections.[28]

In July 1992, a petition signed by over two hundred Bahrainis was submitted to the amir, calling for the restoration of the National Assembly (suspended in 1975) through direct and free elections, as mandated by the Bahraini constitution. This short document, addressed as a letter to the amir, emphasized repeatedly the importance of the constitution, as proof of the democratic nature of the country, as the guarantor of citizens' right to petition their rulers, and as the source of authority for the National Assembly. The petition was circulated at a time when rumors were rife in Bahrain that the amir would establish a nonelected consultative council, without legislative powers. The petition stated that an appointed council "to widen the scope of the consultations [the government] wants to undertake" would not conflict with the responsibilities of the National Assembly, but at the same time it "cannot take the place of the National Assembly as a constitutional legislative power."[29]

No similar petitions emerged in the UAE or Oman, but the issues raised in the other Gulf states were discussed in both countries, particularly in the UAE.[30] In March 1993, at a public meeting held with members of the UAE Federal National Council, the consultative council appointed by the rulers, a number of political and intellectual figures supported the writing of a permanent constitution for the state, an expanded legislative and oversight role for the Federal National Council, and direct election of its members.[31]

Common Themes

Some common themes run through these participatory exercises. The rule of law is a very prominent one. In states with established constitutions—Kuwait and Bahrain—appeals to rulers stress the importance of the constitution as the only acceptable basis of politics. In Qatar, with a "provisional" constitution, the demand was for a constituent legislative body to draw up a permanent constitution. In Saudi Arabia, where there had been no formal constitutional document, both Islamist and liberal petitions emphasized the importance of implementing *shariᶜa*, though they held very different notions of how it should be implemented and to what effect, as their different positions on judicial reform indicate. Along with the Shiᶜi petition, they called for stronger guarantees of personal rights and equal treatment under the law.

Another important common theme is the need for institutionalized mechanisms for political participation. In Kuwait and Bahrain, with a history of elected legislative assemblies, demands were for restoration of those bodies. In Qatar this sentiment was voiced through the request for a new consultative body, with more independence and wider powers than the current consultative council. In Saudi Arabia, all three petitions expressed support for the idea of a *majlis al-shura*, as promised by the king in November 1990. In three of the four countries, the need for greater freedom of expression through the media was raised as an issue; in Bahrain, though not mentioned in the petition to the amir, the need for greater press freedom has been voiced frequently.[32] The Saudi liberal petition called for sanctioning more civil society organizations like professional syndicates, as well as consultative councils on municipal and provincial levels.

The issue of the accountability of rulers and government officials to society was an important element of all these efforts. Demands both for the rule of law and formal institutions of participation (including a more independent press) can be seen as responses to the perception among many of the arbitrary nature of government in these systems. The Islamist petition in Saudi Arabia was explicit in criticizing practices of nepotism, favoritism, and official interference in judicial proceedings, and called for purging corrupt officials. The liberal petition was more oblique, but in its emphasis on the need for due process and its call for the ruling family to avoid becoming a means for circumventing government rules and regulations, it made the same points. In Kuwait worries about monopolizing of state finances by royal family members, a trend that accelerated during the Iraqi occupation, were an important factor in demands for restoration of the *majlis al-'umma*. Calls for a return to constitutional rule, or for constitution-drafting (in Qatar and the liberal Saudi petition), and for independent legislative, judicial, and supervisory bodies all have as one of their aims curbing executive power.[33]

It must be noted that none of these petitions questioned the basis of the political systems in their countries. All expressed support for the ruling families, even when calling for limits on their powers. None advocated the kind of radical change that Arab nationalist groups called for in past decades; none called for the Islamic revolution supported most seriously by underground Shi'i groups in Kuwait and Bahrain in the 1980s, and by Juhayman al-ʿUtaybi's group in Saudi Arabia in 1979. These were reflections of mainstream opinion, at least among politically involved strata of these societies. Taken together, this trend demanding reform and increased political participation is compelling testimony that the rentier state does not "depoliticize" citizens or reduce their desire for responsible government and participatory institutions. It also challenges the theory that societies in which tribalism and Islam are important elements of the social fabric are immune to more "modern" forms of political debate and organization.

GOVERNMENT RESPONSES

Kuwait

Kuwait went furthest among the Gulf monarchies in responding to popular demands for more accountable government and broader participatory institutions. This outcome is not surprising, for two reasons. First, Kuwait had the most extensive past experience with more open political life. Demands were not for change, but for a return to the constitutional status quo. Social institutions and organizations, independent of the government, had longer histories and stronger roots there, and were available as the bases of political organization. Second, the Kuwaiti government and ruling family were severely shaken by the experience of the Iraqi invasion. Particularly while in exile, they were in desperate need of support from their own people and from the United States. Their bargaining leverage with social forces demanding the restoration of the constitution was minimal. The commitments they made at the Jidda Conference, with one eye on Kuwaitis and another on American policymakers and public opinion, set limits on their freedom of maneuver after liberation.

The promises made in Jidda were redeemed in October 1992, with elections to a new *majlis al-'umma*. It must be noted that the electorate in Kuwait is a small percentage of the total Kuwaiti population. Only Kuwaiti men, twenty-one years of age or older, whose families were identified as Kuwaiti residents in 1921, were eligible to vote. The total number of eligible voters was somewhat more than 80,000, about 15 percent of the adult population. Turnout in the October election exceeded 80 percent.[34] The elections themselves were conducted in a very open manner. Campaigning was intense. Government authorities observed strict formal neutrality, though there were persistent rumors that ruling family members supported friendly candidates indirectly. Polling was observed by the international press and outside monitors. Interpretations of the results differ in various accounts because identifying the political leanings of candidates, particularly independents, was a subjective exercise. Even given these caveats, the results were a startling rebuff for the government and an expression of widespread popular support for political groups' basic demands for return to constitutional government and a strong assembly to check executive power.

By the author's count, thirty-three of the fifty seats were won by candidates identified with the "opposition": those on the ticket of one of the seven political groupings, independents supported by one or more of the groupings, and those who identified themselves during the campaign with the "opposition." No single political group dominated the results. The largest identifiable group of winners were members of the Representatives' Bloc (ten of twelve running), members of the *majlis* suspended in 1986, which was not an ideological group at all. Most of the members of the National Assembly convened in 1990 who sought election, lost. By far the majority of those who did win seats were not identified directly with the more ideological political groups—the three Islamist groups, the Democratic Forum, and the Constitutional Alignment. Twenty of the thirty-three "opposition" winners were independents.

The Islamic groups represent the largest ideological bloc in the *majlis*. Again, by the author's count: four Islamic Constitutional Movement (Muslim Brotherhood) members; three Popular Islamic

Alignment *(salafi)* members; and eight independents supported by either one or both of these Sunni Islamist groups. Three members of the National Islamic Coalition (Shi'i) won seats. Included in this overall group were four *imams* of Kuwaiti mosques. It would be a mistake, however, to see this "Islamic Bloc" as monolithic. The Sunni groups did not cooperate with the Shi'i Islamists; observers speculate that some Shi'i voters sided with more secularist candidates in districts where Sunni Islamists were leading candidates. The two Sunni groups also competed against one another. One Kuwaiti analyst, after review of the total vote, wrote that five more Islamic Constitutional Movement candidates would have won if there had been district-level cooperation with the Popular Islamic Alignment.

Democratic Forum members won two seats. The only Constitutional Alignment candidate who stood for election, Jasim al-Saqr (the son of Chamber of Commerce President 'Abd al-'Aziz al-Saqr), was elected. A number of interesting deals were made at the district level. For example, the Islamic Constitutional Movement (ICM) supported Jasim al-Saqr in his district, and the Constitutional Alignment supported some ICM candidates in other districts. The election was as notable for who did not win. A number of well-known former parliamentarians, known as "services representatives," went down to defeat. These politicians made their careers by taking care of their constituents' personal interests, and were willing to support almost any government policy in exchange for access to resources ("pork" does not seem the proper term in a Muslim country) to meet constituent needs. Tribal identification continued to be an important element in voter loyalty, particularly in the districts outside Kuwait City proper. However, candidates with distinct ideological profiles, particularly Islamists, emerged victorious in a number of the tribal districts. Tribal identity and ideological preference were not mutually exclusive.[35]

The government took the results of the election to heart. Shortly after the polling, the amir met with ten parliamentarians from various groups, telling them that he would meet monthly with the president of the *majlis*, his deputy, and the heads of the major parliamentary committees. Previously, he held formal monthly meetings only with the prime minister. He indirectly pledged not to dissolve this *majlis* as he had the previous one. He also consulted with the deputies on the make-up of the new government. For their part, the deputies reaffirmed the amir's constitutional right to choose the prime minister.[36] Some political groups, including the Democratic Forum and the Islamic Constitutional Movement, had advocated during the campaign formal separation of the offices of prime minister and crown prince. The fact that the political groups were willing to accept a continued link between the position of head of government and the Al Sabah family is an indication of the limited nature of their opposition to the Kuwaiti status quo. With this issue resolved, the amir quickly reappointed Crown Prince Sa'd 'Abdallah as prime minister.

After extensive consultations with deputies, Shaykh Sa'd announced his new government on October 17, 1992. The "national security" positions remained in the hands of the Al Sabah: Defense, Interior, Foreign Affairs. Shaykh Sabah al-Ahmad, criticized by some for his performance as foreign minister in the period leading up to the Iraqi invasion, returned to that post. Shaykh Sa'ud Nasir Al Sabah, a member of the family's younger generation who gained prominence as Kuwait's ambassador to the United States during the Gulf crisis, was brought home to serve as information minister. This ministry in the Gulf monarchies is a sensitive one, given the state's active oversight of the press. What was new about the government was inclusion of six parliamentarians as ministers. Dr. Ahmad al-Rab'i, a Harvard-educated philosopher and independent liberal, was named minister of education and higher education, to the chagrin of many Islamists. Jasim al-'Awn, of the Popular Islamic Alignment, became minister of social and labor affairs; Ju'man al-'Azimi of the Islamic Constitutional Movement, a *khatib* (preacher) in a local mosque, accepted the ministry of *awqaf* (Islamic Endowments) and Islamic affairs. Dr. 'Abdallah al-Hajiri, an independent supported by the Islamic Constitutional Movement, was appointed minister of commerce and industry. 'Ali al-Baghli, an independent Shi'i parliamentarian, received the important post of minister of oil.

In the first year of its term, the new *majlis* exhibited a strong tendency toward independence from the government and assertion of its oversight role. It chose Ahmad al-Sa'dun, leader of the Representatives' Bloc and speaker of the previous *majlis*, as speaker. He had been an outspoken critic of the government since the 1986 dissolution and a driving force in the *diwaniyya* movement. Various parliamentary committees have begun investigations of sensitive issues that are already affecting the workings of government. The military budget is being reviewed by the budget committee, to determine the cost-effectiveness of various arms deals with Western powers agreed to after liberation. A special committee is conducting a closed-door investigation of events leading up to the Iraqi invasion, and has compelled high-ranking officials and ruling family members to testify. Another committee is reviewing security legislation adopted by the government since the dissolution of the last *majlis*. Parliamentary questions about alleged corruption in the Kuwait Investments Office, which manages Kuwait's overseas capital, has led to the suspension of three officials in the office (two of whom are members of the Al Sabah), seizure of their personal assets, and issuing of warrants for their arrest (all three remain abroad). Oil Minister al-Baghli reported significant fraud in the Kuwait Oil Tankers Company during the Iraqi occupation, amounting to nearly $100 million.[37]

A number of very difficult issues lay ahead for the *majlis*: citizenship matters, women's enfranchisement, financing Kuwait's future with its cash reserves largely depleted by the crisis and rebuilding. Social and educational issues will inevitably split the Islamists from more secular tendencies. The beginnings of that fissure emerged in August 1993, when Islamist deputies supported the government's move to close "unlicensed" human rights organizations, many of which were associated with more secularist political trends.[38] Tensions with the government could grow if investigations of corruption reach higher levels. The extremely high hopes attached to the *majlis* by many Kuwaitis will inevitably be disappointed, as the daily grind of politics replaces the exultant atmosphere of the October 1992 elections. But during the first year of its term, the new Kuwaiti *majlis* has acted quickly and responsibly to restore some sense of accountability and participation to that country's politics.

Saudi Arabia

In the other Gulf monarchies, government responses to popular demands for participation were more limited, but still significant.

King Fahd of Saudi Arabia announced on March 1, 1992, three royal decrees that establish important changes in the Saudi domestic political system: a "Basic System of Government" (*al-nizam al-'asasi lil-hukm*), a constitution-like document; the statute for a new consultative council (*majlis al-shura*); and a system of regional government for the kingdom's fourteen provinces. On August 20, 1993 the king issued four more decrees, appointing the members of the Consultative Council, setting out its rules of operation, and amending the charter of the Council of Ministers, the Saudi cabinet. These decrees, taken together, have the potential to be the most far-reaching domestic political reforms in the country since then Crown Prince Faysal's ten-point modernization program of November 1962.

The Basic System specifically states that the constitution of the kingdom is founded on the Quran and the *sunna* (traditions) of the Prophet Muhammad, maintaining the position that Saudi Arabia, as the Islamic state par excellence, has no need for a formal constitution. However, the Basic System is clearly intended to set out the foundations of the state and the distribution of political powers within it. Article 5 asserts that the system of government is monarchical, with rulership (*al-hukm*) resting in the sons and grandsons of King ʿAbd al-ʿAziz Al Saʿud, the founder of the modern kingdom. Article 7 reaffirms Islamic law as the basis of the kingdom, stating that the government draws its authority (*sultatu*) from the Quran and the *sunna* (not, it should be noted, from the people), and that these two sources govern all administrative regulations of the state. In the section on "rights and duties," the first article (Article 23) enjoins the state to "protect the principles of Islam, enforce its *shariʿa*, ordain what is good and forbid what is evil [a Quranic injunction], and undertake the duty of the call to God (*al-daʿwa' ila allah*)."

In terms of specific political powers, the Basic System vests enormous authority in the person of the king. Article 44 defines the powers of the state as the judicial power, the executive power, and the power to issue administrative law (as the immutable *shariʿa* is the legal basis of the state, the Basic System is at pains to avoid reference to "legislative" power). It goes on to identify the king as "the ultimate authority (*al-marjaʿ*) regarding these powers." The king is prime minister, with full power to appoint and remove ministers (Articles 56, 57, 58), and supreme commander of all military forces (Article 60). The judiciary is defined as an independent branch of government (Article 46), but the king appoints judges (Article 52) and "oversees the application of the Islamic *shari'a*, the administrative regulations, and the general policy of the state" (Article 55). In times of emergency the king is granted extraordinary powers (Article 62). The king has the right to choose the crown prince, formerly reserved to informal councils within the Al Sa'ud family, and to remove him by royal decree (Article 5).

It is in the articles that establish citizens' rights that the government has begun to respond to demands voiced in petitions for the rule of law. Guarantees of the sanctity of private homes and private communications from intervention or inspection by state authorities, except by due process of law (Articles 37, 40) were emphasized in reports from the Saudi press about the Basic System.[39] Articles 27 and 31 oblige the state to provide health care to every citizen and support for those "in situations of emergency, sickness, and old age." Freedom from arbitrary arrest and punishment is assured by Articles 36 and 38. Equality of citizens under the *shari'a* is mandated by Article 8; Article 26 states that "the state protects human rights according to the Islamic *shari'a*." The state also "guarantees the freedom and protection of private property. It will not take from anyone his property except for the public good and with the provision of just compensation" (Article 18).

Like most constitutions, the Basic System leaves a number of important questions open to interpretation. It is not clear what legal recourse citizens will have to ensure that these rights are not infringed. The sections of the Basic System on the judiciary are vague as to its organization and the competencies of its various parts. It is clear that there will continue to be different legal tracks within the judiciary—*shari'a* courts and administrative bodies—but their relationship is not defined. Nothing is said of judicial power to review actions of the government. The ultimate recourse is appeal to the king. The Basic System does provide that the *majlis* (public meeting) of the king and the crown prince be open to any citizen for petition for redress of grievances (Article 43).

The Basic System contains a number of provisions meant to ensure accountability in dealing with the public treasury, another major theme in the Saudi petitions. Article 16 states that "public funds are sacrosanct. The state must protect them." Article 73 forbids disbursement of public money except according to the budget or by royal order. Oversight agencies are mandated by Articles 79 and 80 to monitor the treasury and government agencies, to investigate financial and administrative violations, and to prepare yearly reports for the prime minister on these matters. It is clear from Article 39 that the press will remain an organ of the government, subject to its guidance and ultimate control.[40]

The issue of accountability also comes up in the amendments to the charter of the Council of Ministers issued in August 1993. The royal decree reaffirms the Council's central role as both the legislative and executive organ of the Saudi government, setting out the policy of the country in all areas. However, the decree explicitly prevents ministers from having any business dealings with the state, engaging in private business, or serving as a director of any private company during their tenure. The government will also not be permitted to arrange for loans without the explicit approval of the Council. In an effort to encourage upward mobility among Saudi technocrats, the decree set a four-year limit on the service of any minister in one position, unless specific permission for an extension of service is given by the King. No one expects that senior princes who have held ministerial positions for decades, like Amir Sultan (Defense) and Amir Na'if (Interior), will be shunted aside in the next cabinet shuffle, but the new regulation should encourage the appearance of new faces in the Saudi cabinet.[41]

Article 68 of the Basic Law mandates establishment of a Consultative Council (*majlis al-shura*), following on the king's promise of November 1990. The king issued by royal decree the founding statute of the council at the same time as he announced the Basic System. That statute sets the membership of the Council at sixty members and a president, all appointed by the king (Article 3). Councils will have four-year terms, and at least one-half of the membership of every council must be composed of new members (Article 13). No member of the government can sit in the council (Article 9), and from the composition of the first council it is clear that ruling family members will not be appointed.

The council has a wide mandate to comment on affairs of state, including "the general plan for economic and social development" and "administrative statutes and regulations, treaties and international agreements, and concessions" (Article 15). Article 18 seems to imply that administrative regulations and treaties must be submitted to the council for review. Ministries and state agencies are required to submit annual reports to the council for review, and the president of the council may request attendance of any government official at council sessions related to his responsibilities (Articles 15, 22). The king or his representative will present a yearly address to the council "setting out the domestic and foreign policy of the kingdom" (Article 14). Any ten members of the council together have the right "to recommend a new administrative regulation, or an amendment to an existing regulation" to the president of the council, who is then "obligated to submit the recommendation to the king" (Article 23). It is clear what the council is not: it is not an elected representative body; it is not a legislative body; it has no powers other than those of recommendation. The Council of Ministers remains the legislative body in the kingdom. Only the king can issue administrative regulations; he is free to accept and reject proposals from either the Council of Ministers or the Consultative Council.[42]

King Fahd appointed the sixty members of the first Consultative Council in his August 20, 1993, decrees; its president, former minister of justice Shaykh Muhammad ibn Jubayr, was chosen in September 1992. Based on the very sketchy biographical information available about them, the members seem to represent a cross-section of the Saudi elite, including important regime constituencies like the religious establishment, technocrats, and merchants. Approximately one-third of the members are university professors, from both the more secular and the Islamic universities in the kingdom. Eight members are current or former top-ranking civil servants, four are retired military officers, eight are members of various regional chambers of commerce in the country. There are two engineers, three doctors, and seven journalists/writers in the group.[43] Of the forty-eight members for whom background information was available, twenty-three had received Ph.D.s: sixteen from Western universities, one from Cairo University (in engineering), and six from Islamic universities. A substantial number had studied abroad for undergraduate and master's degrees. Information on the regional background of the members is more difficult to come by. At least ten Hijazis were appointed, at least four ʿAsiris, and at least two Saudis from the Eastern province. The Council includes one Saudi Shiʿi, businessman Jamil al-Jishi.[44]

The third statute announced by King Fahd on March 1, 1992, regarded the system of regional governance for the kingdom's fourteen provinces. The statute established greater autonomy for provincial governors (all of whom are currently members of the royal family) on spending and development priorities in their regions, and authorized the establishment of provincial consultative councils on the model of the national Consultative Council.[45] It is billed by the regime as a major effort to decentralize authority in the kingdom. In September 1993 the king appointed the local councils—twenty-member councils for the major cities of Riyad, Mecca, and Medina; fifteen-member councils for the other ten regions. Included in the local councils are the regional representatives of major government ministries.[46]

These constitutional innovations in the Saudi political system are an attempt on the part of the king to respond to various constituencies important to his rule. The popular ferment generated by the Gulf crisis, represented by the petitions discussed, was regarded by the king as a powerful social trend to which response was due. Saudi rulers had in the past, during previous crises like the Egyptian military deployment in Yemen in 1962 and the takeover of the Grand Mosque in 1979, committed themselves to these kinds of changes, only to delay their implementation indefinitely.[47] In this case, the king actually followed through. Within the general desire for some type of reform there were, as the petitions evidenced, two major and competing strands of opinion, the liberal and the Islamist. The king also had to keep in mind his primary constituency, the ruling family itself.

Much of what was new in the proposals seemed to come from the liberal agenda: a consultative council, recognition of some limited civil rights, administrative devolution, and greater local participation. The fact that they came at a time when the government was confronting some of the more vociferous Islamist elements led some observers to view these reforms as a victory for the liberals, or the beginnings of a liberal–ruling family alignment against the Islamists.[48] That is an overstatement. King Fahd went to great lengths, in his speech of March 1, 1992, announcing the three royal decrees, to emphasize the central role of Islam and the *shari*[c]*a* in the history of the kingdom and in the changes he was announcing. "The keystone of the Basic System and its source is the Islamic *shari*[c]*a*. . . . Our constitution in the Kingdom of Saudi Arabia is the Book of God and the *Sunna* of His Prophet. . . . When we differed on any issue we returned to those sources. They governed everything which the state decreed in these systems of governance." He related the peace, prosperity, and stability of the kingdom to its adherence to Islam, frequently mentioning the duty of the state to ordain the good and prohibit evil (*al-'amr bi al-ma*[c]*ruf wa al-nahya* [c]*an al-munkar*), a phrase closely associated with the Wahhabi [c]*ulama*. He was also at pains to highlight the continuities between the Saudi past and the proposed Consultative Council: "The new system for the Consultative Council is an updating and development of what exists already."[49]

Even though the king used harsh language on other occasions against Islamists whom he saw as transgressing the bounds of permissible dissent, he has made it plain that Islam remains the core of the state's legitimacy. He has repeatedly pointed to the unique role of the kingdom in the Muslim world, based on the history of the Al Sa[c]ud's connection with the Wahhabi movement and the family's custodianship of the holy sites of Mecca and Medina. He explicitly rejected Western democracy as an inappropriate basis for politics in the peninsula in an interview published shortly after his March 1 speech: "The nature of our people is different. . . . The democratic system prevailing in the world does not suit us in this region."[50] His desire to maintain a balance between more liberal and/or techno-cratic elements and the broad Islamist current is reflected in his appointments to the Consultative Council.

While attempting to appeal to both liberal and Islamist cur-rents in Saudi society, these changes were also meant to reassure members of the ruling family that their position was not being challenged. The Basic System vests rulership in the Al Sa[c]ud, and explicitly includes the "third generation" of princes—the grandsons of King [c]Abd al-[c]Aziz—in that ruling circle. The panoply of powers conferred on the king by the Basic System demonstrates that the changes are not meant to derogate from the ruler's prerogatives. There is some speculation that the changes were aimed at solidifying the political power of some groups within the family, particularly those closest to King Fahd, at the expense of others, like those close to Crown Prince ʿAbdallah and the sons of King Faysal. These analyses are based on little but rumor. King Fahd explicitly reconfirmed Crown Prince ʿAbdallah in his position when he promulgated the decrees of March 1.[51] There is no evidence as yet of any substantial political fallout within the Al Saʿud as a result of these changes.

It is impossible to predict to what extent these changes will affect politics in the kingdom. As with all constitutions, the most important aspect of the Basic System will be how it is implemented, not what it actually says. Precedent will be extremely important in determining just how significant these new laws and institutions will be. If the king and the government take the Consultative Council seriously in its first sessions, and its members push to play an active role in the political process, it could become a check on the power of the executive and an avenue for some degree of public input into decision-making. If it exercises its oversight functions with diligence at the beginning, the council could also open up the Saudi decision-making process to greater public scrutiny and accountability. Likewise, if the civil rights articles of the Basic System are immediately enforced and clear judicial procedures to address them are established, they could mark a milestone in the constitutional history of the kingdom. On the other hand, history is replete with constitutions honored more in the breach than in the observance and assemblies that are no more than rubber stamps. These next few years will be crucial in establishing which way the Saudi experiment will go.

Oman

The Saudi strategy of responding to demands for greater political participation—an appointed *majlis al-shura* with advisory and oversight roles but no independent legislative powers—has been echoed or anticipated in other Gulf monarchies since the Gulf crisis. The experiment in Oman is the most interesting in the remaining four states—and in many ways the most unlikely. The sultan's regime was subject to intense military and ideological pressure during the Dhufar rebellion of the early 1970s. With the defeat of the rebellion, overt political opposition all but disappeared. The regime fostered an apolitical public ethos since that time, built on commitment to economic and infrastructural development under the leadership of the sultan and a self-consciously technocratic governing elite. A State Consultative Council was appointed in 1981. It was dominated by government members, met infrequently, and had few powers.[52] By the time of the Gulf crisis, the political atmosphere in Oman was the most tranquil (or dull, depending upon one's perspective) in the entire region.

It thus came as something of a surprise to outsiders when the sultan announced in November 1990 that Oman would have a new Consultative Council, filled through indirect election on a provincial basis, with expanded powers. There appeared to be no great public demand for this initiative akin to the petitions that appeared in Saudi Arabia, Bahrain, and Qatar. Rather, the initiative came from the top of the political system. It was explained by Sultan Qabus and other government sources as the natural evolution of the State Consultative Council experiment, unrelated to the regional ferment set off by the Gulf crisis. Given the political and geographical removal of Oman from the crisis, it is difficult to dispute the official reasoning. Perhaps the timing of the announcement was affected by the crisis, but it appears that the changes had been in the sultan's mind for some time.

Two aspects of the new Omani Council are worth noting. The selection process was innovative. Oman is divided into fifty-nine administrative provinces (*wilayat*). In May–June 1991 the provincial governors convoked the "notables" (usually between one hundred and two hundred people) in their areas to recommend three potential council members to the sultan, who then chose the member for that province. In some of the urban provinces, ballots were cast among attendees to determine the three nominees.[53] Although the debates were spirited in many of the provincial meetings, and some horse-trading, usually along tribal lines, occurred among the electors in some provinces, Omani sources were unanimous in reporting that no country-wide political organizations or ideological currents emerged during the nominating process. Former government officials make up the largest group in the council, with tribal leaders and businessmen also heavily represented.[54] Clearly, this system of indirect nomination by province has its drawbacks from the perspective of democratic theory. It is not direct election. The designation of notables is in the hands of the government, calling into question the representative nature of the electorate. The provinces do not have equal population, so urban areas are underrepresented in the Council. All that granted, the willingness to bring some of the citizenry into the process of nominating its representatives was an important departure in recent Omani politics.

The second new aspect of the Omani Council is the greater powers it enjoys, compared with its predecessor. The sultan asserted in his opening address to the council in December 1991 that it was "a complete and equal branch of government," not part of or subject to the executive branch.[55] Whereas members of the bureaucracy dominated the State Consultative Council, government officials are not permitted to sit on the new council. Twelve such officials resigned their positions to take seats on the new council. The council has greater legislative powers than its predecessor. It has the right to review all legislation regarding cultural, educational, social, and economic issues, and state development plans, and to recommend amendments by a two-thirds vote. It also has the right to question "service" ministers (those who head ministries delivering public services, like Health, Education, Housing, Information, Electricity and Water, etc.), who must submit a yearly report to the council. The council has no right to review foreign and defense policy issues, or to interrogate ministers in those areas.[56]

The new council ended its first year of operation in October 1992. Unlike its predecessor, which was a rubber stamp, this council has displayed a spirit of independence from the government. Its most notable activity was its questioning of ministers. In sessions televised to the entire country, members of the council subjected ministers from the "service" ministries to sharp questioning about their activities and, in the eyes of the members, their shortcomings. It was a new experience for the ministers, many of whom had spent two decades in government without ever having to answer in a public forum for their activities. By all accounts, Omanis liked the show.[57] No major legislative initiatives were produced by the council during this first year.

Bahrain, Qatar, and the UAE

An appointed Consultative Council has also been established in Bahrain. In his national day address of December 16, 1992, Shaykh ʿIsa, amir of Bahrain, announced his intention to establish such a body. By the beginning of 1993, thirty members were appointed. They are evenly divided between Sunnis and Shiʿis, with the presidency of the council held by Ibrahim Hamidan, a Shiʿi and former minister of transportation. The dominant socioeconomic background of the members is private business. Eighteen of the members are merchants and/or contractors. Lawyers, religious judges, and doctors are also represented, as well as one prominent journalist, one university professor, and the head of a Shiʿi religious institution.[58] The council held its first session in January 1993. Like its Saudi and Omani counterparts, the Bahraini Council's powers are limited to review of legislation sent to it by the Council of Ministers and to oversight of government activity through questioning of ministers.[59]

Unlike the proposed Saudi experiment and the ongoing Omani one, the changes in Bahrain do not have the same character of being a step forward, however limited that step may be. The original National Assembly in Bahrain, suspended in 1975, was directly elected and had extensive legislative powers. The petition to the amir previously mentioned specifically stated that an appointed consultative council could not take the place of the constitutionally mandated National Assembly. However, worries about the strength of Islamic political currents, in both Sunni and Shiʿi communities in the country, led the regime to take the appointive route favored in Saudi Arabia and Oman, rather than risk elections on the Kuwaiti model.[60]

As of late 1993, neither Qatar nor the UAE has followed the path of the four other Gulf monarchies in offering new opportunities for political participation. In Qatar the Consultative Council appointed in 1972 still sits, its term periodically extended so as to avoid the stipulation in the provisional constitution for elections to the next council. Opposition sources report that some of the signers of the Qatari petition to the amir have been harassed and detained by the authorities.[61] In March 1993 the UAE Federal National Council resumed meetings after a two-year hiatus. Seventy percent of its members, appointed by the rulers of the seven emirates, are new, but rumors that they would be chosen by direct election and that the powers of that body to initiate legislation and oversee government ministries would be expanded proved to be groundless.[62]

CONCLUSIONS

There are a number of important conclusions to be drawn from the experience of the Gulf monarchies during the last few years in the areas of political participation and representation. First and foremost, there are no inherent cultural or historical impediments inhibiting the populace from wanting a say in how their countries are run. When permitted by governments, citizens form organizations to advance their interests. Some such organizations form around what are usually referred to in the West as "traditional" bases—tribal ties and Islamic institutions. Those "traditional" institutions have shown remarkable flexibility in adjusting to the circumstances of large bureaucratic states, modern technologies, and dramatically changed economies. Other civil society organizations have developed along more "modern" functional lines—chambers of commerce, professional syndicates, social clubs, newspapers, even ideological groups that are political parties in everything but name. The Kuwaiti elections of October 1992 were a stark demonstration that, given the opportunity, Gulf citizens take to "modern" politics as well as anybody. The tension in the area of social and political organization is not between "tradition" and "modernity," but between newly powerful governments that seek to dominate and control the public sphere and social, economic, and political groups working to maintain some degree of autonomy.

The growing role of the state in the life of citizens over the past twenty years has called forth the new demands for political participation and government accountability these states have recently witnessed. As the state means more in people's everyday existence, they naturally want to have some control over its actions, or at least an assurance that it will act consistently. The vast expansion of educational opportunities, funded by the states' oil wealth, has produced a much larger cadre of citizens able to articulate such concerns in abstract, theoretical terms rather than as personal appeals for individual favors. While the international movement toward democracy of the late 1980s certainly inspired some Gulf political activists, it is *domestic* pressures and processes that have driven political events in these countries.

Common themes emerged from the various participatory exercises. Those who take an active role in politics in their countries want first and foremost the rule of law. Where there are constitutions, demand was for their restoration (Kuwait, Bahrain). Where there are "temporary" constitutions, demand was for a permanent document developed by a representative institution (Qatar, UAE). Where there was no constitution, demand was for consistency in the application of Islamic law (Saudi Arabia). A number of corollaries follow from this emphasis on the rule of law. Responsible management of public funds was a theme in Kuwait and in the Islamist petition in Saudi Arabia. All petitions requested either establishment or restoration of representative institutions as a check on executive power and to oversee government operations. Judicial reform, though from very different perspectives, was part of both liberal and Islamist petitions in Saudi Arabia.

Desire for greater participatory opportunities was also common. In Kuwait and Bahrain, where there was the precedent of elected legislative bodies, demand was for their restoration. In Qatar and Saudi Arabia, there was no demand for popular elections, but for truly representative and independent consultative councils with real powers. The Saudi liberal petition went further, requesting local and municipal councils and more freedom for civil society organizations. Interest surrounding the Kuwait Chamber of Commerce election was also evidence of the increasing importance attached to nongovernmental social institutions. Complaints in Kuwait, Saudi Arabia, and Qatar about the role of the media indirectly manifested a desire for independent voices in society.

Government responses to these demands also manifested common themes. There was willingness to accommodate the desire for consultative assemblies, though not through direct elections. Saudi Arabia, Bahrain, and Oman all took steps in this direction. The Kuwaiti government also tried something of the sort in its 1990 effort to replace the *majlis al-'umma* with the National Assembly. The Iraqi invasion weakened the government and created circumstances that made restoration of the constitutional *majlis* imperative. On the other hand, real power still lies with the executive in all these countries, with the partial exception now of Kuwait. The ruling families' theme seems to be that consultation is necessary and right, but formal and constitutional sharing of power is not on the agenda.

Governments still hold the trump cards in the political game in these countries. Their economic, bureaucratic, and coercive powers remain enormous. There are divisions in society—tribal, sectarian, ideological—that governments can play upon to deflect demands for reform.[63] The changes that have occurred have been slow in coming; the bias is toward the status quo. Precedents set in the next few years by how governments deal with the new and revived assemblies, and in Saudi Arabia with the new Basic Law, will be extremely important for determining whether these bodies and this document play an effective political role, or are mere window dressing.

It would be a mistake to view the upsurge in political activity in the past few years as a threat to the stability or security of these regimes. The demands discussed above were almost uniformly phrased in the language of loyal opposition—perhaps the word opposition is even stretching a point. But it is clear that the public in these countries wants more responsible government and greater participatory avenues. How governments continue to respond to these desires will set the political agenda in the Gulf monarchies for the next decade and perhaps beyond.

5

Foreign and Defense Policies

T HE FOREIGN AND DEFENSE POLICY DILEMMAS FACED by the Gulf Arab monarchies are a direct product of their domestic realities, discussed in previous chapters. Oil makes them important to the rest of the world, but oil wealth also increases their vulnerability in numerous important ways. Most obviously, it makes them the target of larger, ambitious neighbors, as the Iraqi invasion of Kuwait cruelly demonstrated. On a deeper and less obvious level, the characteristics that oil wealth has elicited in their domestic politics exacerbate their security problems. Their ability to mobilize their populations for defense is limited by the ethos of the rentier state. Demands for military service by the state upon citizens are avoided because such demands could bring forth pressure for citizens to have a say in state policy. The small population, relative to potentially threatening neighbors, of these states complicates their defense planning, and their inability to utilize fully such human resources as they have compounds their difficulties.

The lack of firm, institutionalized political links between these regimes and their societies also opens up a new set of threats in the foreign policy sphere. It is not just military attack that the Gulf monarchies worry about. They also fear *political* intervention origi-

119

nating from abroad, based on powerful transnational ideological platforms of Pan-Arabism and Islam, aimed at stirring up their own domestic populations against them. A succession of ambitious regional figures have used propaganda and subversion, as well as military pressure, against these states: Gamal ʿAbd al-Nasir of Egypt in the 1950s and 1960s, Ayatollah Khumayni in the 1980s, and Saddam Husayn in 1990–1991. None of these challengers succeeded in bringing down the Gulf regimes, but they all frightened the daylights out of the rulers. The irony is that these states, having built up substantial bureaucratic and coercive infrastructures, are less susceptible to this kind of foreign ideological pressure now than they have been in the past. Citizens' interests are much more focused on their domestic agendas than on glorious but impractical transnational ones. But it is difficult for rulers to appreciate this change when little, if any, citizen input into the foreign policy decision-making process is permitted.

Foreign policy is normally the preserve of an elite, even in democratic societies. The lack of institutionalized channels of participation, the family basis of rule, and the power that oil wealth concentrates in the hands of the rulers all combine to narrow even further the circle of those who guide foreign policy in the Gulf Arab monarchies. Foreign policy decisions are the closely held preserve of leading members of the ruling families. Both Saudi Arabia and Kuwait, for example, have as their ambassadors in Washington, their most important foreign relationship, younger ruling family members. Foreign policy makers in these states are for the most part extremely sophisticated players in the international arena, in many cases with decades of experience in dealing with foreign leaders. Their success in forging international alliances to protect them from their neighbors is evidence of their diplomatic skills. However, monopolization of foreign policy decision making in the hands of a few does have its drawbacks.

The focus of foreign policy is on the regime's dynastic interests. State interest is conflated with regime security, and the prism through which events are viewed and analyzed at the top is how they will affect the future of the ruling family. Gulf-state diplomacy remains highly personal. Cooperation among the Gulf monarchies themselves—a natural thing given their common domestic backgrounds,

regional vulnerabilities, and international orientations—is complicated by historical disputes among the dynasties. Though there are
many talented diplomats in their foreign ministries, lines of responsibility for decision making are often muddled by the informal but
central role ruling family members play. These states have yet to
develop the institutionalized, professional diplomatic services found
in neighboring states like Egypt, Iran, or even Jordan, though progress in this direction is being made. Formal agreements mean less
than informal political understandings. While the Gulf states' record in keeping such informal international understandings is excellent, their unwillingness to bind themselves by treaties and formal
agreements is troubling to other regional and international powers.

The immutable effects of geography and demography—small
populations, in some cases vulnerable borders, and valuable natural
resources—combine with these domestic realities to create a Gulf
diplomatic style. This style is characterized by reliance on policies of
balance and maneuver to maintain security. These states have always
exhibited a desire to duck direct confrontation if at all possible. They
have tried to avoid, again when possible, over-identification with
any regional power, both out of fear of offending other regional
players and as a strategy for hedging against the possibility that
today's friend will become tomorrow's enemy. Developing a close
relationship with a major Arab or Muslim power means giving such
a power an entry point into their internal affairs that could come to
be used against these regimes. When confrontation is thrust upon
them, the Gulf states will pick sides and declare themselves. That
was true against Iran during the reflagging of Kuwaiti ships by the
United States in 1987–1988, and against Iraq after the invasion of
Kuwait. But when the crisis passes, they once again seek some
regional middle ground, avoiding, if at all possible, friendships that
are too close and also enmities that are too intense.

The factors that produce this regional diplomatic style also
complicate these states' relations with the United States, their international protector. On the one hand, their need for the U.S. tie is
clear, given their own weakness; it was made even clearer by the
events of 1990–1991. Gulf leaders worry about the credibility of
American commitment to them, particularly given the fate of the
Shah of Iran, and want constant reassurance. Their nervousness

about the Clinton administration, after the defeat of their clearly preferred candidate, is just the latest example of their continuing fear that eventually the United States will abandon them. On the other hand, they worry that their identification with the United States will create problems for them at home with publics who resent other aspects of America's Middle Eastern policy and oppose any relationship that appears to compromise national independence. Many Saudis, who have the longest and closest relationship of all the Gulf monarchies with the United States, continue to think that their country's finest hour was when it defied the United States with the 1973 oil embargo. The Gulf monarchies' traditional desire to keep American forces "over the horizon" encapsulates these tensions—the United States should be close enough to protect them, but not so close as to create problems.

There are, of course, variations among the Gulf states in how closely they fit the pattern described. It is modeled largely on Saudi foreign policy behavior. Kuwait, having suffered from military occupation, has developed a strong public consensus on the need for close military ties with the United States and other foreign powers, setting it apart from its neighbors. Oman, largely because of the steadiness of its ruler, has charted a more consistent and less jittery course than its neighbors over the last two decades, both in terms of regional relations and in its dealings with the West. This chapter concentrates on Saudi foreign policy; where important differences in the other Gulf states' foreign policies arise, they will be noted.[1]

The post–Gulf War period is an interesting test of the resiliency of the style of Gulf diplomacy outlined above. If anything could change that style, the upheaval surrounding the Iraqi invasion of Kuwait, the invitation to the American forces, and then Desert Storm would have done so. Moreover, the destruction of the Iraqi military threat, coupled with the breakup of the Soviet Union, created the most favorable security configuration for the Gulf monarchies since the Iranian Revolution. The time was propitious for sea changes in the Gulf states' foreign policy. While all the Gulf monarchies are now more willing to "go public" with their American relationship, and feel less obligated than previously to support automatically any cause defined as "Arab," the evidence provided by their diplomacy since February 1991 points to remarkable continuity with patterns described above. This chapter will examine how the Gulf monarchies have dealt with questions of self-defense, regional balancing, and relations with the United States during this period.

SELF-DEFENSE

A strategy of self-reliance for defense and security is both inadequate and politically troublesome for the Gulf monarchies. The inadequacy of self-reliance is to some extent a simple matter of numbers. The combined citizen populations of the six Gulf monarchies numbers, by the most generous estimates, no more than seventeen million. Iran's population is around fifty-five million. But numbers are not the whole story. The combined population of the monarchies is close to that of Iraq, but no one in 1990 suggested that they could by themselves handle the Iraqi invasion of Kuwait. It is the political context of the states that renders a policy of self-reliance even less feasible than numbers suggest. The mobilization of citizen manpower into the armed forces would require obligatory military service, a very real demand of the state upon its citizens (one the United States, for example, now chooses to avoid). A ruthlessly efficient authoritarian state like Iraq or Syria can compel a large percentage of its male citizens to serve in the military. States animated by revolutionary fervor like Iran in the 1980s, or by democratic ties of loyalty between citizen and state like Israel (for its Jewish citizens), can call upon their population for military service and receive an enthusiastic response. The Gulf monarchies lack these mobilizational abilities.

The lack is attributable to the fact that the Gulf monarchies are rentier states; their social contract rests upon provision of benefits *to* citizens, not extraction of resources (taxes and service) *from* them. Instituting a national service requirement would upset that implicit contract between state and society. In the West, the need to mobilize citizen armies contributed to pressure for popular participation in government. The ruling families in the Gulf want to avoid exacerbating already growing demand in their societies for greater participation. Moreover, from the perspective of rulers who remember the prevalence of Arab military coups in the 1950s and 1960s, including in the military groups whose loyalty to the regime is questionable would undermine rather than increase security.

Military recruitment strategies in all the Gulf monarchies reflect these social realities. Only in Kuwait is there obligatory service, and before the Iraqi invasion such service was easily avoidable. All the other monarchies rely upon volunteer forces. Discussions in official Saudi circles immediately after the Gulf War about doubling the size of their armed forces, which would probably entail some kind of draft or obligatory service, appear to have been shelved.[2] In Oman, where the rentier state is newest, there is more prestige to military service, the result of the sultan's very personal involvement in the command of the forces and the resources he devotes to them. In the other monarchies, military service is not a socially desirable profession. With economic opportunities relatively plentiful for well-educated young male citizens in these states, incentives to join the military are limited.

Shi'a in Kuwait, Bahrain, and Saudi Arabia rarely join the military and even more rarely advance in the officer corps, as a result of both government discouragement and social custom within those communities.[3] In Saudi Arabia, there are persistent reports, unconfirmed and unconfirmable officially, that those who do not hail from Najd (Central Arabia) cannot advance in the military hierarchy and are barred from certain sensitive positions (such as fighter pilot). Needless to say, half of these states' human resources— female citizens—are not available for military service. Taken together, these factors mean that the Gulf monarchies cannot and will not mobilize their resources for military purposes with the same efficiency as their neighbors. Demographic, social, and political constraints combine to rule out a policy of self-reliance in security matters.

A simple comparison of Saudi Arabia and other regional powers, regarding the size of their armed forces relative to their populations, points out the barriers in the Gulf to military mobilization. The Saudi census completed in 1992 reported the citizen population of the country as 12.3 million (out of a total population of 16.9 million).[4] One suspects that this figure may be an overestimate, so for comparative purposes let us assume the Saudi citizen population in 1990 was ten million. In that year the Saudi armed forces, including active duty National Guard forces, totaled 111,500. Iraq, with less than double the Saudi population, had a military establishment at least five times as large in 1990. Syria, with a population only two million greater, had a standing armed force of over 400,000 in 1991. Jordan, with less than half of the Saudi population, had an active force of 101,000 in 1991, nearly the same size as the Saudi forces. Israel, also with less than half of the Saudi population, had a standing force of 141,000 and a reserve force of over 500,000 in 1991.[5]

One way to compensate for manpower deficiencies is to recruit foreign personnel into the military service. That tactic is most prevalent in the United Arab Emirates, where the International Institute for Strategic Studies estimates that 30 percent of personnel are foreigners (a conservative estimate, according to some observers), and in Qatar.[6] The "Omanization" of the sultan's armed forces is now practically complete, but for decades the officer corps of the Omani army was predominantly British. During the Iran-Iraq War, two brigades of Pakistani troops were stationed in Saudi Arabia in exchange for aid to Pakistan; and after the Gulf War 11,000 Pakistani forces deployed as part of the coalition remained in the kingdom under a Saudi-Pakistani security agreement.[7] In Kuwait, parliamentary sources report that one-third of the army consists of "biduns" (from the Arabic *bidun jinsiyya*, "without citizenship"), Arab tribal inhabitants of the country whose families did not file for Kuwaiti citizenship when it was offered before independence.[8]

The mercenary option is not a realistic answer to the monarchies' security problems. The same traits Machiavelli recognized in mercenary forces in sixteenth-century Italy remain true today: they are expensive in peacetime and unreliable in wartime. If they are units of a foreign army, their role in any conflict is dependent upon that country's policies, no matter what kind of formal agreements exist. If they are individuals recruited into the service, their political loyalties are uncertain and their commitment to the country and the regime variable. Increased reliance on mercenaries also contradicts the efforts of the regimes, through the media and school systems, to increase public identification with and loyalty to the country and the political system. Being unwilling to rely on your own citizens for defense would seem to undermine those efforts.

A large mercenary force could also alienate local public opinion. Particularly in the two countries most affected by the Gulf War, Kuwait and Saudi Arabia, there have been calls for formation of real citizen armies. In Kuwait many members of the new parliament support giving citizenship to the "biduns" who are serving now in the military, and there are calls for a thorough-going reorganization of the military, with reaffirmation of obligatory national service.[9] The Islamist petition of 1991 in Saudi Arabia called for the building of a strong Saudi army, and the subsequent Memorandum of Advice by Islamic activists in 1992 specifically advocated obligatory military training, a 500,000-man army, and a reserve force made up of "all those able to bear arms." If public opinion in these countries is uncomfortable with a large-scale American military presence, as will be discussed, it is safe to assume that any foreign military presence would incite friction with the local population. The regimes appear to recognize all these problems, and have not markedly increased their reliance on mercenary forces since the Gulf War.

Another way to confront the manpower deficiency is to rely on capital-intensive, high-technology weapons. Saudi Arabia in particular has invested billions of dollars in developing its air force and air defense systems. From August 1990 to the end of 1992, Saudi Arabia placed weapons orders in the United States alone worth over $25 billion, and pursued discussions with British officials about implementation of a $30 billion program (the second half of the *al-Yamamah* arms agreement signed in 1985, delayed later by the Saudis) for the air force and air defense. In October 1992, Riyad agreed to purchase three frigates from France at a cost of $4 billion. Kuwait during the same period ordered nearly $7 billion in arms from the United States, and signed weapons deals with other Western countries, though the Kuwaiti parliament has asserted the right to review these deals pending investigations into the organization of the military establishment.[10] In February 1993, the UAE placed an order for over $3 billion worth of battle tanks from France.[11] Defense spending in the other countries, much of it devoted to arms purchases, has also risen in the wake of the war (see Table 7).

Big, expensive weapons systems go some way towards bridging the manpower gap and increasing the Gulf monarchies' deterrent capability. But they are not a panacea. First, such systems increase self-reliance only nominally. They have to be bought from and, more important over the long term, maintained by foreign companies and/or governments. That involves the presence of foreign personnel, though usually in numbers small enough to manage politically, and an ongoing political relationship with the country of origin that limits the autonomous use of the arms. Saudi arms deals with the United States have frequently included provisos limiting the deployment range, basing, and equipment of the systems, in order to mollify Israeli security concerns. Gulf rulers recognize these facts. Splashy arms deals are another way of cementing the commitment of the United States, Britain, France, and other outside powers to their security. That should not be confused with self-reliance.

There is an internal political downside to the current practice of emphasizing expensive high-technology weapons systems. To the extent that they tie the security of these states to Western powers, particularly the United States, they feed charges that these regimes are simply puppets of Washington. That is not currently a problem in Kuwait, where public enthusiasm for formal security links with the West remains high, even among Islamic political currents. But in both Saudi Arabia and Bahrain, segments of the public are uncomfortable with the relationship between their governments and the United States, a topic to be discussed at the end of this chapter. On the issue of arms purchases specifically, both the Saudi Islamist petition of 1991 and the 1992 Memorandum of Advice called for diversification of sources and the development of a domestic arms industry. The latter document was particularly biting about what it saw as Saudi overreliance on the United States, a country that "gives us what it wants, denies us what it does not want us to have, exploits us in times of trouble, and bargains with us during times of calamity."

Defense is the largest component of the Saudi, Omani, and UAE budgets; its share is increasing in the other states. During the height of the oil boom, that was not a problem. There was plenty of money to go around. That is no longer the case. Gulf regimes are having to face for the first time since the early 1970s serious "guns versus butter" choices. The difficulty of these choices is exacerbated by the fact that defense contracting in these states is a major source of recycling public money to influential political figures, through commissions, kickbacks, and graft. In the wake of Desert Storm, informed publics are asking what kind of defense their countries purchased for the billions spent in the 1970s and 1980s, and, like the Kuwaiti parliament, what they are getting in current deals. The Memorandum of Advice from Saudi Islamic activists, for example, complained of the "lack of correspondence" between the vast sums spent in the past and the size and capabilities of Saudi forces now, and advocated strict financial oversight on military projects.

There is also the ultimate question of how effective high-tech weaponry is in providing security for these states. The expenditures of the previous two decades did not protect Kuwaiti and Saudi shipping during the last years of the Iran-Iraq War. Western naval forces had to be called in to safeguard their oil fleets and those of their customers. These expenditures did not deter Iraq from invading Kuwait, nor could the weapons they bought drive Iraq out of

TABLE 7.   GULF ORDER OF BATTLE

Country	Total Armed Forces*	Artillery, Multiple Rocket Launchers, Mortars	Combat Aircraft	Armed Helicopters	Surface-to-Surface Missiles
Bahrain	7,450	20	24	12	—
Iran	528,000	4,130	190	100	130**
Iraq	perhaps 382,500	2,000	260	120	72***
Kuwait	8,200	10	35	10	—
Oman	30,400	100	60	—	—
Qatar	7,500	10	18	20	—
Saudi Arabia	111,500	950	250	—	50
UAE	44,000	175	100	20	—

* Excluding paramilitary and reserve forces, except for Iranian Revolutionary Guard and active Saudi National Guard Forces.
** Source notes "local manufacture of missile reported under development."
*** All in process of destruction under UN Resolution 687, as of end of 1992.

Source: International Institute for Strategic Studies, *The Military Balance 1991–1992* (London: Brassey's, 1991).

Kuwait. Again, the United States and other powers were brought in. It is difficult to see how further increments of spending on sophisticated weapons systems could guarantee security when past expenditures have not. Big-ticket weapons systems are not enough in and of themselves to overcome manpower shortages in these countries and to provide self-sufficient defense.

Another major stumbling block to effective self-defense in the Gulf monarchies is their inability to adopt a unified defense and security posture among themselves. Although talks on military cooperation under the aegis of the Gulf Cooperation Council (GCC) are ongoing, there is very little to show for these efforts as yet. Each state maintains its own procurement policies, with no coordination to promote interchangeability or economies of scale. Each state is forging its own defense agreements with outside powers, rather than negotiating overall GCC deals with them. There are plans to increase the size of the joint GCC force, called Peninsula Shield, stationed at Hafr al-Batin in northeastern Saudi Arabia, but not significantly.

These results are all the more disappointing because the Gulf War was seen by many in the region as the kind of historical turning point that could accelerate the process of GCC integration. The six states stood together during the crisis, their common identity strengthened by the hostility they perceived toward them in the rest of the Arab world. Kuwaitis, who had been relatively dismissive of the GCC before the crisis, discovered its importance in a very personal way, as they were welcomed into the other GCC states for the duration of the crisis. The United States and regional powers started dealing with it, certainly not to the detriment of bilateral ties with the member states, more seriously than in the past. In the heat of the battle, and shortly thereafter, ambitious GCC security initiatives were launched. At the GCC summit in December 1990, the rulers commissioned Sultan Qabus to develop a plan for an integrated GCC military force. In March 1991, GCC foreign ministers signed a security agreement with their Egyptian and Syrian counterparts, called the Damascus Declaration, that appeared to be tantamount to an alliance. The GCC foreign ministers in September 1991 met with Iranian Foreign Minister ʿAli Akbar Velayati and issued a joint statement on principles governing their relations.

The prospects for a unified GCC security approach quickly faded, however. Sultan Qabus' ambitious proposal for a 100,000-man GCC force was shelved at the December 1991 summit and is effectively dead.[12] The ambitious interpretations of the Damascus Declaration emanating from Egypt and Syria were quickly dashed, as each GCC member made its own deals with Arab coalition partners (or chose not to). Joint GCC approaches to Iran deteriorated by the end of 1992 into serious differences of approach toward their large Gulf neighbor, to be discussed in more detail below. Bilateral security arrangements with Western powers preempted the possibility of GCC-American and GCC-European security deals. The GCC remains an institutional forum within which the Gulf monarchies may coordinate policies (in areas like tariff negotiations with the European Community) and work out their differences, but hopes that it would evolve into a real security alliance have not been realized.

The fact remains that the GCC states, united by similar political systems and many common interests toward the outside world, perceive their interests differently on a number of questions. They come together in a crisis, like the combination of the Iranian Revolution and the Iran-Iraq War that gave birth to the organization in 1981, and the Iraqi invasion of Kuwait in 1990. But when the crisis passes, the differing perspectives and disputes among them creep back into the foreground. Each of the states clearly prefers to deal with external powers on security issues directly, not through the GCC. Each of the member states is extremely hesitant to give up any aspect of its sovereignty, and smaller states remain leery of Saudi dominance. Most noticeably, border disputes that shrink into the background in the face of immediate threats tend to resurface when the regional scene quiets down.

Two such border questions resurfaced in 1991 and 1992 to complicate relations among the GCC states. In July 1991, Qatar petitioned the International Court of Justice to rule on conflicting claims between itself and Bahrain to the Hawar Islands and other disputed reefs. Hawar sits just off the west coast of Qatar, about twenty kilometers from Bahrain. As a result of British border demarcations, Bahrain was given the islands, but Qatar has not recognized Bahraini sovereignty. Saudi Arabia attempted to mediate between its two neighbors on the border issue, but was not able to get Qatar to withdraw its case from the ICJ, where, as of August 1993, it was still pending.[13]

In October 1992, an incident took place between a Qatari border patrol and a tribal contingent of the Saudi National Guard in the area where the borders of the two countries and the UAE come together. Two Qatari soldiers and one Saudi tribal shaykh were killed. The Qatari side responded in a harsh and very public way to the incident. The next day the Qatari government "suspended" its 1965 border agreement with Saudi Arabia. Saudi officials accused Qatar of moving border posts into Saudi territory during the Gulf War, while world attention was diverted to Kuwait. Relations continued to deteriorate through the fall of 1992. Qatar refused to participate in the ministerial meetings preparing for the December 1992 GCC summit, and threatened to withdraw its troops from the GCC Peninsula Shield force in Saudi Arabia.

More ominously from the Saudi viewpoint, Qatar also very publicly sought support from both Iran and Iraq in the dispute. A number of Qatari-Iranian economic deals were signed in the summer of 1992, aligning Doha more closely with Iran than any of the other GCC states. In late October 1992, Qatar sent its ambassador back to Iraq, ostensibly to pay "farewell calls," and in exchange received pledges of military support from Baghdad in its "confrontation" with Saudi Arabia. The amir of Qatar, who was out of his country for much of this period, finally met with King Fahd of Saudi Arabia and President Mubarak of Egypt in Medina on December 19–20, 1992. At this meeting Qatar agreed to reaffirm the 1965 agreement, and the two sides accepted a one-year deadline for a final demarcation of their border according to that agreement. With that issue solved, Qatar joined the other GCC states at the December 1992 summit.[14]

The substance of these border disputes is not particularly important; the areas under dispute are not strategic nor rich in oil. They reflect historical tensions among the ruling families and a desire to assert sovereignty. They also point to the problems the GCC has had in developing beyond a forum for yearly summit meetings. The Qatari-Bahraini border issue could not be resolved internally. The Saudi-Qatari dispute was settled through Egyptian mediation. GCC officials admitted that their organization had little to contribute to the settlement of bilateral disputes among its members, and that only frank discussion of such bilateral differences at the highest levels could get the process of Gulf integration, in the economic and security fields, restarted.[15]

The sense of frustration within the GCC secretariat on the lack of progress in a number of areas is also evident in Gulf public opinion. In Kuwait, Saudi Arabia, and Oman, where security issues top the agenda, there is a sense that the GCC is not a relevant player. Some Kuwaitis also resent what they see as pressure from other GCC states to curb their parliamentary experiment.[16] In Bahrain, whose economy depends heavily upon the service sector, there is great resentment that promises of GCC economic integration remain unfulfilled.[17] A number of important issues are under discussion within the GCC, like customs unification, monetary consultation, and joint negotiations with the EC on a range of trade matters. The GCC still provides a forum for cooperation on internal security matters and on diplomatic initiatives. However, there is a palpable feeling in both official and public opinion that the organization is at a turning point and risks sinking into irrelevance unless immediate steps are taken to overcome obstacles to Gulf political and economic integration.

Self-reliance in defense and security matters is a difficult, if not unachievable, goal for the Gulf monarchies. Their narrow demographic bases, political constraints, and problems in cooperating among themselves all work against real self-defense. As small and wealthy states have always done, they seek to play larger regional powers off against one another to maintain local balances and to preserve some freedom of maneuver. The regional balancing game, played with Iran, Iraq, Egypt, and Syria, is the second aspect of these states' security policies.

REGIONAL BALANCING

Since the end of the Gulf War, the Gulf monarchies have walked a tightrope between their Arab coalition partners, Egypt and Syria, on the one hand, and Iran, on the other. Saudi Arabia and the smaller states have attempted to maintain a strong link with their

Arab wartime allies, without allowing that link to become a real military alliance, and without unduly alienating Iran. At the same time they have, with differing degrees of intensity, pursued better relations with Iran while remaining leery about ultimate Iranian intentions. Iraq under Saddam is a special case in this balancing game, unacceptable as a security partner but still seen as an important element of the regional equation. The Gulf monarchies have adopted different approaches for dealing with it.

With the end of the Gulf War, Egypt and Syria were poised to play a major role in Gulf security issues. In March 1991, the foreign ministers of the GCC states and their Arab coalition partners met in Damascus and agreed on a framework for security cooperation among the eight states. The "Damascus Declaration" seemed to be the basis for a permanent Egyptian and Syrian military presence in the Gulf, what regional observers dubbed the "6 + 2" security structure. One Saudi newspaper said at the time that the declaration considered the Egyptian and Syrian forces as "the nucleus of an Arab peacekeeping force for guaranteeing the security and safety of the Arab states in the Gulf region."[18] Four days later, the eight foreign ministers met in Riyad with U.S. Secretary of State James Baker. They endorsed President Bush's broad framework for Middle East security, and Secretary Baker in turn expressed U.S. support for the Damascus Declaration and for an Egyptian and Syrian military role in the Gulf.[19]

Almost immediately, however, Saudi Arabia and other Gulf states began to back away from these far-reaching readings of the Damascus Declaration. At a time when the Saudi and Kuwaiti treasuries were stretched to their limits by financial commitments undertaken during the Gulf War, the idea of taking on a greater, open-ended commitment to Egypt and Syria, which would be the quid pro quo for their troop deployments, was viewed with trepidation. Moreover, there were fears that existing good relations with the Asad and Mubarak governments might change over the long term, either because of domestic political changes in Syria and Egypt or because of regional realignments. In that case, the presence of the troops in the Gulf would become at minimum an irritant, and perhaps even a threat, to the Gulf monarchies.[20]

Another reason for this reassessment was the very negative Iranian reaction to the Damascus Declaration. Iranian officials condemned what they saw as efforts to isolate their country in the Gulf and reiterated their view that Gulf security was a responsibility limited to the states in the Gulf themselves.[21] Oman, which enjoyed much better relations with Teheran during the 1980s than did its upper Gulf neighbors, expressed caution about formal security arrangements that could be interpreted as aimed against Iran.[22] In June 1991, Iranian and Egyptian officials engaged in a public war of words over the Iranian insistence that Egypt could not play a major role in Gulf security affairs.[23]

Saudi Arabia saw the end of the Gulf War as an opportunity to improve relations with Iran. In the Saudi view, Iran had acted responsibly during the crisis over Kuwait. Moreover, since the death of Ayatollah Khumayni, the Islamic Republic had downplayed its desire to spread its ideological message across the Gulf by propaganda and subversion.[24] Kuwait shared the Saudi view that Iran's behavior in the crisis made it a responsible partner, and if anything pursued a rapprochement with Teheran more vigorously that did the Saudis. Oman, the UAE, and Qatar, which had advocated better relations with Iran for years, encouraged this trend within the GCC.

In early June 1991, Saudi Foreign Minister Prince Sa'ud al-Faysal visited Teheran, assuring his hosts that Riyad had no intention of hosting a permanent foreign military presence and that the Damascus Declaration was not aimed against Iran. The two sides agreed on a framework for cooperation on Gulf, Islamic, and economic issues, and on continuing the GCC-Iranian dialogue on security matters.[25] Saudi Arabia also agreed to allow an Iranian delegation of over 100,000 to attend that year's *hajj*, in June 1991. Since the Islamic Revolution came to power, the *hajj* had come to be a barometer of Saudi-Iranian relations. The 1991 *hajj* was very quiet, with the Iranian delegation refraining from the provocative political demonstrations that characterized past years. The head of the Iranian pilgrimage delegation praised the Saudi government's efforts to provide for the needs of the Iranian pilgrims, and Iranian Foreign Minister Velayati, who accompanied the Iranian pilgrims, said that Saudi-Iranian relations were "developing and going in a very positive direction."[26]

The improvement in Saudi-Iranian relations opened the door for the previously tentative process of GCC-Iranian contacts to proceed at a new level. In August 1991, Iranian Foreign Minister Velayati said in an interview that the GCC states "have invited us to reassess the status of the members of the Council. . . . They have somehow come to the conclusion that they must seek Iran's co-operation, or else it will be impossible to defend regional security."[27] The GCC foreign ministers and GCC Secretary-General ʿAbdallah Bishara met with Velayati in New York in late September, during the United Nations General Assembly meetings. They issued a statement setting out the principles upon which their relations would be based, including the inviolability of recognized international boundaries, no resort to force or the threat of force in relations, and noninterference in the domestic affairs of others.[28] In November 1991, Bishara declared that "Iran is an essential participant with the GCC states in the security of the waters of the Gulf. It is impossible to guarantee that security without an understanding with Iran."[29]

Improved relations with Iran both required and allowed the Gulf monarchies to move away from ambitious Egyptian and Syrian interpretations of the Damascus Declaration. As early as May 1991, the dissatisfaction of Cairo and Damascus with the reluctance of their Gulf partners to implement the declaration became apparent. On May 8, Egypt announced plans to begin withdrawing its troops from Saudi Arabia. Syria announced its intention to withdraw in early June 1991, and completed that operation by the end of July 1991.[30] The "final version" of the Damascus Declaration issued at the July 1991 "6 + 2" foreign ministers meeting in Kuwait contained no mention of a permanent Egyptian-Syrian military presence in the Gulf.[31] At his July 1991 summit meeting with Asad, Mubarak told reporters: "A permanent presence is not requested, and we will not impose ourselves."[32] Egyptian policy began to shift from the Damascus Declaration framework to bilateral arrangements with individual GCC countries, particularly the smaller ones.[33]

When it appeared that a stable equidistance between the Arab pole and Iran had been established, Iranian actions pushed Saudi Arabia back toward Cairo and Damascus. In April 1992, Iranian authorities on Abu Musa, which Iran jointly administers with Sharja, one of the United Arab Emirates, expelled about eighty Indian workers in the employ of UAE agencies on the island because they failed to obtain Iranian visas. Their expulsion paralyzed public services to the Arab community on the island, most of whom returned to the UAE.[34] In August 1992, Iran again asserted itself on Abu Musa, turning away a number of third country nationals, mostly Egyptian teachers, who worked on the island for the UAE government. Iranian foreign ministry sources were quoted as saying that continued foreign involvement in the Gulf made it necessary for Iran to strengthen its position on the island.[35]

The GCC states made a public issue of this second Iranian move. Their worries about Iran's geopolitical ambitions were heightened by what they viewed as a major Iranian rearmament program, though its dollar value was far below the weapons sales they themselves were negotiating (Iran's rearmament program will be discussed in more detail in Chapter 6). Saudi Arabia was also particularly concerned at increasing Iranian influence in Qatar, seeing it as part of an Iranian plan to split the GCC and challenge Saudi influence in the small shaykhdoms. The UAE brought the issue of Iran's role, not only in Abu Musa but also in the two Tunbs islands occupied by the Shah in 1971, to the United Nations. Gulf media emphasized the story, in contrast to their treatment of the April 1992 incident. The December 1992 GCC summit expressed its strong support for the UAE, accusing Iran of occupying Arab land and saying that improved relations with Teheran depended upon a "strengthening of trust" that precludes actions like those taken by Iran on Abu Musa.[36] Improvements in Iranian-Saudi relations suffered a further setback during the 1993 *hajj*, held in late May. Iranian pilgrims clashed with Saudi security forces over the holding of what Saudi authorities considered a "political" rally. The incident touched off a new round of media accusations between the states.[37]

The GCC states reacted to the Iranian moves on Abu Musa by reviving their "6 + 2" dialogue with Egypt and Syria. Egypt had been pressing the GCC states for concrete implementation decisions on the Damascus Declaration, but the GCC dragged its feet, postponing the "6 + 2" foreign ministers meeting scheduled for May 1992. However, after the second Abu Musa incident, the eight foreign ministers quickly convened in Qatar on September 10, agreeing to support the UAE in its position on the islands and to hold regular consultations at the foreign minister level.[38] At the December 1992 GCC summit, the leaders set a May 1993 target date for the founding of the Arab development fund promised in the Damascus Declaration. $6.5 billion of the promised $10 billion had been committed by GCC members as of the end of 1992, though concrete plans to implement the fund had yet to be completed by the fall of 1993.[39] Yusif bin ʿAlawi, the straightforward, acerbic Omani minister of state for foreign affairs, joked to Egyptian journalists during a visit to Cairo in July 1993 that the failure to implement the Damascus Declaration fully "is typical of Arab programs. . . . The results will appear after five centuries."[40] The Egyptians were not amused.

The key element for the Gulf states in this balancing act between Iran and Egypt (with Syria as a somewhat secondary actor) is fluidity. None of them now perceives Iran as an implacably hostile enemy, as many of them did during the height of the Iranian Revolution and the Iran-Iraq war. They therefore want to maintain friendly relations with Teheran and not commit themselves fully to an Egyptian-led Arab alignment against Iran. As early as February 1993, Saudi-Iranian tensions over the Abu Musa incidents were beginning to fade.[41] In late January 1993, UAE officials on Abu Musa said that conditions on the island had "returned to normal," with no Iranian interference in UAE institutions.[42] Even after the tensions over the 1993 *hajj*, a Saudi official took pains to attribute the problem to "extremists" in Iran who were trying to sabotage the "reasonable people" who have worked to improve relations with Iran's neighbors.[43] On the other hand, they remain wary of ultimate Iranian intentions, and thus want to maintain their "Arab option" of turning to Egypt and Syria for political, and if need be, military support. The two poles of this Gulf game were graphically displayed in May 1993, when President Mubarak and Iranian Foreign Minister Velayati each visited the GCC states within the space of two weeks. These two trips illustrate how successful the GCC states have been at maintaining the balancing act since the end of the Gulf War. There is no reason why that success should not continue.

The Gulf monarchies' dealings with Iraq are not governed by such neat geopolitical principles. Hatred of Saddam Husayn among the ruling elites, particularly in Kuwait and Saudi Arabia, is real. They want him out. The question is: at what price and with what consequences? The answer for Kuwaitis, rulers and citizens, is clear: at any price and with any consequences. For the other small shaykhdoms, farther from Iraq and less affected by the Gulf War, the answer is also clear, but different. They are unwilling to do much of anything to bring Saddam down, and want to see Iraq remain a counterweight to Iranian and even Saudi influence. The dilemma of how to deal with Iraq is greatest for Saudi Arabia, the only Gulf monarchy with the resources and geopolitical weight to affect events there. The Saudis are anxious to see Saddam replaced, but also worried about the possibility of the breakup of Iraq, by the character of any successor regime, and by the prospect of increased Iranian influence in Iraq.

During the crisis, the Saudis began publicly to support a group of exiled Iraqi opponents of the regime called the Free Iraq Council.[44] More significantly, Riyad began to reach out to the Iranian-supported Iraqi Shi'i opposition.[45] On June 6, 1991, during his visit to Teheran, Saudi Foreign Minister Prince Sa'ud al-Faysal met publicly with Muhammad Baqir al-Hakim, the head of the Supreme Assembly of the Islamic Revolution in Iraq, the Shi'i Islamist "government-in-exile" supported by Iran during its war with Iraq.[46] It was, in part, fear that such groups would gain preponderant influence in Iraq that led Saudi Arabia to support Saddam Husayn during his war with Iran.

The Saudis, along with Syria and Iran, actively encouraged their various Iraqi clients to put aside substantial differences and agree to a common program for opposing Saddam and organizing for the post-Saddam transition period. On March 11–13, 1991, twenty-three Iraqi opposition groups, ranging from Shi'i Islamists and Kurdish nationalists to liberals, dissident Ba'thists, tribal leaders, and Communists met in Beirut. They issued a "lowest common denominator" statement of their intention to cooperate on the ouster of Saddam and to form a new regime based on free elections. Kurdish and other minority rights were also affirmed.[47] Whether this disparate group could have held together and managed a post-Saddam transition is an open question. What is important from the Saudi perspective was Riyad's willingness to support it, demonstrating how far the Saudis were willing to go to get rid of Saddam Husayn.

Saudi support for Iraqi popular forces opposed to Saddam was called into question during the uprisings against the Iraqi regime centered in Shiʿi and Kurdish areas in March–April 1991, immediately following the Gulf War. The Saudis seemed hesitant about openly supporting the rebels, reflecting a fear that Iran would reap most benefits from the chaos in Iraq. Western news sources implied on occasion that Saudi fears led the United States to withhold support for the rebels.[48]

The evidence that has come to light up to now paints a far more ambiguous picture of the Saudi role in the events of those months. It seems that, while Riyad was certainly nervous about prospects of increased Iranian influence in Iraq, it was the Bush administration which took the lead in backing away from the Iraqi rebels, whose prospects for success were doubted in Washington.[49] In order to respond to American public opinion, which questioned why, after portraying Saddam Husayn as the equivalent of Hitler, the United States was refusing to support his own people as they rose up against him, administration spokespersons tried to shift the blame to the Saudis. However, a senior member of the staff of the Senate Foreign Relations Committee asserted in a published committee report that Saudi leaders told him that they were willing to support the Iraqi uprisings, but that the United States would not.[50] Given their actions previous and subsequent to the Iraqi uprisings, it appears that the Saudi fear of a "Shiʿa-dominated Iraq" has been exaggerated in the West, and that the Saudis would have followed an American lead in supporting Iraqi rebels in March–April 1991.

With the failure of the rebellion against Saddam, Saudi Arabia continued to support elements of the Iraqi opposition, including prominent Shiʿi groups. Riyad hosted a (largely unsuccessful) meeting of the groups that participated in the March 1991 Beirut meeting in February 1992. Muhammad Baqir al-Hakim attended the meeting, and was publicly received by both King Fahd and Crown Prince ʿAbdallah. Western sources reported at the same time renewed Saudi efforts to get the United States involved in covert activities aimed at bringing down Saddam.[51] As 1992 wore on, serious splits emerged within the Iraqi opposition, and the Saudis very visibly cooled toward it. The Iraqi National Congress (INC), a Kurdish-dominated group formed in the summer of 1992, has received the backing of Western powers, but is looked upon with suspicion by some Iraqis, Syria, Iran, Turkey, and Saudi Arabia. This group sponsored a meeting of Iraqi oppositionists in the Kurdish areas of northern Iraq in September and October 1992, attended by many important Iraqi Shi‘i representatives but boycotted by pro-Saudi Iraqi figures and criticized by the Saudi government.[52] The INC has tried to mend fences with Riyad, and King Fahd received an INC delegation in Riyad in June 1993.[53]

Saudi ambivalence about the Iraqi National Congress stems primarily from the fear that it is a cover for a Kurdish independence drive that will lead to the fragmentation of Iraq, and Iranian dominance of the remaining rump state. Riyad's position toward the INC reflects the current Saudi ambivalence about Iraq. That Saddam must go is a given, but not at the cost of the breakup of Iraq or Iranian dominance of southern Iraq. The Saudis are willing to deal with Iraqi Shi‘i groups to a much greater extent than the United States, but still worry about their links to Teheran. Their fears of Iraqi disintegration are probably exaggerated, and not shared by Washington, but they are real. The status quo is not the preferred Saudi option, but it ranks higher than many of the alternatives.

RELATIONS WITH THE UNITED STATES

The third, and most important, aspect of the GCC states' security strategy is their link with Western powers in general and the United States in particular. In many ways it is the simplest element: the GCC states want to be protected, and the United States wants to protect them. Their shared interests are clear: oil and political stability. The Gulf regimes and Western powers have a history of cooperation. Even the 1973 Arab oil embargo against the United States did not alter that pattern of cooperation; in fact, the oil revolution of the early 1970s strengthened it by raising the importance of Gulf oil exporters for Washington. Any residual hesitations among the rulers about being openly identified with the United States, because of their broader Arab loyalties or because of American-Israeli ties, were put aside during the Gulf War. Yet even now their American connection presents difficulties for Gulf regimes, largely in the realm of domestic politics, complicating what most Americans assume should be a straightforward relationship based upon mutual interest.

There is no doubt, in the wake of the Gulf War, that the Gulf monarchies look to the United States as their primary security ally. Saudi and Kuwaiti arms purchases are intended as much to cement the political relationship with the United States as to provide for self-defense. Kuwait, Bahrain, and Qatar have signed defense agreements with Washington since the war, the details of which have not been made public. Some of the smaller states have also signed such agreements with Great Britain and France; Kuwait has also signed one with the new Russian Republic. American naval forces have had port facilities in Bahrain since World War II, and Oman has provided access to military facilities since the early 1980s. American ground and naval forces have held a number of exercises in Kuwait since the end of the war. At the beginning of 1993, nearly two years after the Gulf War, sixty American air force planes were still stationed in Saudi Arabia.[54]

For the Gulf monarchs, problems in security relations with the United States arise from their potential domestic consequences. There is still much suspicion within Gulf public opinion about America's ultimate intentions in the region, and opposition to anything that smacks of "colonial"-style foreign military presences. Foreign military bases remain, as they have been since the advent of colonialism in the Arab Middle East, lightning rods for potential domestic opposition. Moreover, politically activist currents in the Gulf, particularly more secular and liberal tendencies, were disappointed that the United States did not use its leverage with their regimes during and immediately after the crisis to promote political freedom and democratization. The refrain in some intellectual circles in the Gulf is that the United States is in the region to protect the rulers, not the people.[55] Even though public support for the Palestine Liberation Organization decreased in the Gulf as a result of Yasir ʿArafat's pro-Saddam stance during the Gulf War, identification with the Palestinian cause in general remains high among politically active Gulf citizens (with the exception of Kuwaitis). The close American-Israeli relationship, while obviously not an absolute bar to American-Gulf security cooperation, remains an irritant in the public perception of the United States in Gulf.

Among Islamist groups, the opposition to a high-profile American military presence is compounded by fear of Western cultural penetration. The Islamist petition in Saudi Arabia called on the Saudi government both to avoid foreign alliances that run counter to Islamic legitimacy and to diversify its sources of arms. The Memorandum of Advice composed by Islamic activists was even more explicit in its criticisms of Riyad's relations with the United States. It called the stationing of equipment and troops from "untrustworthy" countries on the country's soil a derogation of sovereignty, and advocated diversification of arms sources and the development of a domestic arms industry. The Memorandum identified Western regimes as being "opposed to Islam," and called on the regime to "avoid any form of alliance or cooperation which serves imperialist goals or infringes on independent decision-making," and to "cancel all military treaties and conventions which impinge on the sovereignty of the state and its independence in administering and arming its military."

These public opinion sensitivities have led the Saudis to be very cautious, particularly in public, about how they have portrayed their security relations with the United States. In late November 1990, King Fahd, in a speech to the country, denied that Saudi Arabia had made any agreements for the permanent stationing of foreign forces in the kingdom.[56] In a statement to the press immediately after the war, Saudi Defense Minister Prince Sultan referred to a commitment on the part of the United States to withdraw its forces from the kingdom once their mission was completed.[57] In September 1991, during one of the American confrontations with Iraq over application of the U.N. resolutions, Prince Sultan expressed misgivings about the very public way in which the United States was using Saudi Arabia as a military staging area against Iraq, and urged Washington to spread its deployments out to Kuwait and even to capture an airfield in Iraq itself to use as a base.[58] The desire to avoid inflaming public opinion also explains why the Saudis have been more hesitant than their smaller neighbors to negotiate a formal defense agreement with the United States in the wake of the war, a hesitation that dates back decades in the U.S.-Saudi relationship.[59] None of the smaller states have been willing to host the regional headquarters of the U.S. Central Command, though immediately after the war there was speculation in Washington that CENTCOM would move from its current Tampa, Florida, base to the Gulf, in part for the same public opinion reasons.

The only Gulf country where public opinion does not constrain the rulers in their pursuit of security ties with the United States is Kuwait. Understandably, Kuwaitis have a heightened sense of security fears, and the United States remains enormously popular among Kuwaitis of all political stripes. The Islamic Constitutional Movement, the political grouping of the Kuwaiti Muslim Brotherhood, publicly supported the September 1991 U.S.-Kuwaiti defense agreement. *Salafi* and Shi'i political activists in Kuwait, while worrying about American cultural influences in the country, also see no alternative to a strong security link to the United States.[60] A poll commissioned by the Kuwaiti News Agency in early 1993 found that 72 percent of respondents supported defense agreements with Western countries, though only 43 percent were in favor of a permanent American force in the country, with more people preferring an international force of some type stationed in Kuwait.[61]

These constraints within public opinion obviously do not prevent the Gulf monarchies from maintaining close security relations with the United States. Naval and ground force exercises are conducted regularly. Equipment is pre-positioned. American ships and aircraft have access to facilities in these countries on a continuous basis. Military consultations at the highest levels are ongoing. The United States has been very cautious about high-profile military presence in the postwar period, understanding the political sensitivities of the region. President Bush told Congress immediately after the Gulf War that the United States had no plans for a permanent ground force presence in the Gulf, and no such plans have emerged since. There is an understanding between the United States and the Gulf monarchies about the potentially negative political import of their security relationship.

Despite that understanding, there is a risk that the United States will stumble, unintentionally, into a position where it feels compelled to maintain a larger military presence in the Gulf than the Gulf monarchies might want or feel comfortable with. The political and military obligations that the United States took on in postwar Iraq—enforcing compliance with U.N. resolutions on ridding Iraq of weapons of mass destruction, protecting Iraqi Kurdish areas in the north, establishing a no-fly zone in the Shiʿi areas of southern Iraq—require a substantial American military commitment. The Clinton administration's focus on potential Iranian threats to American interests in the region increases incentives for more substantial American military deployments in the Gulf. Gulf rulers take a different view of these issues than Washington does. They are also constrained by public opinion from simply following along with American military and security plans. The potential for misunderstandings between the United States and its Gulf allies grows as the memory of the Gulf War recedes. The need to be at least somewhat solicitous of public opinion limits Gulf rulers' freedom to be what most Americans would consider "good allies."

CONCLUSION

There are problems with each element of the security strategy of the Gulf monarchies. Self-reliance is politically difficult and militarily ineffective. Today's regional allies could be tomorrow's threats, and are expensive to keep friendly. The Americans are considered more reliable than before the Gulf War, but too close an embrace could have negative consequences domestically. As is usually the case with small and weak states, none of the foreign policy options available looks particularly good.

On the other hand, similar problems faced these states before August 1990, and they weathered Desert Storm. The security picture for the Gulf monarchies is far better now than it has been since the Iranian Revolution of 1979. It must be remembered that for all the GCC states except Kuwait, their security policies have been remarkably successful. They survived the Iranian Revolution, the Iran-Iraq War, and the Gulf War with their domestic political systems and their international standing intact. It is only in Kuwait that a radical rethinking of foreign policy is taking place, reflected in its much greater willingness than its GCC partners to be publicly identified with American security plans. The Gulf monarchies can be expected to continue to rely on a flexible and reactive mix of these three security elements—self-reliance, regional balancing, and their Western connection—for the foreseeable future. There are few attractive alternatives to this policy of "muddling through."

6

Challenges

IT WOULD BE FOOLISH TO PREDICT THE COURSE OF political development in the Arab monarchies of the Gulf or to venture guesses about their overall political stability. The epitaphs of these regimes have been written many times over the last four decades, by different generations of Middle East observers. The dominant view that they would fall to a triumphant Pan-Arabism was replaced by an equally strong view that they would be toppled by a resurgent Islamic current. The sense that they are anachronisms, just waiting to be swept away by the next crisis, remains prevalent in the West, even though they have weathered the storms of the modern Middle East better than many of their more "modern" neighbors. It would be a serious mistake to underestimate their staying power, or to assume that the only support for their rule is the protection of the United States.

That being said, it is also important to recognize that these regimes must evolve if they are to survive into the next century. These are not static polities. Social and economic change is occurring that will have political consequences. Such change could be gradual and evolutionary, largely guided from above but driven along by sustained popular pressure, or it could be revolutionary, potentially disrupting domestic oil production or bringing to power governments that see confrontation with the West as either in their domestic interests or part of their ideological duties. If the United States does have an interest in the stability of the Gulf (a question that will be examined in Chapter 7), then it is in the American interest that domestic change in the Gulf monarchies be gradual and evolutionary. To that end, it is necessary to think about scenarios that could lead to political instability, in order to identify and possibly remedy problems before they occur.

DOMESTIC CHALLENGES AND POLITICAL STABILITY

In oil states such as the Arab monarchies of the Gulf, where the government is the primary actor in and motor for the economy, economic issues are particularly central to the political agenda. These regimes over the last few decades have taken upon themselves the responsibility of providing their citizens with jobs, services, and a relatively high standard of living, as part of a social contract that ensures political stability. Were the Gulf monarchies to find themselves unable to meet their end of the economic bargain with their citizens, the future of their political systems could be called into question. While both the fiscal position of the governments and the problem of unemployment are troubling issues, it does not appear that any of these states faces that kind of severe economic crisis in the foreseeable future.

The most noteworthy economic consequence of the past ten years has been the drawing down of the enormous financial reserves built up by these states during the oil boom years of 1970–1982. The precipitous decline in world oil prices in the mid-1980s led more to deficit spending than to belt-tightening in the Gulf monarchies. Governments preferred to dip into principal than to cut their budgets for military expenditures, bureaucratic jobs, and social services. Then, as oil prices were beginning to turn up again, the invasion and liberation of Kuwait faced these states with enormous costs that could only be borne by further expenditure of state reserves.

Kuwait and Saudi Arabia have been the states most affected by these financial pressures. Kuwait's foreign reserves, thought to be over $100 billion before the invasion, have been substantially drawn down by the expenses of the war and the rebuilding. Some estimates put Kuwaiti expenditure since the invasion at $65 billion. On top of that, revelations of corruption and ineptitude in the management of Kuwait's overseas reserves that have come to light since the re-establishment of parliament indicate that a further $10 billion may have been squandered.[1]

Saudi Arabia has been meeting deficits by drawing on its reserves since the early 1980s and by borrowing on the domestic market since the late 1980s. The oil windfall brought by increased prices and the near doubling of Saudi production during the Gulf crisis was more than absorbed by the expenses the Saudis incurred during the war and the arms purchases they negotiated during and afterwards.[2] The International Monetary Fund (IMF) estimated the direct costs of the Gulf War for the Saudis as $55 billion, a figure that Saudi officials have not challenged. Saudi government reserves, which totaled more than $100 billion in the early 1980s, have fallen by at least 75 percent since then. Some estimates put Saudi liquid reserves at below $10 billion.[3]

For the first time in decades, the Saudi government went to the international capital markets for loans in February 1991, and the *New York Times* reported that both the U.S. Federal Reserve Bank and the Bank of England have serious concerns about Saudi credit worthiness.[4] Domestic borrowing through the issue of government bonds to cover deficits has become common practice in the kingdom. Saudi Finance Minister Muhammad Aba al-Khayl, in a detailed response to the *New York Times* report, said that Saudi Arabia's public debt does not exceed 52 percent of Saudi GDP, and of that only $4.5 billion is foreign debt. If we take the 1990 Saudi GDP figure of approximately $105 billion, that would put the government debt at about $50 billion, about $45 billion of that debt domestic, all of it taken on within last ten years.[5] The Saudis have even resorted to an indirect income tax through payroll deductions for the social security fund to increase government revenue. (Riyad's Ministry of Finance must have learned some tricks from the U.S. Treasury Department.)

Government spending continues to exceed revenues, despite the stabilization of world oil prices after Desert Storm. All six Arab

Gulf monarchies are planning on deficits in their 1993 budgets: Kuwait of $3.2 billion, Saudi Arabia of $7.4 billion, Bahrain of $170 million, Qatar of $940 million, the UAE of $708 million, and Oman of $170 million.[6] This deficit spending, financed mostly from reserves in Kuwait, Qatar, and the UAE and by borrowing in Oman, Saudi Arabia, and Bahrain, continues a decade-long trend that shows no signs of ending soon. Only a dramatic upturn in world oil prices, something not foreseen by oil experts in the near future, could change the situation. In fact, the $3 per barrel decline in world oil prices in the summer of 1993 probably means that the actual deficits in each country will be greater than those planned. None of the governments has demonstrated the ability or the will to cut back significantly on either social services or military spending. Given growing populations that will make continued demands on the state budgets, the Gulf states face hard political choices ahead about their priorities. It is difficult to imagine, particularly in Saudi Arabia, that current levels of defense spending can be maintained while continuing both to provide the same level of social services to an increasing number of citizens and to support the ever-growing ruling families in the style to which they have become accustomed.

It needs to be emphasized that this gloomy financial news does not mean that these countries are poor—far from it. Most developing countries would love to have their problems. The governments have a valuable natural resource, good credit ratings, and in some cases still substantial international reserves. In fact, since the end of the Gulf War Saudi Arabia has enjoyed something of an economic boom, with a large amount of capital coming back to the country, the local stock market surging (largely on the strength of bank shares), and an increase in private sector investment. The Saudi boom is not region-wide, however, as neither Bahrain nor Kuwait has seen much of the capital that left during the war return. This probably marks the end of the Bahraini off-shore banking industry that drove economic growth there in the 1980s.[7] The Gulf monarchies are not now in the midst of an immediate fiscal crisis. Some may face such a crisis in the coming years if they cannot discipline their spending, increase oil production, or find some way to increase oil prices. What the current financial picture does mean is that the Arab Gulf monarchies are not in a position to absorb another economic blow like the collapse of oil prices in the mid-1980s or the Iraqi invasion of Kuwait. Their economic margin of safety has disappeared.

The other troublesome economic issue on these states' agendas is unemployment. The problem is particularly acute in Bahrain, where it is estimated by some that 25 percent of the male citizen labor force is without jobs, and is growing more important in Saudi Arabia. All the states will face this problem eventually, if current labor practices continue. It seems astonishing that countries where expatriates make up such a large proportion of the labor force, in some cases the majority of the labor force, face an unemployment problem. This unusual situation is the result of a mixture of demographics, economics, and culture.

The demographics are simple. The population growth rate in these six states is among the highest in the world. The lowest growth rate is in the UAE, 3.1 percent; the highest is in Qatar, 4.0 percent (for the period 1985–1991). By comparison, total Asian population growth during that period was 1.9 percent, total world growth was 1.7 percent. The population pyramids in these countries are heavily weighted toward the younger end of the age spectrum. For example, 1991 figures show that in Bahrain 43 percent of the population was under the age of twenty (compared with 28 percent in the United States).[8] Larger and larger numbers of citizens are coming onto the job market every year. Many of these are graduates of the new university systems in these states, and are looking for jobs of a status and salary commensurate with their educational attainments. During the boom years, every citizen college graduate who wanted one was virtually assured of a government job. Those days are over.

The simple answer, if the goal is to employ nationals, is to restrict labor immigration and perhaps even send some foreign labor home. The economics, however, are more complicated. For private sector employers, it is much more economical to hire foreign workers. They can be paid lower salaries than nationals, will perform tasks that nationals try to avoid, and do not require the same level of benefits that nationals demand. In upper-level management positions, private sector employers in the Gulf also contend that expatriates frequently bring more skills and better training to their jobs than do products of the local school systems. So powerful local business interests oppose immigration restrictions. Some powerful political interests also oppose such restrictions. For those who control foreign worker permits, labor immigration is a lucrative business. Access to visas and other necessary documents comes at a price, in some cases a fixed percentage of the foreign worker's salary.

The cultural issue is an important one, but the source of much confused thinking. There is a prevalent notion in the West that the citizens of the Gulf Arab monarchies are "soft," and that there is a cultural disposition against hard work. That is a racist canard. For years the people who lived in these countries performed the most arduous physical labors to secure their daily bread (pearl-diving, fishing, long-distance trade, nomadic pastoralism, oasis farming). The military prowess of the Arabian tribes was fabled. This region has produced some of the shrewdest and most successful merchants the world has ever seen. There are no "cultural" barriers between Gulf residents and hard work.

However, the oil riches of the last two decades have changed expectations among people in the Gulf monarchies about the kind of work they should and should not do. It is not unique to the Gulf to pay other people to do menial labor. Not many U.S. citizens pick lettuce in California. Access to great wealth has allowed Gulf countries the luxury of paying other people to do their (literally) dirty work. That luxury has come to be taken as an immutable fact of history by some in the Gulf, and by gullible outside observers. Changing attitudes about what is "appropriate" work for nationals is a difficult, but not an impossible task. Economic factors drove the purported "cultural" distaste for some kinds of jobs; economic factors will have to play a major role if such attitudes are to be shifted.

Labor issues are now at the top of the agenda in Kuwait and Saudi Arabia. Both countries, for political not economic reasons, effectively expelled large contingents of foreign laborers as a result of the Gulf War—Palestinians from Kuwait and Yemenis from Saudi Arabia. Particularly in Kuwait, there was much talk of taking advantage of that event to alter population policy and avoid a return to dependence on foreign labor. In both cases, the evidence to date is that the expelled labor is being largely replaced by foreign workers from other places, not by citizens. South Asian and East Asian workers are filling many jobs left by Palestinians in Kuwait. Egyptians are taking the place of Yemenis in many areas of the Saudi economy; South and East Asians are also a growing percentage of the Saudi expatriate labor force.[9] How these countries deal with the effects of these politically induced labor shortages will determine population policies for the future.

The issue of citizen unemployment is embedded in the larger issue of generational change facing the Gulf monarchies. That change is occurring and will continue to occur over the next decade, on two levels. The first, discussed above, is generational change in society at large. The population explosion in these countries means that the political and economic systems will have to support much larger populations in the near future. That presents challenges beyond simply employing new entrants into the workforce. Growing populations have to be provided with health care and other social services. Enough water must be provided to support urban, middle-class life-styles, an increasingly difficult and environmentally damaging task in an arid climate. The children of the new generation must be educated. Finally, the new generation needs a political framework that will allow them to participate in, and thus identify with, their political system. The economic repercussions of population growth are obvious, but given the natural resources of these states, they can be managed if the right economic decisions are made. Politically, the growth of literate and politically aware populations is already straining the old patron-client networks in the Arab monarchies of the Gulf; that strain will only increase over the coming years. It will be more difficult for regimes to deal with the political than the economic consequences of population increases.

The second level on which generational change presents specific political challenges to these states is in the ruling families themselves. In most families, the younger generation, those who have come of age since the oil boom, is numerically much larger than the circle of their fathers and uncles who are ruling now—Oman is the exception. They are better educated, at least as measured by academic degrees. They are now demanding, and will in the future continue to demand, increased roles in the governing of their states, which many of them see as their birthright. Some faces are familiar to the West: Saʿud al-Faysal, the son of King Faysal and foreign minister of Saudi Arabia; Bandar bin Sultan, the Saudi ambassador in Washington and son of Defense Minister Prince Sultan; Saʿud Nasir Al Sabah, former Kuwaiti ambassador in Washington and now information minister. Many more are less familiar to us, but very important at home. The importance of this new generation to the ruling families was recognized by King Fahd in the Saudi Basic System of Government issued in March 1992. Every ruler of the kingdom since the death of the modern founder, King ʿAbd al-ʿAziz, has been one of his sons. Article 5 of the Basic System states that rulership now resides in the sons of ʿAbd al-ʿAziz and in *their sons.*[10]

Succession questions are part of the generational change issue. In Bahrain, Qatar, and many of the UAE emirates, father-son succession patterns assure that generational change is a regular feature of ruling family life. In Kuwait and Saudi Arabia, succession has recently passed laterally among brothers and cousins from different branches of the ruling family. The switch to the next generation in these countries will not come soon, and establishing the principle by which that generational change takes place will be the subject of some very hard bargaining in the future.

In the past two decades, succession in all these states has been remarkably smooth. The assassination of King Faysal in 1975 and the death of King Khalid in 1982 hardly disrupted Saudi governance. Amir Jabir picked up the reins in Kuwait upon the death of his cousin Sabah in 1977. Shaykh Rashid, the long-time ruler of Dubai, was succeeded by his son Maktoum upon his death in October 1990. The next succession in five of the six states, as matters now stand, is established and agreed upon. Kuwait's Crown Prince Saʿd ʿAbdallah of the Al Salim branch of the family will follow his cousin Amir Jabir of the Al Jabir branch. Crown Prince ʿAbdallah of Saudi Arabia is slotted to succeed his half-brother King Fahd, with Prince Sultan, Fahd's full brother and defense minister, standing next in line. In both Bahrain and Qatar, the crown princes, sons of the amirs, appear to be firmly in place for succession. Succession in the UAE is complicated by the federal nature of the state. Shaykh Zayid is both ruler of Abu Dhabi, and in that capacity will most likely be succeeded by his son Khalifa, and president of the UAE. Given Abu Dhabi's stature in the federation, it is unlikely that any other ruler would challenge Shaykh Zayid's successor as president. Only in Oman is there no clear succession line established. Sultan Qabus has no issue, and no designated heir.

The relatively settled nature of the succession at this time should not obscure the fact that this issue has been extremely contentious at various times in all the Gulf monarchies. The last two successions in Qatar have been *coups de famille;* recently, rumors of differences between the crown prince and his father have circulated. British pressure led to the successions of Shaykh Zayid and Sultan Qabus from their hidebound predecessors. The shaykh of Sharjah in the UAE removed his older brother from the position of crown prince in February 1990, after the latter launched an unsuccessful coup attempt in 1987. The contest for power in Saudi Arabia between then King Sa'ud and Crown Prince Faysal, from the late 1950s until Sa'ud's deposition in 1964, hampered Saudi efforts to meet the challenges of Egyptian President Gamal 'Abd al-Nasir and the Yemeni civil war. While no serious succession crisis now looms, this topic cannot be ignored when assessing the political scene in these countries.

Also related to the generational change issue in the ruling families is the larger question of political participation. At a time when demands for a greater say in political affairs are being voiced in these countries' societies, rulers are being pressured to reserve more political positions and power levers for members of their families. Just as the increasing involvement of ruling family members in business in some of these countries is leading to resentment, so also claims by the younger generation of ruling families to a greater share of political power could lead to resentment among commoners who want broader access to the political system. How to accommodate the political ambitions of the younger princes and politically ambitious commoners—as the numbers of both are increasing rapidly—is a difficult problem for the rulers.

The regimes in the Arab monarchies of the Gulf face important challenges in terms of economic management and political development, but an examination of prospects for political stability in these states cannot be limited to the "government" side. Opposition is an equally important part of the stability equation. For most of their recent history, these regimes' most formidable challengers came from the Arab nationalist and leftist camps. As in the Middle East as a whole, the power of such groups has declined precipitously in the Gulf over the past two decades.[11] The most significant potential oppositions in the area are now Islamic groups; their origins and importance were discussed in Chapter 2. In discussing the "Islamic challenge" to these regimes, it is important to recognize that the agendas of the various Islamic groups differ, with only some openly challenging the legitimacy of existing political systems. It is also important to recall that these governments continue to have a number of tangible and intangible resources in dealing with Islamic opposition groups.

The character of Islamic political groupings, and thus the nature of Islamic political challenges, differs among the countries. In Bahrain, where Shiʿis form a majority of the citizen population and the ruling family is Sunni, the period since the Iranian Revolution has been characterized by relatively high sectarian tension. Iran supported an effort by dissident Bahraini Shiʿis to stage a coup against the government in 1981, and the primary Islamic opposition to the government, up until very recently, has been exclusively Shiʿi and led by the Islamic Movement for the Liberation of Bahrain. The substantial Shiʿi minorities in Kuwait and Saudi Arabia were also the target of Iranian propaganda in the 1980s, and Iran provided support to local opposition movements in those communities. It must be pointed out that, while Iranian moral and material support for all these groups was very important, there would have been no Shiʿi opposition to the governments had there not been real discontent among these communities. Iran could not simply manufacture opposition. Oman and Qatar, with few Shiʿi citizens, were largely immune from this pressure, and the United Arab Emirates maintained cordial relations with Teheran throughout the Iran-Iraq war, avoiding the kind of Iranian pressure faced by the states of the upper Gulf.

The efficacy of purely Shiʿi Islamic opposition has been limited. The Gulf monarchies were able to contain Shiʿi groups during the 1980s through a combination of increased internal security measures and more attention to the material needs of the Shiʿi communities. Improved relations with Iran, particularly since the Iraqi invasion of Kuwait, have lessened the intensity of (though not completely ended) Iranian support for Shi‘i opposition groups in the Gulf monarchies. Given demographic realities, it is only in Bahrain that exclusively Shi‘i groups can pose a realistic and sustained challenge to ruling regimes.

Since the late 1980s, political activism among Sunni Islamist groups in the Gulf has grown in prominence. The end of the Iran-Iraq war mitigated the sectarian tone of Islamic politics in the Gulf, allowing Sunni groups to become more vocal without being perceived as either pro-Iranian or pro-Shi‘a. Populist Sunni groups grew in importance during the 1980s, as Gulf governments supported their development as a counterweight to Shi‘i groups and Iranian pressure.[12] *Salafi* groups, followers of the Saudi Wahhabi Islamic tradition, have become important players on the Kuwaiti, Bahraini, and Qatari political scenes, as well as adopting more independent and critical positions in Saudi Arabia itself. The Muslim Brotherhood in Bahrain has taken a higher public profile on political issues, and the Kuwaiti branch of the Brotherhood forms the basis of the Islamic Constitutional Movement political party.[13] Increased Islamic activism, centered on Sunni mosques, has also been noticed in the UAE, though to a lesser degree than in Kuwait and Bahrain. Only Oman has been relatively immune to public manifestations of increased Sunni activism.

The organizational advantages enjoyed by Sunni Islamic political groups in the Gulf states are clear: relatively benign, if not openly supportive, relations with the governments; the organizational structure of the mosque and other religious institutions; strong financial support from followers and in some cases from the governments; more access to media and other means of communication than other political groups; and a political vocabulary with deep roots and broad appeal in society. They are now and will be in the near future the most important mass-based political forces in these states. However, that does not necessarily make them threats to the political stability of these regimes. The last Sunni group to publicly call for the overthrow of an existing regime were the followers of Juhayman al-‘Utaybi, who took over the Grand Mosque in Mecca in 1979.

There are still close ties between some of these groups and the Gulf governments. Breaking those ties would have enormous costs for Islamist organizations, including political suppression by the regimes' internal security forces, loss of official and unofficial government financial support, and restriction of their access to various means of communication with the population. The close organizational, financial, and ideological relationship between the Saudi government and its religious establishment remains. It is important to note that the more critical Memorandum of Advice composed by Saudi Islamic activists in 1992 had only a quarter of the number of signatures of the less critical Islamist petition of 1991, indicating that the Saudi religious establishment is far from united in a confrontational strategy against the government. Quite the opposite, as the government has been able to mobilize senior clerics to condemn the signers of the Memorandum of Advice and to replace those in official positions perceived to be sympathetic with this trend. In Kuwait, the amir has openly appealed to Islamic groups, setting up in 1991 an advisory committee on the implementation of *shariᶜa* and in March 1993 publicly calling for full application of *shariᶜa* in the country.[14] Sunni and Shiᶜi Islamic groups in Kuwait participated in the October 1992 elections on platforms of support for the 1962 Kuwaiti constitution and limitations on the power of the ruling family, not its overthrow.

Not only do the governments have the resources to work with and/or co-opt many segments of Islamic opinion in their countries, but they also have political strategies to counter the influence of Islamic movements in society. Repression is, of course, a major tool in this effort, but not the only one. Governments can also rely upon the only other significant, organized constituency in their countries—the business community—to act as a counterweight to Islamic currents. It would be a mistake to regard business interests as absolutely opposed to the Islamist agenda; some prominent businessmen are major financial supporters of Islamic movements. In general, however, there are significant differences between the two groups, particularly on economic questions. Islamic movements oppose the pillar of the modern banking system—earning interest on investments and paying interest on loans. Gulf businessmen play in international capital markets and have founded local banks built on the concept of interest. More generally, Gulf business communities, tied into international networks of trade and finance, are opposed to political changes that might isolate their countries from the rest of the capitalist world.

Gulf governments can also appeal on the ideological level to tribal sentiment and heritage to counter Islamic groups, though it is a risky strategy. Tribal identification and ethos remain a very important element of personal identity in all these countries, even while the socioeconomic bases of Gulf tribalism have changed markedly and these regimes have successfully subordinated tribal autonomy to state control. While Gulf governments have worked in their official ideologies to portray tribal and Islamic heritage as mutually compatible and reinforcing, in fact there has historically been a great deal of tension between tribes and Muslim religious authorities. The Gulf regimes could try to play the "tribal" card, in terms of mobilizing public opinion against Islamic movements, much as they played the Islamic card against leftist and Arab nationalist groups in the 1950s and 1960s, though that strategy would be tantamount to abandoning their own propaganda efforts of the past decades. The effectiveness of such appeals is hard to gauge. What is clear is that if Gulf governments do start to make such appeals, adopting a conscious policy of pitting Islamists against tribalists, it will be a signal that a serious political crisis is brewing.

The importance of government policy in dealing with the Islamic resurgence, even in terms of how the Islamic movements themselves develop, can be seen in a comparison of Kuwait and Saudi Arabia. In Kuwait, the relative openness of political life has allowed Islamic groups to play a major role in the political arena. But, at the same time, it has allowed the development of other important social groups and institutions that prevent the Islamists from monopolizing the political field. Opposition to government policies did not have to be expressed through Islamic means, for there are other avenues of political expression open to Kuwaitis. To achieve their political goals, Kuwaiti Islamic groups have had to engage in dialogue, not just with the Kuwaiti government but with other organized forces in Kuwaiti society as well. Also, the relative freedom of political association that characterizes Kuwait encouraged the various elements of the Kuwaiti Islamic movement to establish their own independent organizations. Where repression is the major government strategy and open political organizations are banned, the tendency is for Islamic groups to consolidate their efforts. In Kuwait, where the movement is open and above-ground, it has split into three major elements—*salafi*, Muslim Brotherhood, and Shi'i—which share some common goals but also exhibit numerous differences.

The contrast with Saudi Arabia is instructive. The relatively limited nature of Saudi political life has not permitted civil society organizations (with the exception of chambers of commerce) to emerge. Therefore, the Islamists in effect have a monopoly on organized political activity, and thus dominate political discourse in the country. They do not have to deal with other social organizations to get what they want in the political sphere. They can thus avoid the kind of compromises with other social forces, and the ameliorating effects of the political dialogue that produces such compromises, that have characterized the Islamist experience in Kuwait. They confront the government on many issues as the only organized representatives of popular opinion in the kingdom, so the government's ability to deflect their agenda and their popular appeal is more limited. By refusing to countenance more open political activity, Islamist or otherwise, the government also encourages a blurring of distinctions within the Islamic current generally, giving the most radical elements a disproportionate amount of influence and encouraging a "government versus Islamist" polarization of public opinion.

The Gulf regimes have numerous resources to draw upon in dealing with the phenomenon of Islamic resurgence. As the preceding comparison shows, the choices they make in using these resources can have a profound impact upon the development of Islamic movements in their countries, and thus upon the nature of the Islamic challenge to the regimes themselves. How they choose to use their resources—the choice between policies that rely primarily upon repression and the stifling of debate, on the one hand, and those that take the gamble of greater political openness and freedom, on the other—will greatly affect the political future of these states.

It is unlikely that any one of the challenges discussed above—economic crisis, generational change in its various manifestations, or Islamic opposition—by itself could threaten the stability of the Gulf monarchies. More likely scenarios involve a combination of such issues coming to a head at the same time.[15] For example, if there were a contested succession, and the contestants in that succession looked for allies in society like Islamic groups, the likelihood of political instability would grow. Similarly, if a particularly acute economic downturn were accompanied by a closing off of avenues of political debate, more and more people might be attracted to extremist opposition groups. If, in such a situation, the regime were unable to respond to a particular domestic crisis or event, opposition groups might be able to polarize society, attract support from within the security apparatus, and mobilize a serious challenge to the regime. A third scenario would be serious disputes within a regime—over succession or distribution of power—exploited by one or more regional powers seeking to expand their influence. Factions within the regime might then request more active support from the outside, risking escalation into international conflict.

Any scenario of potential political instability would probably include either a weakening of the will and/or the ability of the regime to resist, or an overt split in the regime itself. These governments have too many resources in their hands for them to be seriously threatened by domestic opponents, as long as the ruling elite has the capacity to use those resources in a coherent way. Weakening of the regimes would exacerbate other problems, and open the door to exploitation by potential enemies, domestic and foreign. For that reason, it is particularly important to recognize *intra-regime* crises like succession fights or serious personal splits among top officials as potential first steps toward a more general political crisis. One of the best ways to avoid such internal crises is to institutionalize political processes, including participatory processes for the citizenry as a whole. However, the long-term benefits of greater political institutionalization are weighed in the minds of the rulers against short-term instabilities that opening up the political system could cause. There are no guarantees in such matters, only probabilities. In the next chapter, the dilemmas facing American policymakers in dealing with issues of political stability and political participation in these states will be discussed.

LONG-TERM CHALLENGES

A number of issues face the Arab monarchies of the Gulf that are extremely important for the future of these states, but do not pose any kind of threat to their political stability in the near term. They merit discussion both because of their long-term effects on society and culture in the region, and because some analysts have incorrectly identified them as potential sources of immediate political instability.

The first is the overwhelming number of foreign workers in these states. The link between this fact and the problem of unemployment has already been discussed. There are also cultural issues raised by the prominent role of expatriate labor in these countries. Some Gulf intellectuals worry about the effect of South Asian and Filipino nannies, who speak no Arabic, playing such a large role in raising middle and upper-class Gulf children. Another worry frequently expressed is dilution of Arab cultural values generally, and in Saudi Arabia of puritanical Wahhabi Islamic values particularly, by the presence of so many foreigners in these countries—both South and East Asian workers and Western expatriates.

These concerns are authentic, but should not be confused with more immediate questions of political stability. Foreign workers pose no threat to the Gulf regimes. The incapacity of those workers to have any political impact on these countries was brought home by the Gulf crisis. Analysts who saw foreign workers as a potential threat usually pointed to two groups as the most likely candidates— Palestinians in Kuwait and Yemenis in Saudi Arabia. Both groups were very numerous, making up substantial parts of the total population of the two countries. Both were Arab, and thus linguistically and culturally closer to local nationals than other foreign workers. If any two groups could build ties to the local population, insinuate themselves into local political life, and eventually have an impact on the politics of Kuwait and Saudi Arabia, it was the Palestinians and the Yemenis, respectively.

Yet during and after the Gulf crisis, somewhere between 750,000 and one million Yemenis were forced to leave the kingdom and 300,000 to 400,000 Palestinians were forced to leave Kuwait as a result of political decisions taken by the two governments. These communities were unable to resist these moves themselves, or to mobilize any significant support among Kuwaiti and Saudi citizens to pressure their governments to reverse the decision. Their years of work in these countries, their common linguistic and cultural heritage, the political power of their home countries and of the PLO in the Arab world, did them no good, indeed maybe more harm than good. If Kuwait could expel so many Palestinians, and Saudi Arabia so many Yemenis, with barely a ripple of political consequences, then foreign workers from non-Arab countries, who represent an increasing percentage of the Gulf labor force, are certainly not going to pose any political threat to these regimes.

The second important social issue facing these states is the role of women in their political and economic life. There are important differences among the states in terms of women's issues. Social freedom is greater in Bahrain and the UAE than elsewhere. Access to the work force is easier in Bahrain than the other states. There was discussion during the Kuwaiti election campaign about giving women the vote, on the same restricted citizenship basis as men, but that does not appear likely now.[16] In all these states, the role that women can play economically, politically, and socially is limited by law and convention, particularly in comparison to the roles and rights of women in these spheres in the United States.

Women's issues in the Gulf were highlighted for the American audience by the now famous "women's driving incident" in Saudi Arabia during the Gulf crisis. In November 1990, some forty Saudi women challenged the unwritten law prohibiting women from driving by publicly forming a convoy of cars and driving through the streets of Riyad.[17] Elements in the religious establishment vehemently protested the act. The women drivers lost their jobs (most were teachers in women's schools), had their passports confiscated, and experienced unofficial house arrest for months after the event. The Interior Ministry issued an official ban on driving by women, backed up with a *fatwa* from the kingdom's highest religious authorities to the same effect.[18] King Fahd subsequently quietly rehabilitated the women, restoring their passports and eventually their academic positions, without changing the policy.[19] At a time when relations with the religious establishment and Islamic groups were already tense, the regime would not be pushed into confronting this sensitive issue, despite persistent rumors that the women drivers claimed sympathizers at the highest levels of the ruling family.

This episode is not in its details representative of the Gulf as a whole; only in Saudi Arabia are women legally prohibited from driving. It is, however, emblematic of the dilemma these countries face regarding the larger issues of women's participation in their societies. All the Gulf monarchies provide education for women, actively encouraging parents to educate their daughters as well as their sons. Many women of the younger generation are university graduates; many have also lived abroad or traveled extensively. Their horizons are much broader than those of their mothers and grandmothers, in part as a result of government policy, but their opportunities to work and socialize (in the broadest sense) outside the home are almost as limited, again as a result at least in part of government policy. The debate about how women can contribute to economic and social development in their countries without sacrificing their roles as mothers (a sacrosanct element in both official and popular discourse), offending local customs, or contravening local interpretations of Islamic law, is actively joined in all the Gulf monarchies.

While extremely important, women's issues are not in any way threatening political stability in the Gulf monarchies. One can speak of an organized women's movement only in Kuwait, and even there it is small. While there is no consensus on how the dilemma described above should be handled, there is widespread agreement among the politically relevant strata in these societies (almost exclusively male) on cultural boundaries currently circumscribing the social and political roles of women in Gulf societies. Debate exists, but there is little pressure from within society for a more liberal approach to these questions. In fact, it is more common for issues regarding women to be raised by Islamic groups, as a way of attacking what they see as the Westernizing tendencies of the governments. The immediate political pressures on the regimes are all in the direction of maintaining restrictions on women's roles in society.[20]

The third general issue facing the Gulf monarchies is the question of political identity, in particular the tension between identification with the state and with groups based upon sectarianism, regionalism, and tribalism. From the end of World War II right up to the recent Gulf War, the major challenges to political identity in the Gulf states have been transnational: Pan-Arab and Pan-Islamic. Efforts by outside powers to shake the domestic stability of these states by appealing to their citizens on the basis of transnational loyalties have failed.[21] The Arab Gulf monarchies have been able to provide their citizens with enough carrots, and to threaten them with enough sticks, to frustrate such appeals by outsiders. The centrality of these states in the everyday life of their citizens, for good and for ill, has focused political agendas there very much on internal issues, not on grandiose international designs. It was clear from the issues raised by the various petitions that circulated during and after the Gulf War, and in the Kuwaiti election campaign, that local issues are uppermost in people's minds.

But the importance of subnational identities remains. It would be a mistake to think that loyalty to the country and loyalty to what Burke called our "little platoons" are necessarily contradictory. Loyalty to state identities in the United States was a dangerous political phenomenon in the 1860s; in the 1990s, it is not. In the past, serious threats to political stability in the Gulf monarchies have been raised on sectarian, regional, and tribal bases. The Dhufar rebellion in Oman, discussed in Chapter 2, continued into the mid-1970s, and challenges to Muscat's authority from Inner Oman, based on the institution of the Ibadi Imamate, have been a recurrent aspect of Omani history for centuries. The Saudi state, the first Arabian political entity to encompass most of the peninsula since the time of the Prophet, faced serious regional and tribal separatist tendencies in the early decades of its history, particularly in the former Hashemite Kingdom of the Hijaz. Ayatollah Khumayni appealed to Shiʿi sectarian loyalties in Bahrain, Kuwait, and Saudi Arabia in the 1980s.

The states were able to meet these challenges to their political integrity and stability, but they are indicative of continuing problems of integrating state and subnational political loyalties of Gulf citizens into a coherent political identity. Regional, sectarian, and tribal prejudices and discrimination remain, though they do not present immediate threats to the political order today. Sunni-Shiʿi differences continue to be important in employment practices, in both the public and private sectors, in Kuwait, Bahrain, and Saudi Arabia. Recruitment into the military and intelligence services in many of these states is restricted on tribal, regional, and sectarian bases. Certain government offices become known for their restrictive hiring policies, as ministers and directors build patronage networks based on ascriptive ties.

The picture is not completely negative on these issues. Gulf governments recognize the problem, and some have taken steps to alleviate it. Sultan Qabus has been in the forefront. After the Dhufar rebellion, he committed considerable resources to the region and recruited numerous Dhufaris, some of whom were active in the rebellion, into his government. The new Bahraini consultative council is carefully balanced between Sunnis and Shiᶜis. After the Iranian Revolution, the Saudi government began to funnel more government money into the Shiᶜi areas of the Eastern province. Some social trends in the area are also contributing to ameliorating prejudices based on ascriptive characteristics. The experience of the Iraqi occupation in Kuwait, where Sunni and Shiᶜi Kuwaitis worked together against the occupiers, has helped lessen communal tensions exacerbated by the Iranian Revolution and Iran-Iraq war.[22] Sunni-Shiᶜi intermarriage is increasingly common in Bahrain.[23] The process of modern education has provided a path of upward mobility for younger members of more marginal beduin tribes. The general phenomenon of urbanization, while hardly erasing communal identities, has created more cross-cutting avenues of social interaction.

Problems associated with regional, tribal, and sectarian identification are not immediate threats to political stability in the Gulf monarchies. Autonomous tribal and regional power has been tamed, as discussed in Chapter 2. The Iranian appeal to sectarian loyalty in the 1980s failed, and only in Bahrain is there a demographic base for such a challenge. Still, the persistence of these subnational identities is a long-term political problem for these states. It would be impossible and counterproductive for the Gulf monarchies to try to erase these kinds of loyalties. Such ambitious and brutal state undertakings almost invariably fail. The challenge they face is to integrate these aspects of personal and social identity with a larger sense of citizenship that, in the political realm, transcends these narrower identifications. Such a definition of citizenship implies rights and responsibilities—to equal opportunities for political participation, to equality before the law, to an equal opportunity to serve the state in its civilian and military bureaucracies—that Gulf regimes have serious qualms about adopting. Defining just who citizens are, and what their rights and responsibilities should be, beyond the right to share in oil money largesse, is the central issue for the long-term political future of these states.

REGIONAL SECURITY CHALLENGES

Chapter 5 concluded with the assertion that the regional security environment for the Arab monarchies of the Gulf is the most benign it has been since the Iranian Revolution in 1979. The only significant potential military threat in the near future is from Iran. The nature of Iranian intentions, both in the Gulf and in the Middle East, has been the subject of much debate since the end of the Gulf War. A host of unlikely Middle Eastern bedfellows, from the governments of Israel and Egypt through those of Algeria and Tunisia all the way to Saddam Husayn, have publicly identified Iran as the next "big threat" in the region. Some American analysts have joined the chorus.[24] They point to Iranian rearmament, to the weakening of the Iraqi counterbalance to Iranian power, to Iran's ties with the Islamic government in Sudan, to Iranian support for Islamic groups in North Africa, Egypt, Lebanon, Central Asia, and among the Palestinians. That analysis has been adopted by the Clinton administration. In March 1993, Secretary of State Warren Christopher told a Senate committee that Iran was an "international outlaw."[25]

How do the Gulf monarchies view Iran? In terms much more complicated than those set out above. There is worry about Iran's weapons purchases and its actions on the Gulf islands in 1992. Gulf leaders fear that, unconstrained by a powerful Iraq, Iran is pursuing a policy aimed at regional hegemony. But fears of Iran are not new for the Gulf monarchies. They feared the Shah and his grandiose intentions, also. The realities of geography and demography dictate that the Gulf monarchies will always view Iran warily, as at least a potential threat. However, they see Iran now as *less* threatening than it was during the 1980s, when it was at war with Iraq, attacking

Gulf states' shipping, and actively encouraging export of the Islamic revolution to the Arab side of the Gulf.

The shrill ideological tone that characterized relations during the Khumayni period has been replaced by more normal diplomatic exchanges. Meetings between Gulf and Iranian officials are now part of the regular diplomatic scene in the region. There has been a marked reduction in open Iranian support for underground Islamic opposition groups in the Gulf monarchies since Khumayni's death, and a subsequent decline in acts of political violence and protest attributed to these groups. Important differences exist, but they are seen more in geopolitical terms than as apocalyptic clashes between opposed political systems. Iran must be watched, and other relationships cultivated to provide counterweights to Iranian power (with the West, Turkey, Egypt, and Syria), but there are also areas where dialogue and cooperation are possible, like oil issues, limited security understandings on Gulf maritime issues, and even the future of Iraq. The relationship is not one of outright conflict.[26]

The Gulf monarchies differ on the extent to which cooperation with Iran is possible. Ideological issues will continue to trouble Saudi-Iranian relations, because both regimes claim to be the interpreters of what "Islamic politics" means for the rest of the Muslim world. The smaller states, lacking that element in their foreign policies and self-conceptions, have an easier time dealing with Teheran. Saudi officials express worries about Iranian connections with Islamic movements in the Arab world, particularly as the Gulf War demonstrated the limits of their own influence with these groups, many of whom the Saudis had been cultivating for decades. The Saudis also fear that a powerful and less overtly threatening Iran will compete with them for influence in the smaller monarchies.[27] They view the development of Iranian-Qatari relations during 1992 in this light. Bahraini officials, constantly concerned about political opposition in the majority Shiʿi community, tend to regard Iran in a more threatening light than do their neighbors.

A view from the other end of the Gulf spectrum was expressed by the Omani Minister of State for Foreign Affairs, Yusif bin ʿAlawi, in January 1993. When questioned about the threat posed by Iranian rearmament, he responded: "The size of Iran's armament is not new. . . . I do not believe that things will develop to a point where anyone could imagine that Iran would launch a military attack on the Gulf region. . . . What is said about this possibility is nothing but political propaganda." The interviewer followed with a question about the threat posed to domestic stability in the Gulf monarchies by Iranian support for Islamic opponents of the regimes. Bin ʿAlawi answered: "I think this is also political propaganda." In the same interview, he said that, despite differences on some issues like Abu Musa and the other Gulf islands, "there remains the firm truth that there are common interests between Iran and the Arab states of the Gulf."[28]

It is useful when assessing the Iranian threat to the Gulf monarchies to consider the extent of Iranian rearmament and the overall military picture in the region. Iran has been spending about $2 billion per year for the last five years to buy advanced weapons, mostly from China, North Korea, and the states of the former Soviet Union. Among its purchases are MiG fighter planes, tanks, Scud missiles, and three Russian submarines. There are also indications that Iran is reviving the Shah's nuclear weapons program, and could develop a nuclear capability by the year 2000, though no confirmed evidence has come to public light that proves this.[29] It is an ambitious program, but in context not as threatening as it appears by itself. During the years of the Iran-Iraq war, Iran had a difficult time acquiring high-tech weapons on international markets. Its ability to pay was limited, and United States pressure kept some sellers from dealing with Teheran. Since the end of that war, Iran has endeavored to replace material lost in that war and to modernize its forces. Given the amount of violence in the region over the past fifteen years, those are not unreasonable goals from a purely defensive point of view. It must also be noted that Saudi Arabia has spent more than twice the amount Iran has for arms, just since the Gulf War.

The level of Iranian armaments is thus not a clear-cut indication of Iranian motives, defensive or offensive. But even if it were assumed that Iranian intentions toward the Gulf monarchies were offensive, there would be very serious limitations on its ability to carry through its intentions. Iran, unlike Iraq, has no land border with any Gulf monarchy. A full-scale attack would necessitate either a move on Iraq first, and then a pivot south, or a highly developed ability to move troops by air and sea across the Gulf. The first scenario is very unlikely, given the recently demonstrated consequences of cross-border military actions in the region. An Iranian military move on Kuwait or Saudi Arabia through Iraq would not only have to overcome Iraqi resistance, but would also give other powers much more time to mobilize against it than was the case with the Iraqi invasion of Kuwait. Such a move would entail risk of enormous proportions and be almost guaranteed to fail.

The second scenario is virtually impossible. Iran does not have the sea and air lift capabilities to move large numbers of troops across the Gulf even if it controlled the sea and air, which it does not. For the foreseeable future, the United States of America will control the sea and the air in the Gulf. Given the devastating might of American air power in the Gulf War and its overpowering naval superiority (something that three Iranian submarines cannot threaten), any kind of Iranian amphibious or air assault on the Gulf monarchies would be madness. No one has ever suggested that the leadership in Teheran has taken leave of its senses. There is only one realistic, direct military threat posed by the Iranians to the Gulf monarchies. If an "Islamic" group seized power in any of these states, through coup or revolt, it might invite Iranian forces to come to its aid. That scenario depends as much upon internal as regional factors.

Iranian nuclear ambitions warrant special consideration. Setting aside the accuracy of the various reports about Iran's nuclear development, which cannot be confirmed from public sources, what would be the consequences of Iran acquiring a small nuclear capability? The likelihood of a direct Iranian-Israeli confrontation would be very high, as the Israelis have made no secret of their policy of preventing potential enemies from developing the nuclear option. Whatever possibilities there might be in the region for arms control, however slim they are, would disappear. Iranian prestige would grow. Tensions between Saudi Arabia and Iran would increase.

None of this is to the good, of course, and anything the United States can do to prevent third countries from supplying the Iranian nuclear program should be done. At the same time, it is difficult to see how Iranian nuclear weapons could be translated into Iranian control over the Gulf monarchies. The first impulse of these states, faced with a nuclear Iran, would be to strengthen their ties with the United States and the West even more. Iran could not contemplate the use of such weapons against the Gulf monarchies. They would destroy the very assets that Iran presumably would want to control, and the chances of nuclear fallout doing substantial harm to Iran itself, given how close the states are, would be great. The risk of escalating conflict with the United States, which under the Carter Doctrine has committed itself to use all means at its disposal to prevent a hostile power's control of the Gulf, would also be considerable. With Iranian use of nuclear forces highly incredible, the threat of their use would carry less impact. Would Teheran threaten to "nuke" Riyad over oil price disputes? Unlikely, because incredible. Would it matter if they did? The probable effect would be to solidify Saudi-U.S. relations. It is hard to see how Iran acquiring a small nuclear capacity would substantially alter power relations between Teheran and the Gulf monarchies, or the Gulf monarchies' current international alignments.

Another potential regional threat to the Gulf monarchies emanates from Iraq—not of a military attack but of a further descent into civil war, chaos, and potential fragmentation. The Gulf monarchies, with the exception of Kuwait, are concerned about the territorial integrity of Iraq, and stress on every occasion their commitment to it. GCC states fear increased Iranian influence in a post-Saddam Iraq, particularly were it to fragment. They have no love for Saddam himself, but cannot manage a transition with any degree of certainty, and fear the consequences of his fall. Saudi Arabia does have some influence in Iraq and with some Iraqi opposition figures, but not nearly as much as Iran, Turkey, and even Syria can bring to bear. The Iraqi issue is now largely on hold for the Gulf states, as Saddam remains ensconced in Baghdad. Were he to fall, they could not remain aloof from the subsequent struggle for power in Iraq, though their capacity to influence it would be limited. (Iraq presents special dilemmas for U.S. policy in the Gulf that will be discussed in the next chapter.)

It is a mistake to view the Arab-Israeli conflict as a threat to the physical security of the Gulf states. Their positions on this matter are a political issue of importance to their people and to the United States, but none of these states has a direct strategic role in the Arab-

Israeli arena. It is a domestic issue because their publics, with the possible exception now of Kuwait, care about the Palestinian issue. Americans sometimes assume that Arab governments cynically exploit the Palestinian issue and whip up concern about it. That is occasionally true, as Saddam demonstrated during the Gulf War. But more often than not the causal links are reversed. Arab governments would happily shed themselves of the Palestinian cause. It complicates their relations with each other and the outside world, and places upon them responsibilities they would rather avoid. They cannot ignore the issue because substantial and important segments of public opinion in these countries demand that they play a role, or at least be seen as playing a role, in support of the Palestinians. Ignoring that opinion would create too many easily avoided headaches at home. Thus, even though their ire at the PLO position on the Gulf War remains hot, the Saudis have consistently expressed their continued commitment to the Palestinian cause.

The United States also wants Saudi Arabia to play a supportive role in the ongoing peace process. It was as a result of their American relationship, not out of any desire to take a high profile on Arab-Israeli issues, that Saudi representatives attended the opening session of the Madrid peace talks and the signing of the Israeli-PLO agreement at the White House. It is for this same reason that Riyad funded the multilateral peace talks talks in Moscow, when the cash-strapped Russians could not. It is to support American policy in the region, not because they have forgiven Yasir ꜤArafat for his stance during the Gulf War, that the Saudis will provide some financial support for the "Gaza-Jericho first" plan. The problem for the Saudis is that the Americans tug one way on Arab-Israeli questions and public opinion pulls the other way. This makes American pressure on Riyad to be more forthcoming toward the Israelis, particularly on very public symbolic issues like diplomatic relations and the Arab boycott, a delicate point in U.S.–Saudi relations.

Two other regional issues, less concerned with immediate security and more with identity, face the Gulf monarchies. The first, concerning Saudi Arabia mainly, is how to deal with the Islamic resurgence. In one sense, the upsurge in Islamic political activity in recent years in the Middle East is the successful culmination of a decades-long Saudi policy. In order to confront the challenge of

Arab nationalism in the 1950s and 1960s, the Saudis encouraged the growth of Islamic political groups throughout the Arab world. They proposed the establishment of the Islamic Conference Organization in the 1960s to widen the scope of regional politics, in response to Nasir's domination of the Arab League. With the oil boom of the 1970s, the Saudis funded the development of Islamic schools, presses, and institutions throughout the Muslim world, and provided scholarships to many Islamic activists for study in the kingdom. The Islamic element of Saudi foreign policy has always been extremely important in the regime's self-conception and in its portrayal of itself to its own citizens and the outside world.

The reaction of Islamic movements, not only in the Arab world but throughout the Muslim community, to the Saudi decision to invite in American troops was thus very shocking to Riyad. It has led to a reassessment of close Saudi relations with Islamic movements like the Algerian Islamic Salvation Front and the Muslim Brotherhood. Riyad seems to be aligning, however cautiously, with the Arab front, spearheaded by Egypt, Tunisia, and Algeria, that sees domestic Islamic movements supported by Iran and Sudan as the major regional security challenge. In April 1993, the Saudi Interior Ministry banned any Islamic civic or religious group from soliciting donations in the kingdom without specific authorization from the ministry, in an effort to get some control over private Saudi donations to such groups.[30] At the same time, it is clear that Islamic opposition groups in the region continue to have sympathizers within Saudi Arabia. The Memorandum of Advice strongly criticized the Saudi government for abandoning such groups, and personal ties between Saudi activists and these groups remain strong. The Saudis are not going to renounce the Islamic element of their foreign policy, because it is too intimately tied up with their whole notion of their own domestic legitimacy and regional role. How they reconfigure their Islamic strategy in the region in light of the Gulf War experience and their own internal Islamic challenge is a major issue before the regime.

The second issue of regional identity that all the Gulf monarchies have to confront is their role in the Arab world. During and immediately after the Gulf War, there was rejection of the Arab political identity in these states, in reaction to what was seen as the hostility of Arab public opinion toward them. That rejection was clearest in Kuwait, and became less intense the farther from Kuwait one went. It was represented in official circles by the open embrace of the United States and the unwillingness to accept an "Arab" responsibility to provide substantial aid to poorer Arab states. Official and popular opinion (again, more in Kuwait and Saudi Arabia than elsewhere) was vehemently anti-PLO, and in a few circles the need to make any commitment at all to the Palestinian cause was questioned.

With the passage of time, both official and popular opinion have come back to the inevitability of some kind of Arab identification in the foreign policies of these states. What that identification means is still a matter of debate. Questions about the kind of responsibility these states and societies have to the Palestinian cause, to the poorer Arabs, to the Arab League, to reconciling the splits created by the Gulf War, are debated in the press and among intellectuals. Even in Kuwait, where bitterness is greatest, this debate is fully engaged. What is clear is that these states do not have the choice of "opting out" of the Arab world.

CONCLUSIONS

The challenges the Arab monarchies of the Gulf face are substantial, but none now threatens the political stability of these regimes. Their financial, administrative, and ideological resources remain substantial, despite the shocks of the last fifteen years. The regional environment is comparatively benign. There are economic problems, but not nearly as many as when oil prices plunged below $10 a barrel in 1986. The threat from violent underground Islamist groups that was particularly acute in Kuwait and Bahrain in the 1980s seems to be reduced. Demands for political participation are being voiced throughout the region, but these demands are generally couched in terms of a greater role within existing systems, not for overturning of these systems. The long-term future of these states will turn largely on the question of whether such desires can be met through evolutionary political changes managed by the existing regimes.

In the future, substantial threats to political stability could emerge only if there were a concatenation of crises: a simultaneous breakdown of regime will and/or authority, emergence of organized opposition forces seeking radical political change, and mobilization of popular opinion around some defining issue, like a severe economic crisis or charismatic personality. Such occurrences are rare. An important indicator of the possibility of such instability arising is the cohesion and political will of the regimes themselves. Regime crises can be the first steps to more general political instability.

7

American Policy

DESPITE THE ENORMOUS MILITARY SUCCESS OF DESERT Storm, no stable security arrangements for the Gulf emerged from America's victory of 1990–1991. U.S. policymakers confront a number of dilemmas in their relations with the Arab monarchies of the Gulf, including how to reconcile the global American policy of support for democracy and human rights with our close relationships with these states, what role arms sales and military presence should play in those relationships, and how to deal with the Gulf monarchies in the context of other regional issues—Iran, Iraq, and the Arab-Israeli conflict. But before these questions are addressed, a larger issue needs to be faced: is the Gulf, and are the Gulf monarchical regimes, still important to American interests?

IS THE GULF IMPORTANT?
ARE THE REGIMES IMPORTANT?

At first glance, such questions seem foolish. The world economy still runs on oil, and the Gulf is by far the largest reservoir of oil in the world. The GCC states themselves account for 46.3 percent of proven world reserves of oil; add Iran and Iraq, and the Gulf has

175

65.6 percent of the world's proven oil reserves.[1] The United States recently sent half a million troops to the Gulf to liberate Kuwait and protect the other Gulf regimes. How can they not be important? On the other hand, the United States sent just as many troops to Vietnam, and lost tens of thousands of them, and no one now argues that Vietnam is central to American interests. A case must be made for America's continued involvement in the area. One might start by examining the case against such involvement.

The argument that the United States should disengage from the Gulf does not deny the importance of oil, but questions whether intense American political involvement in the region is necessary to assure access to that oil. American strategy in the Gulf has been premised, in large measure, on the need to deny the region to the Soviets and to limit Soviet influence there. The demise of the USSR has ended that. The assumption now is that market forces, not political variables, will dictate oil supply and price. No matter who governs the Gulf states, they will have to pump oil to maintain their governments and their economies. Even if they are ideologically opposed to the United States, they will have no choice but to sell oil on the world market. After all, Libya and Iran do not refuse to sell oil to the United States—the United States refuses to buy it. Even if these states wanted to use oil as a political weapon, market forces would frustrate the effort. The bottom line of this argument is that even if Saddam Husayn had stayed in Kuwait, he would have had to sell its oil on the market, and market forces would have dictated its price.

The extension of this argument holds that Gulf oil is declining in importance for the world oil market as a whole. Investment in Russian oil production and new finds in Central Asia will, over the next decade, increase the amount of available oil, decreasing the market leverage of the major Gulf producers. They will be less able to affect the market by their own decisions, and thus less able to use oil for political purposes. Even unintentional disruptions in Gulf production, because of political upheaval, war, or natural disaster, are not as destabilizing to the market as they once were. The combination of new finds outside the Gulf, energy-sharing institutions among industrialized countries under the International Energy

Agency, and the U.S. Strategic Petroleum Reserve provide enough cushion to ride out temporary market fluctuations.

These arguments receive some support from recent events. The political disruptions of the last decade have had very little long-term impact on oil prices, unlike those of the 1970s. At the beginning of the Iran-Iraq war and during the Iraqi occupation of Kuwait, Saudi Arabia and other producers increased their production to make up for the combatants' oil taken off the market. Spot oil prices shot up for a short time, and then fell back to levels roughly similar to those before the wars began. During the Iran-Iraq war, oil prices fell to their lowest point (in current, not constant dollars) since 1973, when the supply glut of 1986 pushed prices below $10 per barrel. The oil market is slack now and will be for the short term. OPEC output, with Kuwaiti production just coming back on line and very limited Iraqi production, easily meets current demand. With the eventual return of Iraq to the market, and the current unwillingness of Saudi Arabia to revert to its previous role of "swing" producer, the prospects for a substantial glut of OPEC oil in the next few years are high.[2] Moreover, many of the major oil producers, including Saudi Arabia and Iran, have announced plans to expand their production capabilities and are seeking the capital to do so.

While these arguments cannot be dismissed out of hand, and the importance of structural market forces is much greater than short-term political considerations over the long haul, there remain reasons why an isolationist stance toward the Gulf poses risks for the United States. First, the importance of short-term disruptions of oil supply depends upon a number of factors. Overall world supply is critical, but so is overall world demand, the speed with which unused capacity elsewhere can be brought on the market, and the amount of supply affected by the disruption. The Iraqi invasion of Kuwait took somewhere between four and five million barrels per day (bpd) off the market. Oil demand was slack because of the world recession, and Saudi Arabia had much excess capacity it could bring to the market immediately. Had circumstances been different— with world demand much stronger, or with some Saudi production taken off the market because the Iraqis continued marching south— the impact of the Gulf War on world oil markets might have been much greater.

The importance of Gulf oil for short-term market stability is underlined by production statistics for the first eight months of 1992. Total Gulf production (excluding Oman) averaged 15.7 million bpd, which was 26.4 percent of total world production. Saudi Arabia itself produced 8.4 million bpd, 14.1 percent of the world total. The Saudis are now the largest producer of crude oil in the world, overtaking the states of the former Soviet Union.[3] With other world producers pumping at capacity, any disruption of Saudi production could not be made up immediately elsewhere, particularly if Iraqi oil is kept off the market. Likewise, with Saudi Arabia pumping at or very near current capacity, its ability to make up for shortfalls resulting from production interruptions elsewhere is very limited. Oil markets are not nearly as tight (in terms of amount of excess potential production capacity) as they were preceding the price shocks of 1973 and 1979, but they are tighter than they were in 1990, again assuming that Iraqi oil is kept off the market.

The world economy's vulnerability to short-term supply disruption is potentially greater than the isolationist argument contends, and thus avoiding such disruptions is important for the United States. Global economic recovery, particularly if it extends to Eastern Europe, Russia, and the Indian subcontinent, will increase the world demand for oil. It will take years of work and billions of dollars in investments to increase production capacity significantly outside the Gulf—in Russia, Central Asia, Latin America, or elsewhere. Whether and how much U.S. demand will fall as a result of government conservation and tax policies cannot be known. The possibility that increases in world demand will accelerate faster than increases in supply is high. Both International Energy Agency sharing plans and the release of Strategic Petroleum Reserve oil are largely untested mechanisms of crisis management. Any disruptions that take substantial parts of either Saudi or Iranian production off the market, particularly if sanctions continue on Iraq, would immediately tighten markets and might lead to the kind of panic buying that drove up prices in 1973–1974 and 1979–1981. Short-term disruptions in Gulf oil production could still have devastating effects on the world's economic circumstances. To the extent that U.S. involvement in the Gulf helps ward off such short-term disruptions, involvement remains in the American interest. To the extent that the stability of the current regimes contributes to avoidance of such short-term disruptions, the U.S. commitment to them makes sense.

Second, it would be a mistake to assume that an isolationist American policy toward the Gulf would insulate the United States from Middle Eastern political pressures on oil questions. To the extent that the politics of the Gulf remain tied to the politics of the Arab-Israeli arena, and that the United States remains involved with and committed to the security of Israel, there is still the chance that the combustible mix of oil and Arab-Israeli conflict could blow up in America's face as it did in 1973, though risks of such linkage are reduced by the recent progress on the Arab-Israeli front. Saddam Husayn did succeed in linking his invasion of Kuwait to the Palestinian question, though not in the way he wanted. The renewed American commitment to the peace process after the Gulf War came in recognition of the fact that the Palestinian issue, enjoying broad support across the Arab world, could be used to damage American interests far from the Occupied Territories. Conversely, the United States hopes to reverse that linkage by pushing the Gulf monarchies to underwrite the emerging Palestinian-Israeli settlement financially. The Gulf states will only do that if they see such support as part of their ongoing political and security relationship with the United States.

The current "disconnection" between Arab-Israeli issues and oil is the product of a particular set of regional political circumstances and world oil market forces, all of which are subject to change. Slack world oil demand combined with the picture of Yitzhak Rabin and Yasir ʿArafat shaking hands make the use of the "oil weapon" seem ludicrous now, but can one be assured that these current realities will be enduring? The implementation of the Israeli-PLO deal remains fraught with pitfalls; Syrian-Israeli talks have not proceeded as far; and the Islamist political currents in the region remain bitterly opposed to peace with Israel. Should the United States pursue an isolationist policy toward the Gulf, the Gulf monarchies' security dependence on Washington would end. To safeguard their regimes, the Gulf monarchs would be more likely to accede to regional and domestic pressures to use oil as part of a regional confrontation involving Israel. Such pressures might be even greater than in 1973, as Iran is now an enthusiastic proponent of confronting Israel rather than, as in the Shah's day, a de facto ally of Israel. Without American power in the Gulf, Israel would have to be more concerned about any regional leader becoming dominant there and turning the power of the area against it. Its predisposition to preempt potential regional threats emerging from the Gulf would increase. An American decision to disengage from the Gulf might, paradoxically, lead to even costlier involvement in the future, if Israel and Iran came to a clash.

This is not to say that every possible Arab-Israeli conflict scenario would involve oil, or that oil could be effectively used in every scenario. It is only to point out that the connection between the two issues remains close in Arab public opinion and regional politics. Saddam failed in his efforts to use the Palestinian issue to break up the coalition against him not because the issue did not resonate throughout the region, but because the Arab states of the coalition were able to manage their public opinions over the short period of the crisis, to count on American support, and to tell their publics that right after the war the Palestinian issue would be addressed. In other crises the pressures to link oil and Arab-Israeli issues could again emerge. To the extent that American involvement in the Gulf prevents this linkage, such involvement serves American interests. The current regimes are less likely to pursue such a linkage strategy than any of their potential replacements. An isolationist stance could protect American interests in Gulf oil only if it were applied to *all* Middle East questions. Such a dramatic reversal of American commitments in the region is highly unlikely.

Finally, the United States enjoys significant financial benefits from its close relationship with the Arab monarchies of the Gulf. Many of the assets of these countries and their citizens are invested in Wall Street and U.S. Treasury bills. When Citibank needed a capital infusion to overcome the problems brought on by the East Coast real estate collapse of the early 1990s, it turned to an investor from the Al Saʿud, Prince Walid ibn Talal, for help. American arms manufacturers are benefiting from Gulf contracts at a time when the Pentagon budget is being cut. At an April 1993 meeting in Washington on American-Gulf business links, sponsored by the U.S. Department of Commerce, the Gulf Cooperation Council, and the American–Gulf Chamber of Commerce, it was reported that direct Gulf investment in the United States totaled $407 billion as of the beginning of 1992.[4] It is unlikely that other types of regimes in these states would commit so much of their financial resources to the West in general and the United States in particular.

Such investments and purchases are, of course, but a small percentage of the overall American economy. Their absence would be felt, no doubt, but would not be enormously damaging to American economic health. What would be immediately damaging to the U.S. economy would be any effort to denominate the world price of oil in anything but dollars. As the world oil price is now set in dollars, the United States is buffered from the effects of currency fluctuations on its energy imports. If oil prices were, however, denominated in Japanese yen, America's energy bill would increase as the value of the dollar against the yen fell, even though nominal oil prices remained unchanged. During another episode when the dollar fell in relation to other major currencies, in the mid-1970s, there was much talk in OPEC about changing the basis of oil pricing from the dollar to a basket of currencies. Loud complaints could be heard from the Gulf about the decline in return from oil sales because the dollar was not worth as much as it used to be. The Iranian Revolution put a halt to such talk by reemphasizing the security dependence of the Gulf monarchies on the United States. The recent decline of the dollar since the Gulf War has not elicited similar comments. Were the security link between the United States and the Gulf monarchies to be broken, their incentive to maintain the dollar as the benchmark currency for oil pricing would be reduced.[5]

Financial and oil questions are likely to be the only areas of serious dispute between the United States and the Gulf monarchies in the context of their current relationship. The Clinton administration's proposed energy tax elicited very public criticism from Gulf oil ministers, who saw it as aimed exclusively at oil imports. They implicitly threatened to defer plans for increasing production capacity until the issue was settled.[6] The involvement of political elites in the UAE and Saudi Arabia in the BCCI scandal now unfolding in American courts is also an irritant. Such issues are not enough to threaten common security and economic interests recognized by both sides in the relationship, but they point out the extent of the economic interconnection of the parties.

Questions about the rationale behind American involvement in the Gulf are necessary and healthy. They force American policymakers to define just what our interests in the area are. Those interests, revolving as they do around access to and the price of oil, are contingent upon a number of circumstances. A political upheaval in the area that could be enormously damaging in a tight oil market might be marginal in a slack one. In some circumstances Gulf producers might be isolated from an Arab-Israeli dispute, as they were during the 1982 Israeli invasion of Lebanon, and in others they might be directly involved. Contingencies need to be evaluated on their specific and individual effects on oil production and pricing, not on received wisdom from the Cold War past. What the above discussion points out is that there are realistic circumstances in which U.S. interests could be damaged by domestic or regional upheaval in the Gulf. American interests are therefore sufficiently engaged in the Gulf, and will remain sufficiently engaged as long as political steps are not taken to restrain America's appetite for imported oil, to justify continued involvement there. So the Gulf, and the Arab Gulf monarchies remain important. How should the United States deal with them?

DEMOCRACY AND HUMAN RIGHTS

Many Americans opposed going to war in the Gulf in 1990–1991 on the grounds that the United States had no business protecting "feudal monarchies." Many Gulf intellectuals were disappointed that the United States did not use its immediate postwar leverage with the Gulf monarchies to pressure them to open up their political systems.[7] There will be tensions in the American relationship with these states, and among Americans concerned with policy toward these states, as long as Washington maintains that its overall foreign policy is based, at least to some degree, upon promoting American democratic principles.

The dilemma facing American policymakers on this question is easy to understand but difficult to manage. The United States is interested in political stability in these states. Regimes that rest on institutionalized procedures for eliciting the consent of the governed are the best bets for long-term stability. But the process of building such institutions and initiating participatory mechanisms can be destabilizing in the short term. Powerful political forces, including in the ruling families themselves, would oppose openings of the political system while other political groups who seek revolutionary political change could exploit them. Also, participatory regimes, if they do evolve, would be more difficult to deal with for Washington, because popular political forces in the Gulf, even when not hostile to the United States, are less likely to be as accommodating to American interests as these regimes now are. For example, in any elections in these states, Islamic political forces would do very well, as they did in the Kuwaiti elections of October 1992.

The simple response to this dilemma, one followed by the Bush and, so far, by the Clinton administration, is to avoid it. The American relationship with these states is good; they are responsive to Washington's desires; there is no question about their immediate political stability. According to the *New York Times*, citing administration officials, President Bush avoided even using the word democracy in his immediate post–Gulf War communications with the amir of Kuwait.[8] But that begs the question of the long-term benefits, in terms of political stability and reliability, of dealing with regimes grounded in participatory institutions. The policy of avoidance risks so alienating local public opinion, important segments of which do look to the United States for support for their political aspirations (as a result of American rhetoric on these questions), as to squander at least some of the goodwill won during Desert Storm. Avoiding the issue makes the United States look either weak or cynical: weak because Washington talks about democracy but cannot get its Gulf allies to do anything about it, cynical because Washington talks about it but does not do anything about it itself.

The United States can manage this dilemma with a policy aimed at encouraging the Gulf monarchies to permit the development of more autonomous social institutions in their countries. Opening up political life in these countries would permit various groups to form, breaking up the effective monopoly Islamist organizations exert in most of these countries on political discourse outside the government and ruling family. Participatory institutions, such as the various consultative councils, even if not elected, need to be encouraged. A freer press would be more critical of the United States on a number of scores, but would also encourage more open internal political debate. The model for such evolutionary change should be Kuwait.

United States policy needs to be subtle, recognizing the different circumstances of the various states and choosing the right occasions to interject its views discreetly. But there are steps that the United States can take to encourage evolution toward more participatory, and thus more stable, polities in the Gulf monarchies. First, washington can encourage its friends to live up to their own constitutions, many of which include elected or appointed consultative assemblies. The United States should also encourage more participatory experiments at the local government level. Second, the United States can support efforts by the regimes to expand participation—the new Omani *majlis*, the Kuwaiti parliament, the Saudi *majlis*, the Bahraini *majlis* (as a step toward restoration of its elected assembly). American officials with responsibilities in the region should deal with these institutions and their members in a serious way, according to their countries' constitutions. For example, the United States should have demanded that its defense agreement with Kuwait be ratified by an elected, constitutional Kuwaiti parliament, as a guarantee of its popular acceptance and legitimacy.

Third, civil society organizations, including political parties, professional organizations, chambers of commerce, and independent organs of news and opinion, can be encouraged to establish relationships with similar American organizations. U.S. diplomatic missions in the area should facilitate such contacts and be willing to provide technical assistance, if asked. A small increase in American resources committed to such efforts, like more Fulbright grants for Gulf citizens active in such organizations to spend time in the United States, could pay dividends in this regard. Fourth, Washington can discourage its friends from backtracking on the path toward more participatory political life. Suspensions of assemblies, suppressions of existing press freedoms, and efforts to exert control over independent social organizations should meet with American disapproval.

Pursuing these aims while still maintaining close relations with the Gulf governments will not be an easy task. It is worth repeating that these issues need to be pursued in a cautious, incremental, mostly private way. At the same time, the United States can recognize the importance of the American tie to these regimes and the leverage this relationship gives U.S. officials. Gulf officials are not hesitant about commenting on American domestic issues, like energy taxes. American officials need not apologize for their interest in the domestic politics of their friends, particularly if such comments are couched in terms of long-term friendships and common interests. The Gulf regimes are not so flimsy that such discussions would shake their stability. The headaches such moves might cause for U.S. policy in the near term would be more than balanced by increased prospects for long-term Gulf political stability.

While encouraging evolution toward more open political systems in these countries, there are a number of points that U.S. policy must approach with extreme caution. First, pushing for political reform during times of acute crisis, domestic or regional, can be counterproductive. Fortunately, the regional environment is now relatively benign and the domestic situations of the Gulf monarchies stable, as demonstrated by their ability to weather the storms of the last decade. The rulers themselves have, in a sense, recognized that the time is now propitious for political reform, in the spate of institutional innovations announced after the Gulf War. Second, the United States must not be seen as combating Islamic organizations or consciously working to develop "secular" alternatives in order to weaken Islamic groups. Getting involved in such a polarizing situation could only damage American interests by alienating large segments of public opinion in these countries. American officials and institutions must be willing to deal with Islamic groups that work within their countries' laws on the same basis as other groups. American policy must neither be, nor be interpreted as, "anti-Islam."

Third, there are some issues seen by many in the United States as integral parts of a human rights agenda that should not be part of American approaches toward the Gulf monarchies. One is penal codes. Many Americans think the imposition of the *hudud* punishments stipulated in Islamic law and carried out in Saudi Arabia contravenes human rights.[9] There is strong support in the kingdom for this system. Public American intervention on this issue would only create a backlash, allowing opponents of the regime and of the

United States to portray it as trying to combat Islamic values. A second issue that American officials should avoid is women's rights. This subject is a particularly difficult one for many Americans, who see the differences between the United States and the Gulf monarchies on women's issues as the largest and most disturbing cultural gap between the societies. However, the fact remains that, as yet, there is no organized constituency to speak of in these states supporting what most Americans would recognize as a women's rights agenda. There are large and powerful forces supporting the status quo on these issues. Any kind of public American pressure on these issues will only to lead to a fierce backlash, as the women's driving incident in Saudi Arabia demonstrated. Change on women's issues has to come from within these societies; it cannot be imposed from the outside if it is to be enduring.

Democracy and human rights are not now an important part of American policy toward the Gulf monarchies. To the extent that they contribute to the likelihood of managed, evolutionary political change, and reduce the chances of violent upheaval, they should be. These issues need to be approached with caution and tact, raised within the context of the friendly and supportive relations the United States enjoys with the Gulf monarchies. The more vigorous political debate these open political systems would encourage should be welcomed by the United States as a sign of healthy and stable polities, even if such openness made it more difficult to achieve American ends on specific issues. To the extent that these issues encourage political instability and promote backlash against the United States, they should be avoided. Drawing that distinction is a difficult task.

ARMS SALES AND AMERICAN MILITARY PRESENCE

American military commitment to the defense of these states is their ultimate protection against outside attack. That commitment was frequently questioned, played down in public, and often denigrated by Gulf leaders before 1990. Kuwait proudly proclaimed its non-aligned status; in the early 1980s, Saudi Arabia sent Reagan administration officials peddling their "strategic consensus" approach packing. Now, the opposite is the case. All the Gulf states are more than willing to acknowledge an open military relationship with the United States. Through the signing of defense agreements with Washington, the smaller states have entered into de facto military alliances with America. But the old reasons Gulf leaders were wary about open military ties with the United States have not disappeared.

On the one hand, it is important not to exaggerate the desta-bilizing domestic impact of American military forces in the Gulf monarchies. The United States has had a naval base in Bahrain since the end of World War II and a military facilities agreement with Oman since 1980. The Gulf states managed to support the vast American naval flotilla sent to the region in 1987 to protect ship-ping during the last year of the Iran-Iraq war. Most obviously, while the American military presence during Desert Storm excited some local antipathy, all the Gulf monarchical regimes survived the crisis of 1990–1991. On the other hand, foreign military bases and presences in the Middle East have historically been lightning rods for domestic opposition to ruling regimes. They call into question the independence of the host country and the nationalist credentials of its rulers. The British experience in Egypt and Iraq in the 1950s and the American experience in Iran in the 1970s, are object lessons that a military embrace can be too strong for a friendly regime's own good. Saudi Arabia's reluctance to sign a formal defense agreement with Washington indicates that, at least in Riyad, those lessons still carry weight.

Recent experience in the Gulf provides the United States with some guidelines for how to go about maintaining a military pres-ence without encouraging local backlash. First, naval presence, kept mostly offshore, is less offensive to local political sentiments than ground presence. Air force units fall somewhere in between. They have a higher day-to-day profile than naval forces, but are relatively small and mostly staffed by officers, in comparison to full-fledged ground force bases. Second, facilities arrangements are more palat-able locally than actual bases. Pre-positioning of equipment and frequent training exercises can provide a number (though certainly not all) of the military benefits that permanent bases can, without the same domestic political risks for the host countries. Third, facilities located away from major population centers are preferable. It is not always possible or practical to follow this policy, but in cases where it is, such as the Omani air facilities at Thamarit, domestic political consequences can be minimized.

American policy since the Gulf War has largely followed these guidelines. The Bush administration exhibited no desire to establish a major, permanent ground force base in the region; neither has the Clinton administration. There is a danger, however, that the United States could be pushed, by force of circumstance, to maintain a much larger and more permanent military force in the area than American decision-makers either plan or desire. Commitments to protect the northern Kurdish area of Iraq and to enforce a no-fly zone over southern Iraq require American air force units, some of which are based in the Gulf. Increasing tensions with Iran, either over the future of a post-Saddam Iraq or as a result of some Iran-Iraq rapprochement against the United States, could lead to larger American air, naval, and even ground commitments in the Gulf. The main point is that the United States needs to be careful about backing, through a series of incremental decisions, into military situations that could have negative long-term consequences.

While there seems to be some consensus in Washington about the need to keep the American military profile in the Gulf as modest as possible, there are no such inhibitions about American arms sales to the region. It is important to consider whether such arms sales may have negative consequences for the overall American policy goal of promoting stability and security in the Gulf.

Arms sales are not damaging to domestic stability and security in and of themselves. If they are seen as an indirect way of pre-positioning equipment, they can be useful instruments for promoting U.S.–Gulf security cooperation. They also, of course, help American arms manufacturers looking to maintain profits and keep production lines operational at a time of cutbacks in American military spending. Arms sales become problematic for political stability when vast resources spent on arms purchases are perceived as cutting into domestic social spending and hurting the local economy. In the more straitened economic circumstances of the Gulf states after the war, there is danger that massive arms purchases will be seen as made at the expense of other, more immediate needs. For example, the Kuwaiti parliament elected in October

1992 has insisted on reviewing arms deals made by the government since liberation. At such points, the issue of corruption that always colors big arms deals could become explosive.

It must also be noted that the volume of American arms sales to the Gulf since the Iraqi invasion of Kuwait makes a mockery of U.S. proposals to control the arms race in the region. Even though a theoretical case can be made that curbing unconventional arms, such as nuclear, chemical, and long-range missile technologies, is unrelated to conventional arms buildups, such assertions by Washington are regarded by other parties, both in the Middle East and elsewhere, as simply hypocritical. The Bush administration listed regional arms control as a major goal of its post–Gulf War policy for the Middle East, but did little if anything to follow through on it. The Clinton administration seems no more eager to take up the cause of regional arms control. Continued American support for the U.N. effort to disarm Iraq and efforts to prevent international supply of the Iranian nuclear program are to be encouraged, but should not been viewed as arms control measures, which must be comprehensive and multilateral to be effective.

The best course for American arms sales policy in the Gulf would be for the United States to encourage its Gulf allies to develop proficiency with the weapons they now have, rather than spend more billions acquiring yet more sophisticated Western weaponry. In the longer term, exploring real arms control proposals with Iran and a post-Saddam Iraq should be on Washington's agenda, as unlikely as that possibility seems now. The conversion of American defense industries in the wake of the Cold War is a large and complicated issue. Encouraging American arms manufacturers to increase their dependence on the Gulf market is no substitute for an effective policy in this area, and could militate against America's long-term interest in a stable Gulf.

GULF SECURITY

While the United States' closest relations in the Gulf are with the monarchies, the eyes of American policymakers are always on Iran and Iraq. Both are regional powers with a demonstrated capacity to challenge U.S. interests in the area. For the first time since the British withdrawal from the region in 1971, the United States lacks any kind of strategic or political relationship with either state. Even during the Iran-Iraq war, the war that so many Americans, in Henry Kissinger's memorable phrase, hoped "both sides would lose," Washington supported Iraq to check the spread of Iranian military and ideological power. Today, the United States considers Iran an "international outlaw" and openly supports the Iraqi National Congress (INC), a group including Arab Shiʿi and Sunni personalities but dominated by the Iraqi Kurdish opposition, which seeks the overthrow of Saddam Husayn. The Clinton administration's Gulf policy of "dual containment" is premised on the view that Iran and Iraq are equally threatening to U.S. interests. The policy seeks to isolate both states internationally, implement fully U.N. sanctions against Iraq in the belief that such implementation will bring down the regime there, and pressure Iran to change its foreign and domestic behavior.[10]

The dual containment policy suffers from a number of logical inconsistencies. Containment of Iran requires a strong Iraq on its western border, but dual containment encourages the creation of a political vacuum in Iraq. Pressure on Iraq cannot be effective if Iran, the country with the longest land border with Iraq, is not cooperating. Dual containment not only discourages Iran from such cooperation, but actively pushes it in the other direction, toward some kind of rapprochement with Saddam. There are some signs that the two old enemies are moving toward a lessening of tension in face of American hostility toward both. It appears that Iran opened its borders with Iraq in late April 1993, in contravention of U.N. sanctions, and has been buying some Iraqi oil. In early May 1993, Teheran announced that it was resuming discussions with Baghdad on political issues between the two countries.[11] In the unlikely event of some kind of Iran-Iraq alignment, the regional balance of forces would be tilted significantly against the Gulf monarchies, and the pressure for the United States to increase its military commitments in the area would grow, with all the problems that could entail.

Moreover, dual containment fails to address adequately the major immediate issue on the Gulf security agenda, which is not military attack by either Iran or Iraq on its neighbors, but rather the political future of Iraq itself. The longer Saddam remains in power, the more likely it becomes that American support for the INC and protection of the Iraqi Kurdish zone will lead to the fragmentation of the country. This is certainly not a U.S. goal; American policy-makers have continually asserted their support for the territorial integrity of Iraq. It could become an unintended consequence of the dual containment policy, however, and lead to geopolitical upheaval in the region.[12] Such fragmentation is not inevitable. The INC insists it does not seek such an end, and the major Iraqi Kurdish groups have limited their publicly stated agenda to regional autonomy in a federal, democratic Iraq. All the regional powers, including Iran and Turkey, which have Kurdish problems of their own, support the territorial integrity of the country. It is, however, a possibility that grows the longer the status quo continues.

It is difficult to see how there can be a successful and stable transition in Iraq to a post-Saddam regime, avoiding the fragmentation of the country and/or a bloody civil war, without the involvement of Iran and its local Iraqi allies in such a process. If Saddam were toppled, it is foolish to assume that Iran would sit idly by while the United States played the major role in reconstructing a post-Saddam Iraq, particularly as one of the major goals of such a role would be to limit Iranian influence and isolate Iran in the region. Iran has an enormous number of assets that it can bring to bear in Iraq. It has the longest border with Iraq of any regional state. It has close relations with the Shiʿi community in southern Iraq and with a number of Shiʿi political organizations. It is the largest regional military and geopolitical power. Iran is well placed at least to frustrate American-sponsored efforts to construct a post-Saddam regime. In a chaotic situation of civil strife, it could directly intervene in Iraq. An American policy that sets up Iraq as the prize in a geopolitical struggle with Iran runs a high risk of failure.

The consequences of an Iranian-dominated, post-Saddam Iraq would be extremely serious for the United States. Such an outcome would increase pressure on Washington to maintain a large military presence in the region to protect the Gulf monarchies. Such a military presence could have negative internal consequences for those countries. An Iranian "victory" in Iraq would also revive the smoldering ideological embers of the revolution, encouraging those in Iran who want to make the "export" of the Islamic revolution their country's top foreign policy goal. The Gulf monarchies would once again be subject to the kind of ideological and subversive pressures that characterized the early and mid-1980s, though this time without the Iraqi military bulwark against Iranian power. The chances of an Iranian-Israeli confrontation would increase enormously, with the subsequent risk that, as in 1973, oil issues would be linked with a political-military confrontation. The Arab-Israeli peace process would be slowed, if not derailed.

There is an alternative policy to dual containment that, though not without its risks, avoids the problems associated with propping up Saddam, encouraging an Iranian-Iraqi alliance, or making Iraq a test case in an American-Iranian battle for regional influence. The United States could launch a dialogue with the Iranian regime about the future of Iraq. Such a dialogue would include Iranian-supported Iraqi Shiʿi groups. The goals of such a dialogue would be to assure Iran that the United States does not seek to make a post-Saddam Iraq a base for anti-Iranian activity, that it does not seek to deny Iran's allies in Iraq a role in reconstructing the political order in the country, and that it does not seek a confrontation with Iran over Iraq. The aim of the dialogue would be to establish the ground rules for dealing with Iraq in the event of the fall of Saddam. This dialogue would have to be contemporaneous with similar discussions with the other regional powers who have some influence in Iraq: Turkey, Syria, and Saudi Arabia. As it is, Turkey, Syria, and Iran have an ongoing dialogue at the foreign minister level on Iraqi and Kurdish issues. The Saudis have opened direct diplomatic channels to Teheran and to Iraqi Shiʿi groups that enjoy Iranian support. In fact, the United States has been the one significant player so far unwilling to consult with Iran on Iraqi issues.

The difficulties with this option are obvious. The United States and Iran continue to exhibit major differences over a number of important regional issues, including the Arab-Israeli peace process. It might not be possible to arrive at an understanding on Iraq, or to separate the Iraqi issue from differences on other issues. The domestic political fallout from dealing with Iran could be damaging to any administration, particularly given the continuing death sentence on Salman Rushdie and the alleged Iranian involvement in terrorist activities. The Iranian side has its own internal problems in dealing with the United States. Any dialogue with Teheran should not be secret, though the preliminary steps toward it and the actual content of the talks would have to be confidential. In the end, it might not work. However, the risks to American interests of engaging in a direct confrontation with Iran over the future of Iraq are clear. Some kind of understanding with Iran and other regional powers over the future of a post-Saddam Iraq offers the best hope of keeping Iraq united and independent of domination by any party, of preventing the escalation of a new regional crisis, and of minimizing the need for new American military and financial commitments in the area. It is an option that is at least worth pursuing.

As direct and open U.S.–Iranian contacts are difficult because of domestic constraints on both sides, such a dialogue might be initiated through a multilateral framework. Such a framework exists through the United Nations. U.N. Security Council Resolution 598, under which the Iran-Iraq war ended, calls for the secretary-general to consult with states in the region on measures to "enhance security and stability." Under those auspices it might be possible for Iran and the United States to explore security issues—at a minimum, confidence-building measures such as prior notification of military exercises. This is not to advocate a formal U.N. role in a Gulf security structure, which would inevitably be unwieldy, over-bureaucratized, and constraining on U.S. options. Any formal U.N. security organization for the Gulf would have to include Iraq, which, while Saddam remains in power, is not a desirable goal. Rather, use of the U.N. as a forum for exploring political understandings with Iran about the "rules of the game" for Gulf security should be encouraged.

THE ARAB-ISRAELI CONFLICT

How should the United States approach its Gulf allies on the Arab-Israeli issue? Very carefully. In general, these governments are more willing to support American initiatives on questions related to Palestinian and Arab-Israeli issues than their publics are. Because the stability and security of these states are of importance to the United States, it does not pay to press them to take positions on these questions that would excite domestic opposition. Behind-the-scenes-support is the best role the Gulf monarchies can play in American initiatives on Arab-Israeli issues. They are, since the Gulf War, increasingly comfortable with and willing to play such a role. Pressuring them to take high-profile public positions on largely symbolic issues is counterproductive.

A good example of such a symbolic issue is the Arab economic boycott of Israel. Increasingly, the secondary and tertiary aspects of boycott—aimed at preventing foreign companies that do business in Israel, and companies that do business with such companies, from entering Arab markets—are breaking down. Enforcement by Gulf state governments of these aspects of the boycott is more lax than it was in the past, to some extent as a result of U.S. pressure.[13] The primary boycott—that no Arab company deal directly with Israel—will remain in effect until some kind of comprehensive peace agreement is reached. Gulf states will not open themselves up to the wave of domestic and regional criticism that would follow their unilateral repeal of the boycott. The economic benefit to Israel of direct business dealings with Gulf countries is hard to calculate, but it is probably marginal. The issue is important to Israel, understandably, for its symbolic content.

Pressing the Saudis in particular to take such a symbolic step is not in America's interests. The real substance of Arab-Israeli negotiations is among the parties themselves, not including the Gulf states. Syrians, Palestinians, and Jordanians who have to make decisions on such issues will not be impressed by public relations moves by the Saudis on matters like the boycott. It is the behind-the-scenes Saudi role, particularly in terms of financial aid, that matters to the other Arab parties. Islamic currents in the kingdom have already been critical of Saudi support for the current round of Arab-Israeli talks. Symbolic gestures on marginal issues like the boycott will only help such currents polarize public opinion, by allowing them to portray the Saudi regime as in complete thrall to the United States. Pushing the Saudis to take high-profile public stands on marginal Arab-Israeli issues could have serious costs for the United States, and would bring few, if any, benefits.

On substantive matters, particularly financial ones, the Gulf states, again particularly the Saudis, have been helpful in pushing the Arab-Israeli peace process. It is this role that the United States should encourage. Gulf leaders are much more reluctant to commit large sums of money to their Arab brethren than has been the case in the past. They discovered during the Gulf War that previous payments did not ensure popularity in Arab public opinion, or (in the cases of Jordan, Yemen, and the PLO) sympathetic positions by Arab states. Their post–Gulf War hesitancy to open up their wallets is thus understandable. But it is also shortsighted.

All the Arab parties to the peace process—Syria, Lebanon, Egypt, Jordan, and the Palestinians—will need help to implement the agreements that have been reached and those that may come in the future. The Saudis and the other Gulf states have an interest in a stable regional order, in a solution that removes the Palestinian issue from the Middle Eastern agenda, and in the stability of governments that take steps in this direction. Their economic assistance, through accepting guest workers from these states, providing concessionary oil, investing in these countries' economies, and providing direct state-to-state aid, can help ensure the success of any Arab-Israeli deal. If there is a continuing reluctance to directly subsidize the PLO, because of its stand in the Gulf War, their aid can be channeled through international financial institutions. These kinds of inter-Arab steps from the Gulf states can do more to encourage Arab-Israeli peace moves than any cosmetic announcements from Riyad or Kuwait City about the boycott or relations with Israel. It is such steps that the United States should urge upon its friends in the Gulf.

CONCLUSIONS

As long as the United States has an interest in oil and in Arab-Israeli matters, it will have to be concerned with events in the Gulf. The overriding American concern about the Gulf is that the world economy have access to its oil at sustainable prices. American policy in the Gulf should therefore be directed at helping to avoid political outcomes that could interfere with market considerations in the production and pricing of Gulf oil.

Obviously, military conquest of the Arab Gulf monarchies by a single state, or military dominance that would accord such a state political control over the oil decisions of the Gulf monarchies, could lead to political interference with market forces. The Carter Doctrine of 1980 codified American opposition to any such efforts. It is for this reason, in the end, that the United States went to war in the Gulf in 1990–1991. Given the outcome of that war, this kind of threat to Gulf oil is most unlikely in the near and intermediate future, particularly as the United States remains actively involved in political and security issues in the area. Neither Iran nor Iraq has the military might to contemplate a direct attack on the monarchies. The indirect influence that they might try to exercise over the Gulf monarchies on oil questions, as part of the normal diplomatic give-and-take in the Gulf, is no threat to major American interests in the area.

The only realistic scenario under which the international political configuration in the Gulf might be substantially altered to the detriment of American interests would be complete Iranian domination of a post-Saddam Iraq. Fear of such an outcome explained the Bush administration's inaction during Saddam Husayn's brutal suppression of the popular uprisings in Iraq in March–April 1991. The chance that Iran could come to control Iraq through a client regime was exaggerated then and remains limited now. Iraqi Shiʿis look to Iran for support; that does not necessarily mean they are mere pawns under Teheran's control. Other regional powers, including Turkey, Syria, and Saudi Arabia, exert influence in Iraq that could be used to prevent Iranian domination.

There is only one remotely plausible way that an Iranian puppet regime could be imposed on Baghdad. Should post-Saddam Iraq fall into absolute chaos, then Iran would hold more cards to play in Iraqi politics than any other outside power. It has the longest border with Iraq and the closest ties with the largest segment of Iraq's population. If the United States and its friends are drawn into a direct, zero-sum confrontation with Iran over the future of Iraq, then Iran would have the incentive to play those cards in the struggle for control over Iraq. The best way for the United States to avoid such an outcome would be to engage the Iranians and the Iraqi Shiʿi opposition, along with other regional parties, in dialogue about the post-Saddam transition in Iraq. That means acknowledging Iranian interests in Iraq, but at the same time circumscribing those interests, and getting Iran to acknowledge the interests of others there. The worst outcome for the United States would be to fall into a confrontation with Iran over the future of Iraq, and lose. The consequences for the Gulf monarchies, for overall Middle Eastern stability, and for American interests there would be grave. The United States should make avoiding such a confrontation a high priority of its Gulf policy.

As matters now stand, there is little likelihood, barring the kind of geopolitical tumult just described, that oil production and pricing decisions will be affected by regional political events. But this conclusion stems from a particular conjunction of political circumstances, not from some permanent change in the political landscape of the Middle East. With the end of the Iran-Iraq war, the Gulf War, and the Cold War, and perhaps the beginning of a comprehensive Arab-Israeli peace, the regional situation is less threatening for the Gulf monarchies than it has been for years, if not decades. However, one can imagine regional scenarios, such as Islamic revolution in Egypt or Iranian dominance of post-Saddam Iraq, that could quickly alter the current favorable climate to the detriment of American interests. Such events could derail the peace process, put new pressures on the Gulf monarchies to distance themselves from the United States, and raise again the potential of a link between oil and Arab-Israeli issues. Thus successful American policy toward the Gulf monarchies is dependent in many respects on avoiding revolutionary upheaval in Egypt and preventing the kind of scenario described above of Iranian dominance over post-Saddam Iraq.

On the domestic side as well, the current outlook for regime stability in the Gulf monarchies is good. They survived the ideological challenges of Nasirist Pan-Arabism, Khumaynist Islam, and the Saddamist mix of the two. They have significant domestic resources—economic, coercive and ideological—with which to maintain their rule. At the same time, their polities are not static. Population growth, the diffusion of higher education, the demand for jobs and services put strains on the political systems, strains that have recently been expressed in public appeals for less arbitrary and more participatory political institutions. While the Islamic idiom dominates political discourse in these countries, both among opposition figures and the regimes, these kinds of appeals have cut across ideological lines in Gulf societies.

The best safeguard of long-term stability, through evolutionary change, in the Gulf monarchies is the expansion of autonomous civil society institutions. Such institutions can serve as the basis for more participatory political life, lessening the risk that any one group or current could monopolize the political arena and threaten revolutionary change. A number of Gulf regimes, recognizing the dynamics at work in their societies, have recently taken steps toward opening up their political systems. The United States should, through careful and judicious steps of its own, encourage such opening up and press its friends in the Gulf to do more. The goal of such steps should not be "democracy" in and of itself, but stable political evolution toward more participatory polities. That means a cautious approach, recognizing and avoiding the dangers of pushing too far, too fast.

Such American initiatives will not be welcomed by many in the Gulf regimes, where entrenched interests, particularly in the ruling families themselves, will resist expanding political freedom and participation. However, they are in the American interest and, in the long run, in the interest of the regimes themselves. Such gradual political development is the only guarantee for avoiding the kind of political upheaval that could paralyze oil production and threaten the regimes' stability. The United States can also take steps on its own to reduce the risks presented by upheaval in the Gulf to its own economy: maintenance of the Strategic Petroleum Reserve, commitment to the International Energy Agency crisis allocation plans, and encouragement of oil investment in areas outside the Middle East. Reducing American consumption of imported oil, through tax and conservation policies, has been talked about since the oil crisis of 1973–1974. Some steps have been taken, mainly in the private sector, but more could be done. A substantial increase in taxes on gasoline at the pump would be the most sensible way to start.

The American relationship with the Gulf states goes back only a few decades. The United States does not have a long history of economic, cultural, and political contact with this area, as it does with Europe. Geography, which dictates sustained American interest and involvement with Latin America and the Caribbean, separates here rather than unites. But the exigencies of geology, technology, and strategy have made the relationship with the Gulf monarchies one of the most important for American foreign policy, as central in the post–Cold War world as it was during the Cold War. In the wake of the Gulf War, America's interests in the region seem secure and American power unchallenged. It is tempting for Americans to assume that this particular garden needs no more tending. One conclusion of this book is that this assumption is wrong. It is only through a thorough understanding of the dynamics of the domestic politics of the Gulf monarchies, and of the regional environment in which they operate, that United States policy can successfully safeguard American interests in the region without having to fight future Gulf wars.

Notes

CHAPTER 1

1. The body of water that separates the Arabian Peninsula from Iran is called the Persian Gulf by Iranians and the Arabian Gulf by Arabs. In order to avoid even the hint of partiality in the dispute, and to avoid the clumsy compound used in the opening sentence, I will refer to the said body of water as the Gulf.

CHAPTER 2

1. The other major institutional framework sanctioned by the Gulf monarchies for popular organization is the chamber of commerce. In every state but Kuwait the national chambers of commerce are very close to the government. Kuwait is the exception among the Gulf monarchies in terms of public space for political and social organizing. Civil society institutions, other than religious and tribal ones—such as political organizations, the press, professional associations—are much more vigorous and independent of the state in Kuwait than elsewhere.

2. On the link between Wahhabism and the Al Saʿud, see: Christine Moss Helms, *The Cohesion of Saudi Arabia* (Baltimore: Johns Hopkins University Press, 1981), chapters 1–3; R. Bayly Winder, *Saudi Arabia in the Nineteenth Century* (New York: St. Martin's Press, 1965); Nadav Safran, *Saudi Arabia: The Ceaseless Quest for Security* (Cambridge: Harvard University Press, 1985), chapters 1–2. For a firsthand and personal account of the history of the Al Saʿud and the development of the twentieth century Saudi state, see the works of H. St. John Philby, the British Arabist who served as adviser to King ʿAbd

200

al-ᶜAziz. Among his better known works are *Arabia of the Wahhabis* (London: Constable, 1928) and *Saudi Arabia* (London: Benn, 1955). For a Saudi view of the importance of the link between Wahhabism and the building of the Saudi state, see Turki al-Hamad, "tawhid al-jazira al-ᶜarabiyya: dur al-'idiulujiyya wa al-tanthim fi tahtim al-bunya al-'ijtimaᶜiyya al-'iqtisadiyya al-muᶜiqa lil-wahda [The Unification of the Arabian Peninsula: The Role of Ideology and Organization in Overcoming the Socio-economic Structure Preventing Unity]," *al-Mustaqbal al-ᶜArabi*, vol. 93 (November 1986).

3. Helms, *Cohesion of Saudi Arabia*, chapter 8; Joseph Kostiner, "Transforming Dualities: Tribe and State Formation in Saudi Arabia," in Philip Khoury and Joseph Kostiner, eds., *Tribes and State Formation in the Middle East* (Berkeley: University of California Press, 1990).

4. On the political history of the Ibadi Imamate, see particularly John Wilkinson, *The Imamate Tradition of Oman* (New York: Cambridge University Press, 1987).

5. Ayman Al-Yassini, *Religion and State in the Kingdom of Saudi Arabia* (Boulder, Colo.: Westview Press, 1985), pp. 70–72, 76.

6. The text of the *fatwa* on the foreign troops can be found in *al-Sharq al-'Awsat*, August 21, 1990, p. 4, and the *fatwa* referring to the war with Iraq as a legitimate *jihad* is mentioned in the *New York Times*, January 20, 1991, p. 18.

7. *al-Hayat*, July 12, 1993, pp. 1, 4.

8. James Bill reports that, in the decade after the 1973 oil boom, the number of mosques in the Gulf Arab monarchies tripled. While some were privately financed, "most of the mosque construction is being planned and financed by governments." "Resurgent Islam in the Persian Gulf," *Foreign Affairs*, vol. 63, no. 1 (Fall 1984), p. 116.

9. In Oman the ministry of religious affairs distributes sample sermons to mosque preachers throughout the country. For a fascinating account of the relationship between the state and religious institutions in Oman, see Dale F. Eickelman, "National Identity and Religious Discourse in Contemporary Oman," *International Journal of Islamic and Arabic Studies*, vol. 6, no. 1 (1989).

10. Eleanor Doumato, "Women and the Stability of Saudi Arabia," *Middle East Report*, no. 171 (July/August 1991), pp. 34–37.

11. For an extensive and interesting discussion of this issue, see Al-Yassini, *Religion and State in the Kingdom of Saudi Arabia*, pp. 67–79.

12. In 1990, the number of foreign pilgrims was 827,236, down from a high in 1987 of 960,386. These numbers do not include Saudis, obviously, or Iranians, who boycotted the pilgrimage that year, and also probably underestimate the number of Yemenis on pilgrimage, as until 1991 Yemenis could enter the kingdom without a passport. Kingdom of Saudi Arabia, Ministry of Finance and National Economy, Central Department of Statistics, *Statistical Year Book—1990*, Table 4-36, p. 223.

13. For a brief discussion of the origin and mission of the *mutawwaᶜin* organization, see Al-Yassini, *Religion and State in the Kingdom of Saudi Arabia*, pp. 68–70.

14. Ibid., pp. 72–73.

15. On the political role of the ᶜ*ulama* in Saudi Arabia, see Alexander Bligh, "The Saudi Religious Elite (Ulama) as Participant in the Political System of the

Kingdom," *International Journal of Middle Eastern Studies*, vol. 17, no. 1 (February 1985), and Joseph A. Kechician, "The Role of the Ulama in the Politics of an Islamic State: The Case of Saudi Arabia," *International Journal of Middle Eastern Studies*, vol. 18, no. 1 (February 1986).

16. On the tribal bases of the various Gulf ruling families, see: Jill Crystal, *Oil and Politics in the Gulf: Rulers and Merchants in Kuwait and Qatar* (New York: Cambridge University Press, 1990), chapter 2; Helms, *Cohesion of Saudi Arabia*, pp. 76–77; John E. Peterson, *Oman in the Twentieth Century: Political Foundations of an Emerging State* (London: Croom Helm, 1978), chapters 1–2; Frauke Heard-Bey, *From Trucial States to United Arab Emirates* (New York: Longman, 1982), chapter 2; Fred H. Lawson, *Bahrain: The Modernization of Autocracy* (Boulder, Colo.: Westview Press, 1989), chapters 1–2. For a general discussion of the role of tribes in the politics of the Arab coast of the Gulf, see J. E. Peterson, "Tribes and Politics in Eastern Arabia," *Middle East Journal*, vol. 31, no. 3 (Summer 1977).

17. For interesting anthropological discussions of Arabian city life, see Soraya Altorki and Donald Cole, *Arabian Oasis City: The Transformation of Unayzah* (Austin: University of Texas Press, 1989), and Madawi Al Rasheed, *Politics in an Arabian Oasis: The Rashidi Tribal Dynasty* (London: I. B. Taurus, 1991).

18. Helms, *Cohesion of Saudi Arabia*, p. 113; Tim Niblock, "Social Structure and the Development of the Saudi Arabian Political System," in T. Niblock, ed., *State, Society and Economy in Saudi Arabia* (London: Croom Helm, 1982); Henry Rosenfeld, "The Social Composition of the Military in the Process of State Formation in the Arabian Desert," *Journal of the Royal Anthropological Institute*, vol. 95, no. 1 (1965), and idem, "The Military Forces Used to Achieve and Maintain Power and the Meaning of Its Social Composition: Slaves, Mercenaries, and Townsmen," *Journal of the Royal Anthropological Institute*, vol. 95, no. 2, (1965).

19. On the economics and politics of the pearling industry in the Gulf, see Crystal, *Oil and Politics in the Gulf*, chapters 3, 5; Heard-Bey, *From Trucial States to United Arab Emirates*, chapters 5–6.

20. Helms, *Cohesion of Saudi Arabia*, chapters 6–7; Al Rasheed, *Politics in an Arabian Oasis*, chapter 9; Yehoshua Porath, *In Search of Arab Unity, 1930–1945* (London: Frank Cass, 1986), p. 27.

21. Peterson, *Oman in the Twentieth Century*, chapter 7.

22. For accounts of these events in Bahrain, see Fuad Khuri, *Tribe and State in Bahrain* (Chicago: University of Chicago Press, 1980), chapters 5, 6 and 11; Fred Lawson, *Bahrain: The Modernization of Autocracy* (Boulder, Colo.: Westview Press, 1989), chapter 2.

23. For a general discussion of British colonial policy in the Gulf, see Malcolm Yapp, "The Nineteenth and Twentieth Centuries" and "British Policy in the Persian Gulf," in Alvin J. Cottrell, ed., *The Persian Gulf States* (Baltimore, Md.: Johns Hopkins University Press, 1980). For a critical account from a local nationalist perspective of the British role, see Khaldun Hasan al-Naqeeb, *al-mujtamaᶜ wa al-dawla fi al-khalij wa al-jazira al-ᶜarabiyya: min manthur mukhtalif* (Beirut: Markaz Dirasat al-Wahda al-ᶜArabiyya, 1987), chapters 4–5. Al-Naqeeb's book has been translated into English by L. M. Kenny: *State*

and Society in the Gulf and Arabian Peninsula: A Different Perspective (New York: Routledge, 1990).

24. Rosemarie Said Zahlan, *The Creation of Qatar* (London: Croom Helm, 1981), chapters 3–5; idem, The Making of the Modern Gulf States (London: Unwin Hyman, 1989), chapter 6; John Wilkinson, *Arabia's Frontiers: The Story of Britain's Boundary Drawing in the Desert* (London: I. B. Taurus, 1991), pp. 41–48.

25. On British policy in what became the UAE, see Heard-Bey, *From Trucial States to United Arab Emirates*, chapters 8 and 9, and Wilkinson, *Arabia's Frontiers*, chapter 2. The most stinging criticism of Britain in this regard can be found in al-Naqueeb, *al-mujtama^c wa al-dawla*, chapters 3, 4.

26. Dale F. Eickelman, *The Middle East: An Anthropological Approach*, 2d ed. (Englewood Cliffs, N.J.: Prentice Hall, 1989), p. 78.

27. These kinds of changes among the Al Murrah beduin of the Empty Quarter (southeastern Saudi Arabia), who inhabit the most isolated and forbidding part of the peninsula, are documented by Donald P. Cole in *Nomads of the Nomads: The Al Murrah Bedouin of the Empty Quarter* (Arlington Heights, Ill.: AHM Publishing Corporation, 1975), pp. 146–63.

28. The quote is from the introduction to an interesting book about how states in Arab oil producing countries attempt to construct and use ideologies to gain the loyalty of their citizens. Eric Davis, "Theorizing Statecraft and Social Change in Arab Oil Producing Countries," in Eric Davis and Nicolas Gavrielides, eds., *Statecraft in the Middle East: Oil, Historical Memory and Popular Culture* (Miami: Florida International University Press, 1991), p. 13.

29. Muhammad Rajab al-Najjar, "Contemporary Trends in the Study of Folklore in the Arab Gulf States," in Davis and Gavrielides, *Statecraft in the Middle East*, pp. 176–201.

30. Crystal, *Oil and Politics in the Gulf*, pp. 161–64.

31. The text of the basic system can be found in *al-Sharq al-'Awsat*, March 2, 1992, p. 4.

32. The text of the king's speech was published in *al-Sharq al-'Awsat*, March 7, 1991, p. 3.

33. *al-Hayat*, December 29, 1991, p. 1; personal interviews in Bahrain, May 1992. For the text of his paper, see ^{c}Abd al-Latif Mahmud Al Mahmud, "dur al-musharaka al-sha^{c}biyya fi siyyagha al-qirar al-siyasi wa mustaqbal al-dimuqratiyya fi al-mintaqa [The Role of Popular Participation in Political Decision-Making and the Future of Democracy in the Region]," *al-Jazira al-^{c}Arabiyya*, no. 12 (January 1992), pp. 20–23.

34. James Bill, "Resurgent Islam in the Persian Gulf."

35. On the 1979 incident and Juhayman al-^{c}Utaybi's political thought, see Joseph Kechichian, "Islamic Revivalism and Change in Saudi Arabia," *The Muslim World*, vol. 80, no. 1 (January 1990).

36. See, for example, remarks against the American presence made by Dr. Safar al-Hawali, Dean of Islamic Studies at 'Umm al-Qura University in Mecca, published in the *New York Times*, November 24, 1990, p. 21. See also the *New York Times*, December 25, 1990, p. 6.

37. Personal interviews, Riyad, May 1991.

38. See the following *New York Times* reports: December 31, 1991, pp. A1, A10; January 1, 1992, p. 3; January 30, 1992, p. A3; March 9, 1992, pp. A1, A7.

39. *New York Times*, December 31, 1991, pp. A1, A10.
40. *al-Hayat*, January 29, 1992, pp. 1, 4. At this same time, in early 1992, opposition sources reported that a number of religious activists were arrested. These reports could not be independently confirmed.
41. *al-Hayat*, January 28, 1992, p. 1; January 29, 1992, pp. 1, 4.
42. The author obtained copies of the Memorandum of Advice in Saudi Arabia— all translations are his. One of the copies was dated Muharram 1413, which corresponds to July 1992, indicating that it was in circulation before the fall of 1992, when Western news organizations reported on it (*New York Times*, October 8, 1992, p. A6). There were 111 signatures on the petition; the *Times* and the *Makka News*, an opposition organ published outside the kingdom, reported 107 signatures.
43. *al-Hayat*, September 18, 1992, p. 4.
44. *al-Hayat*, December 4, 1992, p. 6.
45. *New York Times*, December 15, 1992, p. A14.
46. *al-Hayat*, December 22, 1992, p. 4. See also the *New York Times*, December 22, 1992, p. A10.
47. The author obtained Arabic and English versions of the committee's founding declaration from sources in the Gulf. Accounts of events related to the group can be found in: *al-Hayat*, May 13, 1993, pp. 1, 4; May 14, 1993, pp. 1, 4; May 24, 1993, pp. 1, 4; May 26, 1993, pp. 1, 4; June 2, 1993, pp. 1, 4, 5; the *Washington Post*, May 16, 1993, p. A27; the *New York Times*, May 14, 1993, p. A3; Foreign Broadcast Information Service, Daily Report, *Near East and South Asia*, May 17, 1993, pp. 37–38; May 18, 1993, p. 20.
48. *al-Hayat*, July 12, 1993, pp. 1, 4.
49. Abd al-Rahman Munif, *Cities of Salt* (New York: Vintage Books, 1987); *The Trench* (New York: Pantheon Books, 1991); *Variations on Night and Day* (New York: Pantheon Books, 1993).

CHAPTER 3

1. Much of the discussion in this chapter relies on the important and growing literature on rentier states in the field of comparative politics. Some of the most important works on this concept are: Jacques Delacroix, "The Distributive State in the World System," *Studies in Comparative International Development*, vol. 15 (1980); Hazem Beblawi and Giacomo Luciani, eds., *The Rentier State* (London: Croom Helm, 1987), particularly the Beblawi article "The Rentier State in the Arab World," and the Luciani article "Allocation v. Production States: A Theoretical Framework" [both reprinted in Giacomo Luciani, ed., *The Arab State* (Berkeley: University of California Press, 1990]; Jill Crystal, *Oil and Politics in the Gulf: Rulers and Merchants in Kuwait and Qatar* (New York: Cambridge University Press, 1990), especially chapters 1 and 6; idem, "Coalitions in Oil Monarchies: Kuwait and Qatar," *Comparative Politics*, vol. 21, no. 4 (July 1989); Ghassan Salame, "Political Power and the Saudi State," *MERIP Reports*, no. 91 (October 1980); Khaldun Hasan al-Naqeeb, *al-mujtamaᶜ wa al-dawla fi al-khalij wa al-jazira al-ᶜarabiyya* (Beirut: Markaz Dirasat al-Wahda al-ᶜArabiyya, 1987). Some important work has recently been done questioning some of the conclusions of the earlier rentier

literature: Kiren Aziz Chaudhry, "The Price of Wealth: Business and State in Labor Remittance and Oil Economies," *International Organization*, vol. 43, no. 1 (Winter 1989); idem, "Economic Liberalization in Oil-Exporting Countries: Iraq and Saudi Arabia," in Iliya Harik and Denis Sullivan, eds., *Privatization and Liberalization in the Middle East* (Bloomington: Indiana University Press, 1992); and Eric Davis, "Theorizing Statecraft and Social Change in Arab Oil-Producing Countries," in Eric Davis and Nicolas Gavrielides, eds., *Statecraft in the Middle East* (Miami: Florida International University Press, 1991).

2. Quoted in Robert Lacey, *The Kingdom: Arabia and the House of Saud* (New York: Avon Books, 1981), p. 229. Lacey's book and *The House of Saud* by David Holden and Richard Johns (New York: Holt, Rinehart and Winston, 1981), offer very readable popular accounts of the history of Saudi Arabia.

3. A word of caution is in order when dealing with statistics, particularly government expenditure statistics, in these (or any Middle Eastern) country. The figures should be taken as rough approximations, not exact measures. What they are most useful for is examining the magnitude of change over the past thirty years.

4. *Middle East Economic Digest*, February 2, 1990, pp. 4–5; May 22, 1992, p. 29.

5. For an early discussion of how the Gulf monarchies faced the oil recession of the late 1980s, see Shireen T. Hunter, "The Gulf Economic Crisis and its Social and Political Consequences," *Middle East Journal*, vol. 40, no. 4 (Autumn 1986), pp. 593–613.

6. *New York Times*, May 4, 1992, pp. A1, A6.

7. State of Kuwait, Ministry of Planning, Central Statistical Office, *Annual Statistical Abstract—1989*, Table 265, p. 295; Table 281, p. 307.

8. Much of this information is taken from Table 5 (pp. 188–89) of Khaldun Hassan al-Naqeeb, *al-mujtamaᶜ wa al-dawla fi al-khalij wa al-jazira al-ᶜarabiyya: min manthur mukhtalif* [Society and State in the Gulf and Arabian Peninsula: A Different Perspective], (Beirut: Markaz Dirasat al-Wahda al-ᶜArabiyya, 1987). The information is current to 1985.

9. Sultanate of Oman, Development Council, General Secretariat, *Statistical Year Book 1990*, 19th issue (July 1991), Table 7–4, p. 117. See also Calvin Allen, *Oman: The Modernization of the Sultanate* (Boulder, Colo.: Westview Press, 1987), p. 100.

10. Fred Lawson, *Bahrain: The Modernization of Autocracy* (Boulder, Colo.: Westview Press, 1989), pp. 80–82.

11. Ibid., pp. 79, 81.

12. *al-Hayat*, June 11, 1993, p. 11.

13. Allen, *Oman*, pp. 97–100; personal interview, Riyad.

14. Beblawi, "The Rentier State in the Arab World," in Luciani, ed., *The Arab State*, p. 90; on Kuwait, see Crystal, *Oil and Politics in the Gulf*, chapter 4.

15. *New York Times*, May 4, 1992, pp. A1, A6.

16. *MidEast Report*, November 1, 1991, p. 5.

17. Beblawi in Luciani, p. 94; Abdulkarim Hamoud Al-Dekhayel, "The State and Political Legitimation in an Oil-Rentier Economy: Kuwait as a Case Study," D. Phil. dissertation, University of Exeter, 1990, pp. 403–409; Crystal, *Oil and Politics in the Gulf*, pp. 97–100.

18. *al-Hayat*, December 20, 1991, p. 1; December 22, 1991, p. 4; *New York Times*, May 4, 1992, pp. A1, A6; personal interviews, Kuwait, May 1992.
19. *Middle East Economic Digest*, January 19, 1990, p. 22.
20. Chaudhry, "The Price of Wealth."
21. Personal interviews in the Gulf, May–June 1992, October 1992.
22. Crystal, *Oil and Politics in the Gulf*, especially chapters 1, 6.
23. Personal interview, Oman, June 1992.
24. Personal interviews with businessmen and economists in Kuwait, Saudi Arabia, Bahrain, and Oman. For a fascinating account of some of the prominent merchant families in the Gulf, see Michael Field, *The Merchants* (Woodstock, N.Y.: Overlook Press, 1985). Field has covered the area for a number of years for the *Financial Times*.
25. Kuwait, *Annual Statistical Abstract—1989*, Table 166, p. 168 (for total Kuwaitis in the workforce), and Table 171, p. 172 (for Kuwaitis in the civil service).
26. Sultanate of Oman, Development Council, Directorate General of National Statistics, *Statistical Year Book—1990*, Table 8-2, p. 55.
27. Ibid., Table 1-4, p. 80 (civil service and public corporations employment); Table 9-5, p. 137 (private sector employment).
28. Kingdom of Saudi Arabia, Ministry of Finance and National Economy, Central Department of Statistics, *Statistical Year Book—1990*, Table 10-6, p. 545; Table 12-8, p. 628.
29. For accounts of housing and loan programs, see: Crystal, *Oil and Politics in the Gulf*, pp. 156–57; idem, *Kuwait: The Transformation of an Oil State* (Boulder, Colo.: Westview Press, 1992), pp. 59–62; A. Reza, S. Islami, and Rostam Mehraban Kavoussi, *The Political Economy of Saudi Arabia* (Seattle: University of Washington Press, 1984), pp. 67–68; Lawson, *Bahrain*, pp. 112–13.
30. Bahrain, for example, began its subsidy program on food products in 1974. Lawson, *Bahrain*, p. 80.
31. *al-Hayat*, April 13, 1992, p. 5; *Middle East Economic Digest*, June 12, 1992, p. vii; *New York Times*, May 4, 1992, pp. A1, A6.
32. *al-Hayat*, March 25, 1992, p. 9; *New York Times*, January 13, 1991, p. E2.
33. *Middle East Economic Digest*, May 8, 1992, p. 17.
34. Richard F. Nyrop, ed., *The Persian Gulf States: Country Studies* (Washington, D.C.: U.S. Government Printing Office, 1985), p. 126.
35. Lawson, *Bahrain*, p. 80.
36. Crystal, *Oil and Politics in the Gulf*, pp. 158, 160.
37. For descriptions of health policy in some of the states, see: Allen, *Oman*, pp. 101–102; Crystal, *Kuwait*, pp. 59–61; Fouad Al-Farsy, *Modernity and Tradition: The Saudi Equation* (London: Kegan Paul International, 1990), pp. 269–73. All provide government statistics on the development of the public health infrastructure.
38. Kuwait, *Statistical Abstract-1989*, Table 171, pp. 172–73; Table 260, p. 288.
39. Oman, *Statistical Yearbook*, 1990, Table 3-4, pp. 90–94; Table 4-15, pp. 431–34.
40. Saudi figure calculated from Kingdom of Saudi Arabia, *Statistical Yearbook—1990*, Table 10-3, pp. 535–41; Kuwaiti figure calculated from State of Kuwait, *Annual Statistical Abstract—1989*, Table 260, p. 288; other states

calculated from IMF, *Government Financial Statistics Yearbook—1990.* Saudi budget figures for 1992 from *al-Hayat,* January 3, 1992, p. 5. For a detailed examination of Saudi defense and security spending over time, see Nadav Safran, *Saudi Arabia: Ceaseless Quest for Security* (Cambridge, Mass.: Harvard University Press, 1985), particularly chapters 7 and 17.

41. Figures calculated from IMF, *Government Financial Statistics Yearbook—* 1990.

42. The growth of the coercive arm of the Gulf state governments is emphasized by Khaldun al-Naqeeb in *al-mujtamaᶜ wa al-dawla fi al-khalij wa al-jazira al-ᶜarabiyya,* particularly in chapters 5–6.

43. Personal interviews, Saudi Arabia, May 1991, October 1992.

44. I discuss in greater detail the "un-exportability" of the Iranian revolutionary message in the Gulf in "Revolutionary Fevers and Regional Contagion: Domestic Structures and the 'Export' of Revolution in the Middle East," *Journal of South Asian and Middle Eastern Studies,* vol. 14, no. 3 (Spring 1991), pp. 1–23.

45. Altorki and Cole, *Arabian Oasis City: The Transformation of Unayzah* (Austin: University of Texas Press, 1989), pp. 112–13.

46. Lawson, *Bahrain,* chapters 3 and 4.

47. Crystal, *Oil and Politics in the Gulf,* pp. 139–55.

48. Helen Lackner, *A House Built on Sand: A Political Economy of Saudi Arabia* (London: Ithaca Press, 1978), pp. 95–98, 188–190.

49. For accounts of these family disputes in the five smaller states, see Rosemarie Said Zahlan, *The Making of the Modern Gulf States: Kuwait, Bahrain, Qatar, the United Arab Emirates and Oman* (London: Unwin Hyman, 1989).

50. Crystal, *Oil and Politics in the Gulf,* shows in detail how the amirs in Kuwait and Qatar began to turn more toward family members with the advent of large-scale oil revenues, pp. 62–66, 147–55.

51. *al-Hayat,* November 27, 1991, pp. 1, 4.

52. *al-Hayat,* December 31, 1992, p. 1.

53. Personal interviews in the Gulf, May 1991, May-June 1992, October 1992.

54. Crystal, *Oil and Politics in the Gulf,* p. 160.

55. *New York Times,* January 14, 1992, p. A4.

CHAPTER 4

1. Giacomo Luciani, "Allocation v. Production States: A Theoretical Framework," in Luciani, ed., *The Arab State* (Berkeley: University of California Press, 1990), pp. 76–77.

2. An excellent discussion of the issue of representative institutions in these states can be found in John E. Peterson, *The Arab Gulf States: Steps Toward Political Participation,* The Washington Papers, no. 131 (New York: Praeger, 1988).

3. Shafeeq Ghabra, "Voluntary Associations in Kuwait: The Founding of a New System?" *Middle East Journal,* vol. 45, no. 2 (Spring 1991).

4. Fuad Khuri, *Tribe and State in Bahrain* (Chicago: University of Chicago Press, 1980), Chapter 8.

5. Kiren Aziz Chaudhry, "The Price of Wealth: Business and State in Labor Remittance and Oil Economies," *International Organization*, vol. 43, no. 1 (Winter 1989), pp. 137–40.

6. Personal interviews, Riyad, October 1992.

7. *al-Hayat*, February 8, 1993, p. 9; February 11, 1993, p. 11.

8. Many of them are discussed in Ghabra, "Voluntary Associations in Kuwait," pp. 199–215.

9. On Bahraini clubs, see Fred H. Lawson, *Bahrain: The Modernization of Autocracy* (Boulder, Colo.: Westview Press, 1989), chapter 3; Emile A. Nakhleh, *Bahrain* (Lexington, Mass.: Lexington Books, 1976), pp. 41–58; and Khuri, *Tribe and State in Bahrain*, chapter 8.

10. The only study in English on this organization is Emile A. Nakhleh, "Muntada al-Tanmiyya: Indigenous Scholarship on Development in the GCC Countries," paper presented at the Middle East Studies Association annual convention, San Antonio, Texas, November 1990.

11. *al-Qabas* (Kuwait), May 14, 1992, pp. 1, 4; personal interview.

12. Personal interview with a leader of the group of parliamentarians, Kuwait City, May 24, 1992.

13. Jill Crystal, *Kuwait: The Transformation of an Oil State* (Boulder, Colo.: Westview Press, 1992), pp. 117–119.

14. Ibid., pp. 118–20; *Middle East Economic Digest*, January 19, 1990, pp. 21–22; February 2, 1990, pp. 19–20.

15. Personal interviews in the Gulf, May 1991, May–June 1992, October 1992.

16. *Washington Post*, April 3, 1991, pp. A25, A29; *New York Times*, April 4, 1991, p. A12.

17. *New York Times*, April 9, 1991, p. A13.

18. An example of one of their stronger joint statements, criticizing the crown prince for implicit threats to censor the press and calling for a coalition government to oversee the elections, can be found in *al-Hayat*, March 21, 1992, pp. 1, 4.

19. *al-Hayat*, January 13, 1992, p. 3.

20. The author was in Kuwait during this incident. A talk I was scheduled to give on Gulf security issues, sponsored by the Faculty Association of Kuwait University, was also canceled by the interior ministry.

21. Personal interviews in Kuwait with members of the Muslim Brotherhood and the National Islamic Alliance, May 1992.

22. The final results of the balloting can be found in *Sawt al-Kuwayt*, May 28, 1992, p. 4. The author observed the race in Kuwait and much of the information provided here is based on personal interviews in Kuwait.

23. The author obtained copies of this petition from sources in Saudi Arabia, and all the quotations are my translation. An English translation can be found in *Makka News*, no. 3, January 26, 1991. This broadsheet is published by the "Organization of the Islamic Revolution in the Arabian Peninsula," an Iranian-supported exile group with an American post office box address in Bowling Green, Kentucky. Another English translation can be found in Middle East Watch, "Empty Reforms: Saudi Arabia's New Basic Laws," May 1992, pp. 59–61. Yet a third English translation, from a copy of the petition published in the Jordanian newspaper *'Akhir Khabar*, is in FBIS–NESA, April

29, 1991, pp. 9–10. These various versions are essentially the same, with differences in translation, confirming the authenticity of the document.

24. The author obtained a copy of the "Islamist" petition from sources in Saudi Arabia, and the translations are mine. English language versions of this petition can be found in *Foreign Broadcast Information Service–Near East and South Asia* (hereafter FBIS–NESA), May 23, 1991, p. 21 (translation of a version published in the Cairo newspaper *al-Shaʿb*); *Makka News*, no. 8, June 16, 1991; and Middle East Watch, "Empty Reforms: Saudi Arabia's New Basic Laws," pp. 61–62. All these versions are almost exactly identical, though translations differ somewhat. An "amplification" of the petition, purportedly written by some of the signers of the petition, was published in the London-based Arabic newspaper *al-Quds al-ʿArabi* and translated in FBIS–NESA, August 22, 1991, pp. 22–26. As the author has not seen an original copy of that "amplification," he cannot attest to its validity.

25. See for example *New York Times*, December 31, 1991, pp. A1, A10; March 9, 1992, pp. A1, A7. This trend has been confirmed by Saudi opposition organs like *Makka News* and *Arabia Monitor*, a monthly newsletter published in Washington by the International Committee for Human Rights in the Gulf and Arabian Peninsula, and by the author in personal interviews in Saudi Arabia in May 1991 and October 1992.

26. Practically identical English-language versions of this petition can be found in *Makka News*, no. 7, April 6, 1991; and in *Arabia Monitor*, vol. 1, no. 6, July 1992.

27. An English version of the petition can be found in *Arabia Monitor*, vol. 1, no. 4–5 (May–June 1992). The existence of such a petition was confirmed to the author in interviews in the Gulf, May–June 1992.

28. John E. Peterson, *The Arab Gulf States: Steps Toward Political Participation*, pp. 84–91.

29. A copy of the petition was obtained from sources in Bahrain. The translation is by the author.

30. See, for example, *al-Hayat*, October 28, 1991, pp. 1, 4; December 8, 1992, p. 6.

31. *al-Hayat*, March 2, 1993, p. 7.

32. Personal interviews in Bahrain, May 1992.

33. The themes of responsible government, curbing the unbridled power of the executive, and popular participation were voiced to the author in personal interviews throughout the Gulf in 1991 and 1992.

34. *al-Hayat*, March 2, 1992, p. 5; *New York Times*, October 5, 1992, p. A10.

35. The author based his estimates of the strength of the various groupings in the election on the following sources: *al-Hayat*, October 5, 1992, p. 8; October 7, 1992, pp. 1, 4, 7; October 8, 1992, p. 6; *al-Sharq al-'Awsat*, October 11, 1992, p. 5; *al-Khalij* (UAE), October 7, 1992, p. 1 (provided by Prof. Emile Nakhleh, whom I thank for the reference). Various issues of *al-Hayat* and a number of Kuwaiti newspapers, along with personal interviews in Kuwait, were also used to identify the political leanings of independent candidates. For a detailed account of the campaign and the election, see Shafeeq Ghabra, "Kuwait: Elections and Issues of Democratization in a Middle Eastern State," *Digest of Middle East Studies*, vol. 2, no. 1 (Winter 1993).

36. *al-Hayat*, October 13, 1992, pp. 1, 4.
37. *New York Times*, January 10, 1993, p. 11; June 24, 1993, p. A3.
38. For a detailed account of this issue see the report by Middle East Watch, "Kuwait Closes All Human Rights Organizations," vol. 5, issue 6 (September 1993).
39. See *al-Sharq al-'Awsat*, March 2, 1992, p. 1.
40. The text of the Basic System can be found in *al-Sharq al-'Awsat*, March 2, 1992, pp. 4–5. Translations are by the author. An extremely detailed and very critical analysis of it can be found in Middle East Watch, "Empty Reforms: Saudi Arabia's New Basic Laws," May 1992.
41. The text of the decree on the Council of Ministers can be found in *al-Hayat*, August 21, 1993, p. 6.
42. The text of the founding statute of the Consultative Council can be found in *al-Sharq al-'Awsat*, March 2, 1992, pp. 4–5. Translations are by the author. Chapter 3 of Middle East Watch, "Empty Reforms: Saudi Arabia's New Basic Laws," May 1992, provides an interesting account of the historical background of consultative councils in the kingdom, and a very negative interpretation of the current proposal.
43. The occupational background of the appointees was reported by Saudi political scientist Salih al-Mani^c in an article in *al-Sharq al-'Awsat*, August 23, 1993, p. 4.
44. Biographical information gleaned from: *al-Sharq al-'Awsat*, August 22, 1993, p. 3; and Ghazi al-Qusaybi, "faja'ani bi mithlihim" [They Surprised Me], *al-Hayat*, August 25, 1993, p. 17.
45. The text of the statute on provincial governance can be found in *al-Sharq al-'Awsat*, March 2, 1992, pp. 4–5.
46. *al-Hayat*, September 20, 1993, p. 6.
47. J. E. Peterson, *The Arab Gulf States: Steps Toward Political Participation*, pp. 112–15; Middle East Watch, "Empty Reforms: Saudi Arabia's New Basic Laws," chapter 1.
48. This was the theme of much of the reporting of Youssef Ibrahim in the *New York Times*. See, for example, his reports of November 18, 1991 (p. A3), and March 9, 1992 (pp. A1, A7).
49. The text of the king's speech can be found in *al-Hayat*, March 2, 1992, p. 6.
50. *New York Times*, March 30, 1992, p. A6.
51. *al-Hayat*, March 2, 1992, pp. 1, 4.
52. For a discussion of the Omani State Consultative Council, see Dale F. Eickelman, "Kings and People: Oman's State Consultative Council," *Middle East Journal*, vol. 38, no. 1 (Winter 1984), pp. 51–71.
53. Personal interviews, Oman, June 1992; *al-Hayat*, October 14, 1991, p. 4.
54. Personal interviews, Oman, June 1992.
55. *al-Hayat*, December 22, 1992, p. 4.
56. Personal interviews, Oman, June 1992.
57. Personal interviews, Oman, June 1992; *al-Hayat*, October 30, 1992, p. 6.
58. The author is very grateful to Professor Emile Nakhleh for providing this background information, developed by him from sources in Bahrain, on the members of the Bahraini Council.
59. *al-Hayat*, December 21, 1992, pp. 1, 4.

60. Personal interviews, Bahrain, May 1992.
61. *Arabia Monitor*, vol. 1, nos. 4–5, (May–June 1992), p. 3; ibid., vol. 1, no. 10 (November 1992), p. 6.
62. *al-Hayat*, March 2, 1993, p. 7.
63. For a fascinating argument about the persistence of monarchical forms of government in the Middle East in general, see Lisa Anderson, "Absolutism and the Resilience of Monarchy in the Middle East," *Political Science Quarterly*, vol. 106, no. 1 (Spring 1991).

CHAPTER 5

1. For an account of the regional international politics of the Gulf up to the Iraqi invasion of Kuwait, see F. Gregory Gause, III, "Gulf Regional Politics: Revolution, War and Rivalry," in W. Howard Wriggins, ed., *Dynamics of Regional Politics: Four Systems on the Indian Ocean Rim* (New York: Columbia University Press, 1992).
2. See *New York Times*, October 13, 1991, pp. 1, 18; October 25, 1991, p. A9, for references to the Saudi proposals. Since that time there have been no moves to expand the size of the Saudi military.
3. The Shiʿi petition to King Fahd of Saudi Arabia discussed in chapter 4 complained of a "quarantine" against the entrance of Saudi Shiʿa into the armed forces.
4. *New York Times*, December 18, 1992, p. A8.
5. Figures taken from International Institute for Strategic Studies, *The Military Balance 1990–91* and *The Military Balance 1991–92*, (London: Brassey's for the International Institute for Strategic Studies, 1990, 1991).
6. IISS, *The Military Balance 1990–91*.
7. On the earlier Pakistani deployment, see Nadav Safran, *Saudi Arabia: Ceaseless Quest for Security* (Cambridge: Harvard University Press, 1985), pp. 363–64, 372, 432, 439–40; on the more recent deployment, see *Saudi Gazette* (Riyad), May 22, 1991, p. 2.
8. *al-Hayat*, February 20, 1993, p. 6.
9. *al-Hayat*, December 20, 1992, p. 4; February 20, 1993, p. 6; personal interviews in Kuwait, May 1992. In its electoral manifesto, the Islamic Constitutional Movement (Muslim Brotherhood) called for "strengthening the effectiveness of obligatory military service as one support for the military force," al-haraka al-dusturiyya al-'islamiyya, *al-birnamij al-'intikhabi* [Election Platform], p. 14.
10. *al-Hayat*, December 20, 1992, p. 4.
11. Figures from the Arms Control Association "Fact Sheet," October 8, 1992. Subsequent to that publication, Kuwait placed a $4 billion tank order. British-Saudi discussions on the *al-Yamamah* project were reported by Reuters, January 28, 1993. The Saudi-French naval deal was reported in *al-Hayat*, October 26, 1992, pp. 1, 4. On the general question of arms control and arms spending in the region, see Yahya Sadowski, *Scuds or Butter? The Political Economy of Arms Control in the Middle East* (Washington, D.C.: The Brookings Institution, 1993).

12. Personal interviews in the Gulf, May–June 1992, October 1992. For a report on the summit's resolutions, see *al-Hayat*, December 27, 1991, pp. 1, 3, 4.
13. *al-Hayat*, July 14, 1991, p. 4; July 29, 1991, p. 1; August 16, 1991, p. 4; August 23, 1991, p. 5.
14. See the following sources on this dispute: *New York Times*, October 1, 1992, p. A8; October 2, 1992, p. A8; *al-Hayat*, October 2, 1992, pp. 1, 4; October 5, 1992, pp. 1, 4; October 15, 1992, pp. 1, 4; October 29, 1992, pp. 1, 4; November 15, 1992, pp. 1, 4; November 22, 1992, pp. 1, 4; November 24, 1992, pp. 1, 4; December 21, 1992, pp. 1, 4. Supplemented by personal interviews in Riyad, October 1992.
15. Personal interviews, Riyad, October 1992.
16. Personal interviews, Kuwait, May 1992; Oman, June 1992. For a lengthy discussion of the GCC's problems from a Kuwaiti viewpoint, see the article by Kuwait University political scientist Shamlan ʿIssa in *Sawt al-Kuwayt*, May 28, 1992, p. 9.
17. Personal interviews, Bahrain, May 1992.
18. *al-Sharq al-'Awsat*, March 7, 1991, p. 1.
19. *New York Times*, March 11, 1991, pp. A1, A8.
20. Personal interviews with Saudi and GCC officials, Riyad, May 1991.
21. See, for example, the statement by Iranian Foreign Minister ʿAli Akbar Velayati immediately after the Damascus Declaration in *al-Sharq al-'Awsat*, March 8, 1991, pp. 1, 4. Velayati traveled to Syria two days after the signing of the Declaration to seek clarification of its content.
22. Personal interviews, Oman, June 1992.
23. *al-Hayat*, June 26, 1991, pp. 1, 7; June 27, 1991, pp. 1, 7. See also comments on the subject made by Iranian Foreign Minister Velayati in *Kayhan International* (English edition), August 29, 1991, p. 4; and by Egyptian Foreign Minister ʿAmr Musa in *al-Hayat*, September 26, 1991, p. 5.
24. ʿAbdallah Bishara, then the secretary-general of the Gulf Cooperation Council, said during the Gulf War: "[Iran] has left behind the songs of revolution for the reality of life. . . . I trust that it [good relations] will be very easy to achieve with today's Iran, a country which understands reality, because we are now entering a period of 'new pragmatism' in the Gulf." *al-Sharq al-'Awsat*, February 6, 1991, p. 6.
25. *al-Hayat*, June 8, 1991, p. 4.
26. *al-Hayat*, June 25, 1991, p. 4.
27. *Kayhan International* (English edition), August 29, 1991, p. 4.
28. *al-Hayat*, September 29, 1991, pp. 1, 4.
29. *al-Hayat*, November 28, 1991, p. 4.
30. *al-Hayat*, June 4, 1991, pp. 1, 7; July 30, 1991, p. 5.
31. Egyptian newspapers published this "final version" of the text in early August 1991. For an English translation, see FBIS-NESA, August 7, 1991, pp. 1–2.
32. *al-Hayat*, July 19, 1991, p. 5.
33. *al-Hayat*, June 25, 1991, pp. 1, 7. The "final version" of the Damascus Declaration states: "In this context, any GCC country has the right to employ the services of Egyptian and Syrian forces on its territories if it so desires." FBIS-NESA, August 7, 1991, p. 2.
34. *al-Hayat*, April 19, 1992, pp. 1, 4.

35. *al-Hayat*, September 1, 1992, p. 1; September 3, 1992, p. 5; *New York Times*, September 17, 1992, p. A12.

36. *al-Hayat*, December 23, 1992, pp. 1, 4; December 24, 1992, pp. 1, 4; *New York Times*, December 27, 1992, p. 6.

37. *al-Hayat*, May 30, 1993, pp. 1, 4.

38. *al-Hayat*, September 11, 1992, pp. 1, 4.

39. *al-Hayat*, December 24, 1992, pp. 1, 4; June 14, 1993, pp. 1, 4; personal interviews, Riyad, October 1992.

40. *al-Hayat*, July 6, 1993, p. 6.

41. *al-Hayat*, February 5, 1993, pp. 1, 4; February 6, 1993, p. 4.

42. *al-Hayat*, January 22, 1993, p. 7.

43. *al-Hayat*, June 3, 1993, pp. 1, 4.

44. *New York Times*, February 22, 1991, p. 8.

45. The Saudi media signaled this switch by beginning to feature news on Iraqi Shiʿi organizations. For example, see the following interviews and articles: interview with Muhammad Taqi Mudarrasi, spokesman for the Islamic Action Organization in Iraq, in *al-Sharq al-'Awsat*, March 13, 1991, p. 5; interview with Muwaffiq al-Rubayyaʿ, member of the politburo of al-Daʿwa party, the oldest Islamic opposition group in Iraq, in *al-Sharq al-'Awsat*, March 6, 1991, p. 5; interview with Husayn al-Sadr, nephew of Ayatollah Muhammad Baqir al-Sadr, who was killed by the Iraqi government in 1980, in *al-Sharq al-'Awsat*, February 11, 1991, p. 6; and a very flattering article on Muhammad Baqir al-Hakim, the leader of the Iranian-sponsored Supreme Assembly of the Islamic Revolution in Iraq, in *al-Sharq al-'Awsat*, March 5, 1991, p. 5. See also *New York Times*, March 5, 1991, p. 11, for an account of Saudi support for the Iraqi Salvation Movement, a coalition of opposition forces including Shiʿi groups.

46. *al-Hayat*, June 7, 1991, pp. 1, 7.

47. *al-Hayat*, March 14, 1991, pp. 1, 7; *New York Times*, March 14, 1991, p. A11. For an English translation of the conference's concluding document, see FBIS-NESA, March 14, 1991, pp. 1–2.

48. See, for example, the *New York Times*, March 21, 1991, p. 14; March 24, 1991, p. 18; August 2, 1992, p. 12.

49. In a news analysis story from Riyad as the popular uprisings against Saddam were raging, *New York Times* senior correspondent R. W. Apple said: "Cognizant of Iraq's Shiite [*sic*] majority, and horrified by the prospect of fundamentalist governments in the two most populated countries bordering on the gulf, the U.S. concluded, as one ranking official put it, that 'it's far easier to deal with a tame Saddam than with an unknown quantity.' " In the same article, Apple asserts that Saudi Arabia and Egypt wanted to continue the war until Saddam's downfall, but that the U.S., Great Britain, and France did not. *New York Times*, March 10, 1991, p. 16. See also *New York Times*, March 27, 1991, p. 1.

50. United States Senate, Committee on Foreign Relations, "Civil War in Iraq," Staff Report, 102nd Congress, 1st Session, 1991, S.Prt. 102–27, pp. 16–17. This report contends: " . . . Saudi officials proposed that the United States and Saudi Arabia together militarily assist both Shi'a and Kurdish rebels. The Saudis indicated they had only recently developed contacts with the mainstream Iraqi opposition groups, but said they were prepared to support the

Shi'a foes of Saddam as well as the Kurds. The Dawa [*sic*] party has sent Saudi Arabia a message assuring the Kingdom it has no intention of causing problems among the Shi'a in the strategically sensitive Eastern Province, and the Saudis expressly denied that concerns about the Shi'a would affect their plans to assist the rebellion. According to the Saudis, the United States had not even responded to their proposal by the end of March. If a response came later, it was too late to tip the balance in favor of the rebels." Similar views were expressed to the author by a ranking Saudi foreign affairs official in an interview in October 1992.

51. *New York Times*, January 19, 1992, pp. 1, 10; February 9, 1992, pp. 1, 14; February 25, 1992, p. A6; February 28, 1992, p. A8; *al-Hayat*, February 28, 1992, pp. 1, 4.

52. *al-Hayat*, October 28, 1992, pp. 1, 4; October 29, 1992, pp. 1, 4, 5; October 30, 1992, pp. 1, 4; November 3, 1992, p. 6; *New York Times*, November 2, 1992, p. A7. *Iraq Update* [the English language organ of the Supreme Assembly of the Islamic Revolution in Iraq], December 3, 1992, printed a joint statement by the major Iraqi Shi'i groups represented at the meeting (SAIRI, al-Da'wa, al-'Amal al-'Islami), terming it "a watershed in the activities of the opposition." However, the statement criticized "a number of controversies, mistakes and unhealthy practices" that characterized the meeting.

53. *al-Hayat*, June 2, 1993, pp. 1, 4.

54. *New York Times*, January 13, 1993, pp. A1, A2.

55. That sentiment was particularly strong in Bahrain. Personal interviews, Bahrain, May 1992.

56. *al-Sharq al-'Awsat*, November 28, 1990, p. 3.

57. *al-Hayat*, March 14, 1991, p. 1.

58. *New York Times*, September 30, 1991, p. A5.

59. Personal interview with a ranking Saudi official, Jidda, October 1992. See also *New York Times*, October 13, 1991, pp. 1, 18; October 25, 1991, p. A9.

60. Personal interviews, Kuwait, May 1992.

61. *al-Hayat*, March 6, 1993, p. 1.

CHAPTER 6

1. *New York Times*, May 4, 1993, pp. A1, A6; January 10, 1993, p. 11.

2. For an excellent discussion of the financial impact of the Gulf War on Saudi Arabia in particular, and the Arab world as a whole, see Yahya Sadowski, "Power, Poverty, and Petrodollars: Arab Economies After the Gulf War," *Middle East Report*, no. 170, (May/June 1991), pp. 4–10.

3. It is extremely difficult to find accurate official figures on the liquid reserves of the Saudi government. *Middle East Economic Survey*, January 25, 1993, p. B3, puts usable Saudi government reserves at $7.1 billion at the end of October 1992, though other analysts involved in Gulf financial matters set the figure much higher, closer to $20 billion. The *New York Times* published a two-part series on the Saudi financial situation (August 22, 1993, pp. 1, 12; August 23, 1993, pp. 1, A6) in which they quoted an unnamed Saudi official as estimating the country's liquid reserves at $7 billion. In a response to these articles, the Saudi Finance Minister, Muhammad Aba al-Khayl, wrote that the kingdom

has a $20 billion hard currency fund to support the national currency, and that Saudi banks had hard currency assets in excess of $15 billion. Part of Aba al-Khayl's response was published as a letter to the editor in the *New York Times*, August 26, 1993, p. A18. The full text of the letter can be found in *Middle East Mirror*, September 2, 1993, pp. 20–22.

4. *New York Times*, February 13, 1991, p. 15; August 22, 1993, pp. 1, 12; August 23, 1993, pp. 1, A6.

5. *Middle East Mirror*, September 2, 1993, pp. 20–22.

6. These figures are taken from the following sources: *Middle East Economic Digest*, January 15, 1993, pp. 20, 26 (Bahrain, Oman); January 22, 1993, p. 23 (UAE); February 26, 1993, p. 26 (Kuwait); "Gulf Arab Budget Deficits to Persist in 1993," the *Reuter Library Report*, April 3, 1993 (Qatar); *Saudi Arabia* [newsletter of the Saudi Embassy in Washington], February 1993, p. 3.

7. Personal interviews, Bahrain, May 1992, and Saudi Arabia, October 1992.

8. *United Nations, Demographic Yearbook—1991*, (New York: United Nations, 1992), Table 1, p. 103, Table 3, pp. 106–11.

9. The Egyptian minister of labor told a parliamentary committee that since the Gulf War Saudi Arabia has accepted one million Egyptian workers, *al-Hayat*, May 12, 1993, p. 11.

10. *al-Sharq al-'Awsat*, March 2, 1992, pp. 4–5.

11. For a good historical overview of opposition movements in these states, see Fred H. Lawson, "Opposition Movements and U.S. Policy toward the Arab Gulf States," *Critical Issues 1992*, no. 9 (New York: Council on Foreign Relations Press, 1992).

12. James Bill, "Resurgent Islam in the Persian Gulf," *Foreign Affairs*, vol. 63, no. 1 (Fall 1984).

13. Personal interviews, Kuwait and Bahrain, May 1992.

14. *al-Hayat*, December 2, 1991, pp. 1, 4; March 19, 1993, p. 6.

15. For a interesting account of current Saudi politics, that contends that just such a simultaneous crisis on a number of fronts is occurring, see Helga Graham, "Saudis Break the Silence," *London Review of Books*, vol. 15, no. 8 (April 22, 1993), pp. 6–8. The article is a mix of interesting reporting and gossip, pointing out a number of problems that the regime faces, and takes a more pessimistic view of Saudi prospects than this author does.

16. *al-Hayat*, February 3, 1992, p. 5; personal interviews, Kuwait, May 1992. I am grateful to Eleanor Doumato for updated information on this issue.

17. See the following *New York Times* articles: November 7, 1990, p. 1; November 13, 1990, p. 14; November 15, 1990, p. 19; November 18, 1990, p. 16.

18. Eleanor Abdella Doumato, "Women and the Stability of Saudi Arabia," *Middle East Report*, no. 171 (July/August 1991), pp. 34–37.

19. *New York Times*, November 11, 1991, p. A4; personal interviews, Riyad, October 1992.

20. For a discussion of the role of women's issues in the political discourse of Islamists and the Saudi government, see Doumato, "Women and the Stability of Saudi Arabia."

21. For a discussion of this issue, see F. Gregory Gause, III, "Revolutionary Fevers and Regional Contagion: Domestic Structures and the 'Export' of Revolution in the Middle East," *Journal of South Asian and Middle Eastern Studies*, vol. 14, no. 3 (Spring 1991).

22. Personal interviews, Kuwait, May 1992.
23. Personal interviews, Bahrain, May 1992.
24. See, for example, Daniel Pipes and Patrick Clawson, "Ambitious Iran, Troubled Neighbors," *Foreign Affairs—America and the World 1992–3*, vol. 72, no. 1, pp. 124–41; Patrick Clawson, "Iran's Challenge to the West: How, When, and Why," *The Washington Institute Policy Papers*, no. 33 (Washington, D.C.: The Washington Institute for Near East Policy, 1993).
25. *New York Times*, March 31, 1993, p. A3.
26. This analysis is based upon conversations with officials in Kuwait, Bahrain, and Oman during May–June 1992, and in Saudi Arabia during October 1992. See also the perceptive analysis of Gulf state views of Iran in *al-Hayat*, December 2, 1992, pp. 1, 4.
27. Personal interviews, Saudi Arabia, October 1992.
28. *al-Hayat*, January 24, 1993, p. 5.
29. See the following *New York Times* articles on the Iranian military build-up: August 8, 1992, p. 3; November 7, 1992, pp. 1, 6; November 30, 1992, pp. A1, A6; April 8, 1993, p. A9.
30. *New York Times*, May 1, 1993, p. 4.

CHAPTER 7

1. Figures, accurate to the end of 1991, taken from British Petroleum, *Statistical Review of World Energy*, June 1992, p. 3.
2. For an illuminating discussion of the role of the Gulf in oil market projections, see Paul Stevens, *Oil and Politics: The Post-War Gulf*, A Middle East Programme Report of the Royal Institute of International Affairs, 1992.
3. U.S. Department of Energy, Energy Information Administration, *Monthly Energy Review*, November 1992, Table 10.1a–b, pp. 126–27.
4. *al-Hayat*, April 23, 1993, p. 12.
5. This important point is emphasized by Walter Russell Mead, "An American Grand Strategy: The Quest for Order in a Disordered World," *World Policy Journal*, vol. 10, no. 1 (Spring 1993), especially pp. 29–32.
6. See the statement by GCC oil ministers issued after their March 1993 meeting in Jidda. *Middle East Economic Survey*, March 22, 1993, pp. A1–A3.
7. Personal interviews, Kuwait and Bahrain, May 1992; Saudi Arabia, October 1992.
8. *New York Times*, April 3, 1991, p. 1.
9. It should be noted that a number of Islamic thinkers have also advocated a reinterpretation of the *hudud* punishments. This is part of the general debate in the Muslim world on the meaning of Islam in the modern age.
10. The dual containment policy was set out in a speech by Martin Indyk, senior director for the Near East and South Asia on the National Security Council, to the Washington Institute for Near East Policy on May 18, 1993. See also *New York Times*, May 27, 1993, pp. A1, A8.
11. *al-Hayat*, May 7, 1993, pp. 1, 4.
12. For a bleak assessment of Iraq's future that sees the breakup of the country as likely, see Graham E. Fuller, *Iraq in the Next Decade: Will Iraq Survive Until 2002?*, RAND Note N-3591-DAG, 1993.
13. *New York Times*, May 11, 1993, p. A11.

Glossary of Arabic Terms

amir—Formerly a military title, now used as the title for a prince or various rulers or chiefs.

ᶜashura—The tenth of the month of *muharram*, the first month of the Islamic year. It commemorates the martyrdom of Imam Husayn, one of the sons of ᶜAli ibn Abi Talib, the leader of the Shiᶜa movement, in 680 A.D. and is a day of mourning for Shiᶜa in which ritual self-flagellation takes place as a sign of guilt and grief.

beduin—Nomadic Arabs of the Arabian, Syrian, and North African deserts.

bidun—A resident of Kuwait who does not hold Kuwaiti or foreign citizenship, from "bidun jinsiyya," Arabic for "without citizenship."

diwaniyya—An important Kuwaiti social tradition of holding open house, usually weekly, and most often in private homes, where discussions of current events frequently take place.

fatwa (**Arabic plural** *fatawa*)—A published opinion or decision regarding religious doctrine or law made by a recognized authority, often called a *mufti*.

217

hajj—"The Greater Pilgrimage" is one of the Five Pillars of Islam, and is an elaborate series of rites, requiring several days for their accomplishment, performed at the Grand Mosque of Mecca and in the immediate environs of the city, at a particular moment of the Islamic year. The *hajj* is not absolutely required in Islam, but one should make the trip if one has the means.

hudud—Punishments prescribed by Islamic law.

ikhwan—Literally, "brothers." The term was used to describe the military force raised by Saudi King ʿAbd al-ʿAziz in the 1910s and 1920s, based upon their adherence to the Wahhabi interpretation of Islam, to expand his kingdom. These forces eventually came to threaten ʿAbd al-ʿAziz's position, and he defeated them in a series of battles in the late 1920s. Not to be confused with the "ikhwan al-muslimin," or Muslim Brotherhood, which was founded in 1928 in Egypt and has since spread to numerous Arab countries.

imam—A prayer leader; a title of the head of a community or group; for Shiʿa, the title for Ali ibn Abi Talib and his descendants through Fatima credited with supernatural knowledge and authority.

jihad—Religiously sanctioned warfare to extend Islam into the *dar al-harb*, the "abode of struggle" or of disbelief, or to defend Islam from danger.

majlis—A gathering of notables in a Bedouin tent, the audience of a *shaykh*, an assembly, a ruling council, a parliament. Literally in Arabic meaning a place to sit.

mufti—A legal functionary who may be an assistant to a *qadi* (judge) or a *qadi* himself, empowered to issue *fatwas*.

ma'atim (Arabic singular *ma'tam*)—Particularly in Bahrain, Shiʿi funeary societies that plan the yearly ʿashura celebrations.

mutawwaʿin—Saudi Arabian morality police who enforce Islamic dress, the prohibition of drinking and gambling, and other strictures dealing with religious and moral issues.

salafi—Adjective used in the smaller Gulf monarchies to describe the Islamic political movement that takes its inspiration from the Saudi Wahhabi tradition. Comes from the Arabic word *salaf*, meaning ancestors. Not to be confused with the modernizing intellectual movement, begun at the turn of the century in

Egypt, founded by Jamal ad-Din al-Afghani and Muhammad Abduh.

shaykh—Literally an "old man" or "elder," it is a title of the head of a village, or of a whole tribe, or of a learned religious scholar. The title has come to be attributed to anyone who has authority, spiritual or political.

shura—Literally, "consultation." Used in the name of a number of the appointed consultative councils in the Gulf monarchies (*majlis al-shura*). The Quranic injunction that Muslims should consult among themselves on important issues is seen by modernists as an Islamic mandate for representative institutions.

ᶜulama—Individuals who are recognized as scholars or authorities of the religious sciences. Literally "learned ones," it has come to mean "the men of religion."

waqf (**Arabic plural**—*'awqaf*)—Property deeded by will or by gift in perpetuity for support of a pious cause or institution, such as a mosque. The state now administers these properties.

Bibliography

DOCUMENTS

Arms Control Association, "U.S. Arms Transfers to the Middle East since the Invasion of Kuwait"—Fact Sheet, October 8, 1992, Washington, D.C.

British Petroleum, *Statistical Review of World Energy*, June 1992.

Foreign Broadcast Information Service, *Daily Report—Near East and South Asia*.

al-haraka al-dusturiyya al-'islamiyya [Islamic Constitutional Movement], *al-birnamij al-'intikhabi* [Election Platform]. Kuwait, 1992.

International Institute for Strategic Studies, *Military Balance*. London: Brassey's for the IISS, 1975–1976, 1980–1981, 1990–1991, 1991–1992.

International Monetary Fund, *Government Financial Statistics Yearbook—1991*. Washington, D.C.; IBRD/World Bank, 1992.

International Monetary Fund, *International Financial Statistics*. 1992 Yearbook and May 1993 Monthly. Washington, D.C.: IBRD/World Bank, 1993.

State of Kuwait, Ministry of Planning, Central Statistical office, *Annual Statistical Abstract—1989.*

"Memoradum of Advice," Saudi Arabia, Muharram 1413/July 1992.

Sultanate of Oman, Development Council, General Secretariate, *Statistical Year Book 1990*, 19th issue, July 1991.

Kingdom of Saudi Arabia, Ministry of Finance and National Economy, Central Dapartment of Statistics, *Statistical Year Book— 1990.*

United Nations, *Demographic Yearbook—1991.* New York: United Nations, 1992.

United Nations Development Program, *Human Development Report 1992.* New York: Oxford University Press, 1992.

United Nations Educational, Scientific and Cultural Organization (UNESCO), *Statistical Yearbook*, 1975, 1980, 1991. New York: United Nations, various years.

United States, Department of Energy, Energy Information Administration, *Monthly Energy Review.* Various issues.

United States Senate, Committe on Foreign Relations. "Civil War in Iraq," Staff Report 102nd Congress, 1st Session, 1991, S.Prt. 102–27: 16–17.

World Bank, *Social Indicators of Development—1990.* Washington, D.C.: IBRD/World Bank, 1991.

BOOKS AND MONOGRAPHS

Abir, Mordechai. *Saudi Arabia in the Oil Era: Regime and Elites, Conflict and Cooperation.* London: Croom Helm, 1988.

Al-Dekhayel, Abdulkarim Hamoud. "The State and Political Legitimation in an Oil-Rentier Economy: Kuwait as a Case Study," D. Phil. dissertation, University of Exeter, 1990.

Al-Farsy, Fouad. *Modernity and Tradition: The Saudi Equation.* London: Kegan Paul International, 1990.

Allen, Calvin. *Oman: The Modernization of the Sultanate.* Boulder: Westview Press, 1987.

al-Naqueeb, Khaldoun Hassan [Khaldun Hassan al-Naqib]. *al-mujtamac wa al-dawla fi al-khalij wa al-jazira al-'arabiyya:*

min manthur mukhtalif. Beirut: Markaz Dirasat al-Wahda al-'Arabiyya, 1987.

—— *Society and State in the Gulf and Arabian Peninsula: A Different Perspective.* New York: Routledge, 1990 (translated).

Al Rasheed, Madawi. *Politics in an Arabian Oasis: The Rashidi Tribal Dynasty.* London: I.B. Taurus, 1991.

Altorki, Soraya and Cole, Donald. Arabian Oasis City: *The Transformation of Unayzah.* Austin: University of Texas Press, 1989.

Al Yassini, Ayman. *Religion and State in the Kingdom of Saudi Arabia.* Boulder: Westview, 1985.

Askari, Hossein. *Saudi Arabia's Economy: Oil and the Search for Economic Development.* Greenwich, Connecticut: JAI Press, 1990.

Beblawi, Hazem and Luciani, Giacomo (eds.). *The Rentier State.* London: Croom Helm, 1987.

Bligh, Alexander. *From Prince to King: Royal Succession in the House of Saud in the Twenthieth Century.* New York: New York University Press, 1984.

Clawson, Patrick. *Iran's Challenge to the West: How, When, and Why.* The Washington Institute Policy Papers, No. 33. Washington, D.C.: The Washington Institute for Near East Policy, 1993.

Cole, Donald P. *Nomads of the Nomads: The Al Murrah Bedouin of the Empty Quarter.* Arlington Heights, Illinois: AHM Publishing Corporation, 1975.

Crystal, Jill. *Kuwait: The Transformation of an Oil State.* Boulder: Westview Press, 1992.

—— *Oil and Politics in the Gulf: Rulers and Merchants in Kuwait and Qatar.* New York: Cambridge University Press, 1990.

Davis, Eric and Gavrielides, Nicolas (eds.). *Statecraft in the Middle East.* Miami: Florida International University Press, 1991.

Eickelman, Dale. *The Middle East: An Anthropological Approach* (2nd ed.), Englewood Cliffs, NJ: Prentice Hall, 1989.

Field, Michael. *The Merchants.* Woodstock, NY: Overlook Press, 1985.

Fuller, Graham E. *Iraq in the Next Decade: Will Iraq Survive Until 2002?* RAND Note N-3591-DAG, 1993.

Hardy, Roger. *Arabia After the Storm: Internal Stability of the Gulf Arab States*. London: A Middle East Programme Report of the Royal Institute of International Affairs, 1992.

Heard-Bey, Frauke. *From Trucial States to United Arab Emirates*. New York: Longman, 1982.

Helms, Christine Moss. *The Cohesion of Saudi Arabia*. Baltimore: Johns Hopkins University Press, 1981.

Holden, David and Johns, Richard. *The House of Saud*. New York: Holt, Rinehart and Winston, 1981.

Islami, A. Reza S. and Kavoussi, Rostam Mehraban. *The Political Economy of Saudi Arabia*. Seattle: University of Washington Press, 1984.

Kechichian, Joseph A. *Political Dynamics and Security in the Arabian Peninsula Through the 1990's*. RAND, MR-167-AF/A, 1993.

Khuri, Fuad. *Tribe and State in Bahrain*. Chicago: University of Chicago Press, 1980.

Kostiner, Joseph. *The Making of Saudi Arabia, 1916–1936*. New York: Oxford University Press, 1993.

Lacey, Robert. *The Kingdom: Arabia and the House of Saud*. New York: Avon Books, 1981.

Lackner, Helen. *A House Built on Sand: A Political Economy of Saudi Arabia*. London: Ithaca Press, 1978.

Lawson, Fred H. *Bahrain: The Modernization of Autocracy*. Boulder: Westview Press, 1989.

Looney, Robert E. *Economic Development in Saudi Arabia: Consequences of the Oil Price Decline*. Greenwich, Connecticut: JAI Press, 1990.

Luciani, Giacomo (ed.). *The Arab State*. Berkeley: University of California Press, 1990.

Middle East Watch. "Empty Reforms: Saudi Arabia's New Basic Laws." New York: May 1992.

Munif, Abd al-Rahman. *Cities of Salt*. New York: Vintage, 1987.

———— *The Trench*. New York: Pantheon, 1991.

———— *Variations on Night and Day*. New York: Pantheon, 1993.

Nakhleh, Emile A. *Bahrain*. Lexington, MA: Lexington Books, 1976

Nyrop, Richard F. (ed.). *The Persian Gulf States: Country Studies*. Washington, D.C.: U.S. Government Printing Office, 1985.

Peterson, John E. *The Arab Gulf States: Steps Toward Political Participation*. The Washington Papers No. 131, New York: Praegar, 1988.

—— *Oman in the Twentieth Century: Political Foundations of an Emerging State*. London: Croom Helm, 1978.

Philby, H. St. John. *Arabia of the Wahhabis*. London: Constable, 1928.

—— *Saudi Arabia*. London: Benn, 1955.

Sadowski, Yahya. *Scuds or Butter? The Political Economy of Arms Control in the Middle East*. Washington, D.C.: The Brookings Institution, 1993.

Safran, Nadav. *Saudi Arabia: The Ceaseless Quest for Security*. Cambridge: Harvard University Press, 1985.

Stevens, Paul. *Oil and Politics: The Post-War Gulf*. London: A Middle East Programme Report of the Royal Institute of International Affairs, 1992.

Wilkinson, John. *Arabia's Frontiers: The Story of Britain's Boundary Drawing in the Desert*. London: Longman, 1982.

—— *The Imamate Tradition of Oman*. New York: Cambridge University Press, 1987.

Winder, R. Bayly. *Saudi Arabia in the Nineteenth Century*. New York: St. Martin's Press, 1965.

Zahlan, Rosemarie Said. *The Creation of Qatar*. London: Croom Helm, 1981.

—— *The Making of the Modern Gulf States: Kuwait, Bahrain, Qatar, the United Arab Emirates and Oman*. London: Unwin Hyman, 1989.

ARTICLES AND BOOK CHAPTERS

Al Mahmud, cAbd al-Latif Mahmud. "dur al-musharaka al-shacbiyya fi siyyagha al-qirar al-siyasi wa mustaqbal al-dimuqratiyya fi al-mintaqa [The Role of Popular Participation in Political Decision-Making and the Future of Democracy in the Region]," *al-Jazira al-cArabiyya*. No. 12 (January 1992).

Beblawi, Hazem. "The Rentier State in the Arab World," in Luciani, Giacomo (ed.), *The Arab State*. Berkeley: University of California Press, 1990.

Bill, James. "Resurgent Islam in the Persian Gulf," *Foreign Affairs*. Vol. 63, No. 1 (Fall 1984).

Bligh, Alexander. "The Saudi Religous Elite (Ulama) as Participant in the Political System of the Kingdom," *International Journal of Middle Eastern Studies*. Vol. 18, No. 1 (February 1986).

Chaudhry, Kiren Aziz. "The Price of Wealth: Business and State in Labor Remittance and Oil Economies," *International Organization*. Vol. 43, No. 1 (Winter 1989).

——— "Economic Liberalization in Oil-Exporting Countries: Iraq and Saudi Arabia," in Iliya Harik and Denis J. Sullivan. *Privatization and Liberalization in the Middle East*. Bloomington: Indiana University Press, 1992.

Crystal, Jill. "Coalitions in Oil Monarchies: Kuwait and Qatar," *Comparative Politics*. Vol. 21, No. 4 (July 1989).

Davis, Eric. "Theorizing Statecraft and Social Change in Arab Oil Producing Countries," in Eric Davis and Nicolas Gavrielides (eds.), *Statecraft in the Middle East: Oil, Historical Memory and Popular Culture*. Miami: Florida International University Press, 1991.

Delacroix, Jacques. "The Distributive State in the World System." *Studies in Comparative International Development*. Vol. 15 (1980).

Duomato, Eleanor. "Women and the Stability of Saudi Arabia," *Middle East Report*. No. 171 (July/August 1991).

Eickelman, Dale F. "Kings and People: Oman's State Consultative Council," *Middle East Journal*. Vol. 38, No. 1 (Winter 1984).

——— "National Identity and Religious Discourse in Contemporary Oman," *International Journal of Islamic and Arab Studies*. Vol. 6, No. 1 (1989).

Gause, F. Gregory, III. "Gulf Regional Politics: Revolution, War and Rivalry," in W. Howard Wriggins (ed.). *Dynamics of Regional Politics: Four Systems on the Indian Ocean Rim*. New York: Columbia University Press, 1992.

——— "Revolutionary Fevers and Regional Contagion: Domestic Structures and the 'Export' of Revolution in the Middle East,"

Journal of South Asian and Middle Eastern Studies. Vol. 14, No. 3 (Spring 1991).

Ghabra, Shafeeq. "Voluntary Associations in Kuwait: The Founding of a New System?," *Middle East Journal*. Vol.45, No. 2 (Spring 1991).

―――― "Kuwait: Elections and Issues of Democratization in a Middle Eastern State," *Digest of Middle East Studies*. Vol. 2, No. 1 (Winter 1993).

Graham, Helga. "Saudis Break the Silence," *London Review of Books*. Vol. 15, No.8 (April 22, 1993).

Hunter, Shireen T. "The Gulf Economic Crisis and its Social and Political Consequences," *Middle East Journal*. Vol. 40, No. 4 (Autumn 1986): 593–613.

Kechichian, Joseph A. "Islamic Revivalism and Change in Saudi Arabia," *The Muslim World*. Vol. 80, No. 1 (January 1990).

―――― "The Role of the Ulama in the Politics of an Islamic State: The Case of Saudi Arabia," *International Journal of Middle Eastern Studies*. Vol.18, No. 1 (February 1986).

Kostiner, Joseph. "Transforming Dualities: Tribe and State Formation in the Middle East," in Philip Khoury and Joseph Kostiner, (eds.), *Tribes and State Formation in the Middle East*. Berkeley: University of California Press, 1990.

Lawson, Fred H. "Opposition Movements and U.S. Policy Toward the Arab Gulf States," *Critical Issues 1992*, No. 9. New York: Council on Foreign Relations Press, 1992.

Luciani, Giacomo. "Allocation v. Production States: A Theoretical Framework," in Luciani (ed.), *The Arab State*. Berkeley: University of California Press, 1990.

Mead, Walter Russell. "An American Grand Strategy: The Quest for Order in a Disordered World," *World Policy Journal*. Vol. 10, No. 1 (Spring 1993).

al-Najjar, Muhammad Rajab. "Contemporary Trends in the Study of Folklore in the Arab Gulf States," in Eric Davis and Nicolas Gavrielides (eds.), *Statecraft in the Middle East: Oil, Historical Memory and Popular Culture*. Miami: Florida International University Press, 1991.

Nakhleh, Emile A. "Muntada al-Tanmiyya: Indigenous Scholarship on Development in the GCC Countries," paper presented at the Middle East Studies Association annual convention, San Antonio, Texas, November 1990.

Niblock, Tim. "Social Structure and the Development of the Saudi Arabian Political System," in T. Niblock (ed.), *State, Society and Economy in Saudi Arabia.* London: Croom Helm, 1982.

Peterson, John. E. "Tribes and Politics in Eastern Arabia." *Middle East Journal.* Vol. 31, No. 3 (Summer 1977).

Pipes, Daniel and Clawson, Patrick. "Ambitious Iran, Troubled Neighbors," *Foreign Affairs—America and the World 1992– 1993.* Vol. 72, No. 1 (1993).

Rosenfeld, Henry. "The Social Composition of the Military in the Process of State Formation in the Arabian Desert." *Journal of the Royal Anthropological Institute.* Vol. 95, No. 2 (1965).

——— "The Military Forces Used to Achieve and Maintain Power and the Meaning of Its Social Composition: Slaves, Mercenaries and Townsmen," *Journal of the Royal Anthropological Institute.* Vol. 95, No. 2 (1965).

Sadowski, Yahya. "Power, Poverty, and Petrodollars: Arab Economies After the Gulf War," *Middle East Report.* No. 170 (May/ June 1991): 4–10.

Salame, Ghassan. "Political Power and the Saudi State," *MERIP Reports.* No. 91 (October 1980).

Yapp, Malcolm. "The Nineteenth and Twentieth Centuries," and "British Policy in the Persian Gulf," in Alvin J. Cottrell (ed.), *The Persian Gulf States.* Baltimore: Johns Hopkins University Press, 1980.

NEWSPAPERS AND PERIODICALS

Akhbar al-Khalij (Bahrain).

Arabia Monitor, Monthly Publication of the International Committee for Human Rights in the Gulf and Arabian Peninsula (Washington, D.C.).

al-Hayat (London).

Iraq Update, The Supreme Assembly of the Islamic Revolution in Iraq (London).

Kayhan International, English Edition (Tehran).

al-Khalij (UAE).

Makka News, Newsletter of the Information Bureau of the Organization of Islamic Revolution in the Arabian Peninsula (Tehran).

Middle East Economic Digest.

Middle East Economic Survey.

MidEast Report (New York).

The New York Times.

Petroleum Intelligence Weekly.

al-Qabas (Kuwait).

The Reuter Library Report.

Saudi Gazette (Riyad).

Sawt al-Kuwayt (Kuwait)

al-Sharq al-'Awsat (London).

Voice of Bahrain, Monthly Newsletter of the Bahrain Freedom Movement (London).

The Washington Post.

Index

229

About the Author

F. Gregory Gause III is Associate Professor of Political Science at Columbia University and Fellow for Arab and Islamic Studies at the Council on Foreign Relations.

He received his Ph. D. from Harvard University in 1987, and studied Arabic at the American University in Cairo and Middlebury College. In 1986–87 he was a research fellow at the Brookings Institution in Washington, D.C. He received his B.A. from St. Joseph's University in Philadelphia in 1980.

Gause is also the author of *Saudi-Yemeni Relations: Domestic Structures and Foreign Influence* (Columbia University Press, 1990), as well as a number of articles on the international politics of the Middle East.